Luminos is the Open Access monograph publishing program
from UC Press. Luminos provides a framework for preserving and
reinvigorating monograph publishing for the future and increases
the reach and visibility of important scholarly work. Titles published
in the UC Press Luminos model are published with the same high
standards for selection, peer review, production, and marketing as
those in our traditional program. www.luminosoa.org

D1562568

Recovering Identity

Recovering Identity

Criminalized Women's Fight for Dignity and Freedom

———

Cesraéa Rumpf

UNIVERSITY OF CALIFORNIA PRESS

University of California Press
Oakland, California

© 2023 by Cesraéa Rumpf

This work is licensed under a Creative Commons (CC BY-NC-ND) license.
To view a copy of the license, visit http://creativecommons.org/licenses.

Suggested citation: Rumpf, C. *Recovering Identity: Criminalized Women's Fight for Dignity and Freedom.* Oakland: University of California Press, 2023. DOI: https://doi.org/10.1525/luminos.150

Some excerpts from interviews with research participants appeared previously in Cesraéa Rumpf, "Decentering Power in Research with Criminalized Women: A Case for Photo-Elicitation Interviewing," *Sociological Focus* 50 (1) (2017): 18–35, https://doi.org/10.1080/00380237 .2016.1218214. Copyright © 2017 North Central Sociological Association, reprinted by permission of Taylor & Francis Ltd., http://www.tandfonline .com, on behalf of 2017 North Central Sociological Association.

Cataloging-in-Publication Data is on file at the Library of Congress.

ISBN 978-0-520-37699-1 (pbk.)
ISBN 978-0-520-97635-1 (ebook)

32   31   30   29   28   27   26   25   24   23
10   9   8   7   6   5   4   3   2   1

For my mother, Raelica Rumpf, and my father, Charles Rumpf, who taught me the values of unconditional love, inquiry, and authenticity

CONTENTS

ILLUSTRATIONS

FIGURES

TABLES

ACKNOWLEDGMENTS

This project has slowly unfolded over many years and has been shaped by the generous insights and support of so many people. It is not possible to fully express my gratitude for the many mentors, teachers, colleagues, family members, and friends who have believed in this project and expressed their confidence in my ability to bring it to fruition. I will try, though.

This project would not have been possible without the 36 women who trusted me with their stories and took a chance on an unconventional research process. Their creativity, resilience, and enthusiasm for the project have sustained me over the years as I've developed and refined the writing. I hope I have done their good work justice. I extend my deepest appreciation to Amber, Ann, Ann Williams, Brenda, Carmel, Cathy, Chicken Wing, Chunky, Corrine, Darlene, Denise, Ella, Faye, Ms. Fields, Ida, Iris, Jean Grey, Julia, the Lioness, Lynn, Mae, Maryann, Moon, New Life, Nyla, Olivia, Ranisha, Red, Rose, Sarah, Sharon, Stacey Williams, Susan, Tinybig, Veronica, and Xenia. I also am grateful for the staff members who worked at the recruitment sites and supported this research in various ways.

This project grew out of my dissertation research at Loyola University Chicago, and I was fortunate to benefit from the critical insights and steadfast support of an incredible dissertation committee. Kelly Moore reminded me to keep gender up front and was the first person who encouraged me to develop the dissertation into a book. Lisa Frohmann provided invaluable guidance with the photo-elicitation interviewing method and reminded me to keep race up front. Christine George encouraged me to center women's resilience and empowerment. Judy Wittner did it all. She challenged me when I lagged. She encouraged me when I doubted. She insightfully zeroed in on the moments when women in this research "came together" and guided me in pursuing that line of analysis. Judy's death in February 2022 was an overwhelming loss. I am so sad she will never hold this book in her hands, but I am so thankful for all she gave to make this book possible.

While at Loyola University Chicago, I also benefited greatly from the research assistance of Flannery Bohne, Andrea Gurga, Paul Tran, and Hannah Ramlo. Their transcription work, feedback on interviews, and curiosity about the project were critically important contributions. Additionally, funding from the Graduate School at Loyola University Chicago and the Arthur J. Schmitt Dissertation Fellowship made this research possible.

During my time as a faculty member at Benedictine University, I was fortunate to be part of two writing groups that helped me protect valuable writing time. Steve Burgess, Wilson Chen, Jean-Marie Kauth, Pat Somers, and Beth Vinkler provided critical feedback on early drafts of many chapters. Their insightful questions and comments helped me refine my ideas and clarify my analysis. Rita George-Tvrtkovic and Mary Kate Holman provided good company and endless encouragement. Friday mornings were the highlight of my work week, because I spent it with them. I was lucky to work with an amazing group of colleagues at Benedictine University, who provided a true sense of community. I am particularly grateful for the friendship and support of Jane Boumgarden, Sandy Chmelir, Kristin Clifford, Vince Gaddis, Phil Hardy, Peter Huff, Joe Incandela, Sue Mikula, Dianne Moran, Joel Ostrow, Brian Patterson, Patrick Polasek, Fannie Rushing, Jack Thornburg, and Tammy Sarver. I am especially indebted to Peter for connecting me with Karen Van Fossan and Bonnie Palecek. The conversations the four of us have had have sustained and inspired me, while helping me think through how to ethically and honestly present this work. I also value the hard work of students in my Sex and Gender; Gender, Crime, and Justice; and Inside-Out: Transformative Justice classes at Benedictine University. Their insights on controlling images, transformative justice, and prison abolition, in particular, influenced my thinking as I worked on this book.

This book would not be possible without the incredibly supportive team I've been so lucky to work with at UC Press. Maura Roessner believed in this project from the very beginning and has been nothing but supportive since our first contact. Her patience and guidance have kept me on track and made an at times overwhelming process manageable. I'm especially grateful to Maura for her advocacy to have this book published as part of UC Press's Luminos Open Access Program, which allows the beautiful photographs women took for this project to be printed in color. I also am thankful to Madison Wetzell and Sam Warner for their support, clear instructions, and endless patience. I am indebted to Linda Gorman for her copyediting expertise, which strengthened and clarified my writing.

Tanya Erzen and Melissa Thompson were incredibly generous with their careful, thoughtful feedback on an earlier draft. Their insights strengthened nearly every part of this book, particularly the theoretical framework. They exemplify what it means to be a feminist scholar, and I hope to pay forward the gift of supportive critique they provided to me.

While academia can be a lonely place, I have been fortunate to make fulfilling connections with colleagues who have become good friends. Nicole Kaufman and Megan Welsh have been two of the most influential supporters of this project. It is not possible to state strongly enough how much their ideas and support have helped bring this book to life. They have read and provided detailed feedback on multiple drafts of chapters. They have been a helpful sounding board via phone calls, Zoom meetings, and text messages. Whenever I had a new idea about this project, NK and MW were the first people with whom I shared it. I trust them fully, and if they were on board, I knew I was on the right track. Opportunities to coauthor with Courtney Irby and Quintin Williams sharpened my thinking and pushed my analysis forward. Annmarie van Altena has provided an endless supply of helpful feedback, support, and laughs over the years.

Love & Protect has been my political home for nearly a decade. Thank you Amy Catania, Ash Stephens, Ayanna Harris, Bri Hanny, CAM Morris, Claudia Garcia-Rojas, Deana Lewis, Gail Smith, Jane Hereth, Maya Schenwar, Nnenna Okeke, Rachel Caïdor, Sangi Ravichandran, Sarah Jane Rhee, and Tasasha Henderson for your friendship, care, and commitment to imagining and creating an abolitionist world. I have learned so much from you. Mariame Kaba, who is a founder of Love & Protect, has influenced me more than she knows. I was fortunate to meet Mariame when I was a young carceral feminist working in the domestic violence field in Chicago. I still don't know why Mariame was willing to invest so much in me, but I am thankful she did. I would be a very different person had I not met Mariame many years ago. I also have benefited from the friendship, insights, creativity, and care of a fierce abolitionist feminist community in Chicago, including Alexis Mansfield, Ann Russo, Beth Richie, Chris Rivers, Deane Benos, Debbie Buntyn, Colette Payne, Erica Meiners, Heather Canuel, Holly Krig, Jonice Robinson, LiLi Walker, Monica Cosby, Paris Knox, Rachel White-Domain, Sarah Ross, and Sandra Brown. Thank you for teaching me. I also am grateful for the lessons shared by Tewkunzi Green and Lauren Stumblingbear before their tragic deaths. We love and miss you, Q and Bear.

There were times when the enormity of this project and the responsibility I felt to get it right overwhelmed me. I am lucky for good friends who did not let me drown, particularly Joanne Starer, Cathy Tracy, Sara Powers, Chris Engler, Nikki Ogrin, and Allison Lawton. No matter what they have going on in their lives, they always provide support, perspective, encouragement, connection, and good food. In particular, Sara Powers has listened with unending patience for well over a decade as I have conceptualized this research project and struggled through the writing process. As I have come to expect over our nearly three-decade friendship, Sara always knew exactly what to say and always made clear how much she believed in my ability to share these women's stories in a meaningful, ethical way.

Thank you Aunt Berta, Uncle George, Aunt Mary Lee, Uncle Greg, Aunt Carole, Uncle Jon, Aunt Aline, Uncle Kevin, Aunt Renee, Steve, Marcia, Chuck, Pat, Tom, Jan, Connie, Jimmy, Teri, Rod, Tom Flanders, and Chuck Villette for always rooting for me. Your interest in the book kept me going. Thank you Sue and Christie for your love, care, and support.

My family has sustained me through this process. Their unconditional love and belief in me provide a sense of security and stability that allows me to do the work that I do. Mom, thank you for your unending support and guidance, and for reminding me when I shared the good news about my book contract that Dad would be so proud. Thank you Charlie, Cassie, Chaleen, and Phil for being the strongest, funniest, most loving group of siblings I could ever ask for. Thank you Aaron, April, and Tephany for perfectly fitting in with our wild family. My nephews and nieces have provided me with so much love, joy, fun, and snuggles. Charlie, Addy, Belly, Dutton, Easton, and Brady, I love you so much. Thank you Lois, Bandit, and Vicki for your faithful companionship over the years.

More than anyone else, my husband, Bill Flynn, has lived through the ups and downs of this project. When I have been at my worst, he has provided reassurance. When I have been at my best, he has celebrated with me. He has been patient and generous, as I have devoted hours of our life to this project. Thank you for being a solid, loving partner, Bill. Your support has made all the difference.

Women, Incarceration, and Social Marginality

"Look at the sky," Rose[1] said. She was referring to a photograph she had taken of an alley located behind a homeless shelter where she had stayed off and on for several years (figure 1). Squinting at the photograph, Rose, a 48-year-old Black American[2] woman who had been incarcerated three times, pointed out a few doorways that opened from the shelter onto the alley. She commented that the shelter employees "never used those doors back there, so everybody just did drugs back there . . . They's gettin' high back there for a long time, and they still is. Police will ride through, you know, ask for ID or somethin'. So, if you got anything, you better been done smoked it or tooted it or whatever." Rose laughed, then added, "Get out, they search us and stuff."

Rose and I had been talking for about an hour as part of our second interview for my research on women's incarceration and postincarceration experiences. In preparation for this interview, she had taken approximately 40 photographs to illustrate these experiences. At the start of the interview, she divided the photographs into two piles. One pile documented her life at Growing Stronger, the recovery home where she had been living for nearly a year after serving 18 months in prison for possession of a controlled substance. Photograph after photograph in that pile showed smiling women, posing with one another and some posing with Santa Claus at Growing Stronger's recent Christmas party. The photographs communicated warmth and care, qualities Rose deeply valued. Over the course of my data collection, I observed Rose's care for others, such as the time she brought items back from a local food pantry for a friend who was not able to go because she was busy studying for her adult high school classes. During our three interviews, Rose expressed appreciation for friends, family members, Growing Stronger staff members, and even a parole officer who supported her through multiple attempts to get her life back on the right track, meaning "livin' the rest

FIGURE 1. Rose's alley (Photo credit: Rose).

of my life clean and sober . . . doin' the right things, payin' my bills, goin' to work, helpin' somebody else." In a soft-spoken voice and with a slow pace that put me at ease, Rose said she felt positive about getting things right this time. She had learned from her past mistakes. She knew now to reach out to others when she experienced a challenge, such as a death, relationship problems, or a relapse. "I'm for certain now more than I was then," Rose explained, referring to her previous release from prison five years earlier.

The second pile of photographs documented that earlier time in Rose's life, a time characterized by drug use, homelessness, vulnerability, and run-ins with the police. By the time Rose showed me the photograph of the alley, she had already casually mentioned twice that she had been raped there. Now that our conversation was focused on this photograph, I carefully broached the topic. Rose explained, "I didn't know him. He talked about he had this money and these drugs, so we got in that little gangway, he just grabbed me. You know, had me to do things, you know, do things and then he did things to me and took off runnin'." The alley had been uncharacteristically empty that night, so no one was around to help Rose. I asked her what happened after the man took off. She recalled:

> I mean I was so scared, I, you know, I stood back there for a minute. So, I mean when I did come out, it was a few peoples walkin', but it was cold that night, so there

wasn't too many peoples on the street. So that's why wasn't too many peoples in the alley. But I asked a couple people, "Did you see this guy? This guy runnin' out of the alley or whatnot?" Everybody said, "No." So, and, you know, I never ran into that person again.

I inquired what she did next. Rose replied, "Nothin'. Just walked up and down the street cryin'. I didn't go to the hospital or nothin' because I didn't think it would do any good. I didn't have a description of the guy or nothin'. Only thing I knew that he had on black. I just cried. I, you know, it stayed with me for a long time." Rose eventually confided in an acquaintance about the rape. She recalled, "They'd be like, 'Well, what you doin' up in here in this alley cold as it was? Why didn't you go in the shelter?' You know. Why? 'Cause I was tryin' to get drugs." She sighed before continuing, "I don't know, for some reason didn't nobody come in that alley! I couldn't believe that! I was like, wow. Out of all these times, didn't nobody come in this alley. I stayed in there a good 30 minutes or longer . . . every time I tried to scream, he was like pullin' my hair and hittin' me and stuff, and I was just cryin'. I was hopin' somebody would hear me, but nobody never came that way."

Rose identified a critical tension. She understood this experience as a violent act someone perpetrated against her, despite her verbal and physical resistance. Yet, she suggested she could have prevented the assault. As the person in whom she confided had asked, why had she been in the alley? Reacting to the implicit blame in that question, I commented, "I hope you know, Rose, that it's not your fault and that it's not because you were getting high or because you were in an alley." Rose replied, "I thought it was." When I asked her if she still felt that way today, she explained:

> It's kind of, I don't know. 'Cause I figure if I wasn't gettin' high or wasn't there in that alley, that wouldn't of never happened to me. So, I can't blame nobody, you know, but myself . . . if I was doin' somethin' else . . . it wouldn't of never happened. So I did blame myself for a long time, you know. I did. But I just will say . . . that will never happen again. Only thing what really, really hurt me was that the person that did it didn't get caught or somethin' like that. That's the main part that hurt me. You know. I been raped a lot of times due to my addiction or jumpin' in people cars and stuff. And with the grace of God, I don't have AIDS or anything. You know, that ain't nobody but God.

Without absolving this man of responsibility, Rose held herself responsible. As she reasoned, if she had not been getting high, she would not have been in that alley and thus would not have encountered the man who raped her. For Rose, her addiction was the ultimate cause of that assault and the numerous other rapes she survived. She could not blame anybody other than herself.

Rose also commented on the experience of returning to that alley and taking the photograph in preparation for our second interview. She explained she had stood at "the very beginning of the alley . . . so that's maybe why it got the blue sky like this." Rose stressed, "I will never go down that alley again, and if I do go past it, only thing I can do is just look down there, you know, and be like, 'Wow. Thank you, God.'" She added, "I just couldn't see myself walkin' through there no more. I mean for what? For what?" How Rose positioned herself when taking the photograph indicated how precarious her recovery felt to her. One false step could lead her back to her old lifestyle, making her vulnerable to more violence and even to death.

Each time I looked at the striking alley image, I imagined Rose taking the photograph, balanced not just at the edge of the alley, but also between her past life, in which she bore the *criminal-addict* label, and her current life, in which she was fighting for her recovery from drug use, incarceration, and the countless traumatic experiences she had survived. As she struggled to end the cycle of poverty, interpersonal violence, drug use, and incarceration that had characterized much of her adult life, Rose grounded her postincarceration efforts in her sobriety and faith in God. She credited God for her commitment to her recovery today and for mitigating the consequences of the threats, violence, and overall hardship she had endured while using drugs. Even while looking at a site where she had been raped, she expressed gratitude for God's protection. The photograph and Rose's interpretation of it perfectly represented the personal transformation process described by many women who participated in this research, specifically the tension between the past identities they were working to leave behind and the current identities they were constructing, as well as the centrality of recovery work and religion as mechanisms to facilitate that transformation.

Rose's photograph also brought into focus how these personal transformation processes were deeply gendered and raced. When discussing how she blamed her choices and her drug use for the multiple sexual assaults she endured, Rose indicated the streets were no place for a woman. The risks she encountered while getting high and trying to access drugs were forms of gendered violence. The threat of sexual assault, the multiple rapes, and the risk of AIDS were the costs she bore as an unhoused woman struggling to maintain her drug use. Additionally, Rose's behavior violated conventional notions of femininity, specifically attachment to and responsibility for the domestic sphere and responsibility for monogamous, heterosexual relationships. Feminist criminologists note this violation of both the law and of feminine norms mark criminalized women as "doubly deviant."[3] Yet, Rose's Blackness already violated normative femininity, which is coded White.[4] Like all of the women of color in this study, Rose faced a distinctly gendered stigma related to her status as a *criminal-addict* and to her race.

For these reasons, Rose's photograph provides an apt introduction to this book. It encapsulates the vulnerability and strength, the violence and beauty, and the precarious boundaries between past lives, determined presents, and hopeful futures that characterized criminalized women's lives. The photograph compels viewers to acknowledge a highly traumatic incident that legal and social systems never addressed, while also compelling viewers to understand this incident as but one of many significant acts that have influenced the complex, multifaceted woman Rose is. Perhaps most importantly, the photograph centers Rose's survival. She was able to return to the alley, which represented a portal back to some of the worst times of her life, confront it, and walk away, back to Growing Stronger and the caring community of friends and supporters she found there.

This book examines the identity work of women, like Rose, who fight for their dignity and freedom in the face of criminalization. Based on a series of in-depth, semistructured qualitative and photo-elicitation interviews with formerly incarcerated women living in Chicago, I show how identity is created through and in response to the pervasive violence and punishment that permeated criminalized women's lives. Through their interview narratives and the photographs they took for this project, almost every one of the 36 women who participated in this research conveyed an intense sense of personal responsibility for the challenges they experienced and a commitment to transforming their selves. While women's stories were deeply personal, they seemed to draw from a common script. As I noticed these similar narrative features, I wondered what larger discourses were at work and how women encountered them. To answer this question, I turned to cultural discourses about women of color that date back to colonization and chattel slavery,[5] neoliberal and neoconservative discourses about crime and social control that ushered in the era of mass incarceration in the United States,[6] religious discourses of redemption that have structured prison life since the birth of the penitentiary,[7] and addiction and recovery discourses rooted in the 12-Step model of Alcoholics Anonymous and Narcotics Anonymous that pervade the U.S. correctional system today.[8]

By bringing together these discourses in an original way, I develop a more comprehensive understanding of the lifelong consequences of criminalization for women's identity than previous scholarship that has engaged these discourses individually has produced. I go beyond existing research on redemption narratives by examining how such narratives are constructed in the context of dehumanizing discourses and practices that relegate women to a permanent degraded social status, neither fully accepted or integrated into society. Additionally, I offer new insights about ways the carceral state has merged faith-based and addiction discourses to such an extent that it subjects criminalized women to a lifetime of recovery and rehabilitation work. I also show how, despite these consequences, criminalized women engage these restrictive discourses in innovative ways that allow them to not just survive oppressive systems, but also thrive in the rehabilitated identities they create. In the broadest sense, this book engages fundamental sociological questions about the relationship between agency and structure. More specifically, it adds to our growing understanding of how the carceral state governs socially marginalized groups—inside and outside the prison walls—while centering hopeful signs of resistance.

WOMEN'S CRIMINALIZATION

Over the past 40 years, the United States has experienced an unprecedented expansion of its prison system. Between 1972 and 2007, the rate of people incarcerated in the United States more than quintupled.[9] In the present era of mass incarceration, almost two million individuals are incarcerated in prisons and jails in the United States, and nearly six million people are under some form of correctional supervision.[10] The United States incarcerates more individuals than any other country in the world and incarcerates at a higher rate than any other country.[11] A disproportionate number of incarcerated people are Black or Latino.[12] The racial bias in arrest, prosecution, and incarceration rates has prompted critical analyses of the carceral state as a racialized form of social control.[13] Legal scholar Michelle Alexander, for one, argues that mass incarceration is "the new Jim Crow" in the sense that it supports a racial caste system in the United States not only through incarceration but also through disenfranchisement and the loss of social rights and benefits imposed on individuals postincarceration.[14] Similarly, sociologist Loïc Wacquant argues the present day U.S. prison system is the latest institution that operates to confine and control Black people, following chattel slavery, the Jim Crow system, and the urban ghetto in northern metropolises.[15] An important contextual point about mass incarceration in the United States is that public and private prisons largely have abandoned their past goal of rehabilitation and replaced it with a managerial ethos,[16] as well as "the goals of incapacitation, deterrence, and retribution."[17]

Although men make up the vast majority of the U.S. incarcerated population, the penal system has impacted and continues to impact women in direct and damaging ways. Between 1980 and 2020, women's incarceration rate (including jail and prison) rose twice as quickly as that of men. In 2020, the United States incarcerated more than 150,000 women in state and federal prisons and local jails throughout the country, an increase of 475 percent since 1980. More than one million women live under some form of correctional supervision, such as probation, parole, or serving time in alternative-to-incarceration programs located in community settings.[18] These gendered shifts in the criminal legal system's focus target particular women; incarceration disproportionately impacts women who belong to marginalized groups, particularly women of color and women who are poor, undereducated, survivors of physical and/or sexual violence, and who experience with mental health issues.[19]

This profile indicates most incarcerated women face multiple forms of social disadvantage throughout their lives. Incarceration constitutes a secondary victimization for many women who encounter state violence in the form of inadequate medical and mental health care; shackling during childbirth; separation from children and loved ones; and sexual abuse by correctional officers, the majority of whom are men who perform body searches and have access to women when they undress, shower, and use bathroom facilities.[20] The very experiences that make women vulnerable to criminalization and incarceration continue to impact them while they are in the custody of the state.

Undeniably, the War on Drugs is a leading cause of mass incarceration in the United States. Changes in laws, such as mandatory minimum sentences, and correctional policies, such as revocations of parole and probation, over the past 40 years contributed to more prison admissions, as well as longer prison sentences for a range of drug-related charges.[21] The War on Drugs also is a leading reason for the spike in women's incarceration. Feminist scholars have advanced an understanding of how the War on Drugs has hit women particularly hard, operating, in effect, as a "War on Women."[22] Despite the War on Drugs' clear role in driving mass incarceration, broadly, and increases in women's incarceration, specifically, it does not explain mass incarceration in the United States. Rather, the War on Drugs is a mechanism the state has used as part of a larger project to contain social marginality.

The era of mass incarceration in the United States developed alongside the retrenchment of the U.S. social welfare state.[23] Welfare and penal scholars have documented the convergence of the welfare and the penal states since the mid-1970s, showing how both social welfare policy and penal policy have taken a punitive turn and represent a coordinated effort by the state to regulate social marginality in new ways.[24] Wacquant argues the retrenchment of social welfare policies and the rise of the penal state are linked projects of the neoliberal state that manage and regulate marginal populations, with the Left hand of the state morally reforming poor women of color and their children through Public Aid's bureaucracy and the Right hand of the state morally reforming poor men of color through the penal system.[25] This gendered division of regulation is not as neat as a feminine Left hand and masculine Right hand, however.[26] The Left and Right hands of the state do, in fact, work together to regulate the poor, but women are not immune from the expanding reach of the penal state. Rather, as social welfare assistance, public institutions, and jobs have withered away, the criminal legal system has stepped in to fill the gaps through which women fall.

GENDERED GOVERNANCE

In addition to showing how the expanding carceral system physically contains and monitors socially marginalized groups through correctional interventions, punishment scholars, drawing on the work of French philosopher Michel Foucault, have also shown how this system governs "risky" populations through interventions designed to encourage self-regulation and self-discipline. Rather than manage social problems, the state works to manage individuals. Punishment scholars study how the penal state encourages an inward focus on self-improvement by imposing therapeutic interventions on individuals who are under correctional supervision.[27] In addition to punishing people for their "criminal" behavior, therapeutic interventions claim to help individuals come to know themselves so that they can correct their individual deficiencies that have led to their "criminal" involvement. People learn to regulate their desires, reform their thinking, and modify their behavior in order to come in line with the status quo. Collectively referred to as *responsibilization*, these strategies bracket out structural inequalities in favor of teaching participants to look inward to reform their personal failings.[28]

Feminist sociologists have assessed the gendered nature of these governance strategies when applied to criminalized women. Rather than address the structural conditions that shape women's pathways to incarceration, gender-responsive programming in women's prisons and alternative-to-incarceration programs encourages participants to recognize weak control of flawed selves as the core problem they must address. Women regularly encounter discourses that identify their criminal dependency, dangerous desires, and lack of self-esteem as the causes of their criminalization.[29] These gendered governance discourses intersect with deeply rooted controlling images that frame women of color as inherently deviant and always already in violation of conventional femininity.[30]

CRIMINALIZATION'S CONSEQUENCES

The punitive shift in the state's efforts to contain social marginality has long-term consequences for women. Scholars who study postincarceration experiences have thoroughly documented the range of collateral consequences that follow people long after the end of their prison sentence, permanently subjecting them to discrimination and social exclusion. While research consistently shows the pivotal role education, employment, and safe housing play in helping women end their entanglement with the criminal legal system, systematic barriers prevent formerly incarcerated women from accessing these critical supports.[31] Certain criminal convictions prohibit formerly incarcerated people from accessing a variety of public benefits, such as public assistance, food stamps, and public housing.[32] Lack of supportive, gender-responsive drug treatment and mental health services further hamper women's efforts to navigate the transition from prison to their communities. Complicated and unsafe relationships with family members and romantic partners pose additional barriers that characterize women's postincarceration experiences.[33] Reunification with children is another central and gendered challenge associated with postincarceration life. The majority of incarcerated women are mothers, and most were the primary caretakers of their children prior to incarceration.[34] After their release, women face the challenge of reuniting with their children, which can be particularly difficult if Child Protective Services (CPS) is involved. In addition to meeting parole stipulations, women also must follow

CPS's requirements and prove they are financially, emotionally, and mentally prepared to become the primary caretakers for their children.[35] Healing from the trauma of incarceration is an equally important though less studied challenge of postincarceration life.

In addition to these external barriers, sociologists and criminologists have examined the interior work of postincarceration life, specifically the process through which people change their understanding of their own identity. Criminologist Shadd Maruna's work on redemption scripts has been particularly influential in this area. Based on qualitative research with formerly incarcerated men and women, Maruna showed how people crafted these scripts "to rewrite a shameful past into a necessary prelude to a productive and worthy life."[36] The scripts allowed individuals to make sense of their past criminal behaviors while envisioning the rehabilitated selves they have (or want) to become. Sociologists Andrea Leverentz and Tara Opsal similarly have focused on the narrative strategies women deployed to establish a positive self-identity postincarceration.[37] Identifying markers such as employment, abstaining from drug use, and reconnecting with children helped women distinguish their past and present selves and affirm their continued movement away from criminalization.

These studies of identity narratives provide illuminating insights on criminalization's deep, lifelong impact and encourage appreciation for the degree of visible and invisible work women undertake as part of transitioning out of prison. Some studies examine the available narratives women engage, such as those offered by 12-Step, self-empowerment, and religious programs, to structure their personal narratives of identity change.[38] Yet, such studies seldom connect women's identity work back to larger governance discourses. This gap is significant, since governance discourses focus squarely on presumptions about identity, specifically a gendered, racialized, deviant self that must be managed in perpetuity. To truly understand criminalized women's identity work and the way they see themselves, it is imperative to also understand their perceptions of how the state sees them.

RESEARCH AIMS AND REVISIONS

At the outset of this project, I was not particularly interested in women's identity work. I planned to focus on how the state intervened in women's lives across varied settings. I was curious how women's experiences with service providers, such as domestic violence advocates and public aid caseworkers, compared to their experiences with criminal legal authorities, such as police and correctional officers. To investigate these questions, I conducted a series of qualitative, semistructured interviews and photo-elicitation interviews (PEI) based on participant-generated images with formerly incarcerated women. This type of PEI involves providing participants with cameras to take photographs that will help them tell their stories. The photographs become the basis of a subsequent interview, during which the participant selects the photographs they wish to discuss in the order they want to discuss them and explains what each image communicates. The decision to include PEI was critical, as the photographs women took and their explanations of them completely changed the focus of my research.[39]

PEI provides a number of benefits related to the research process and outcomes. It helps ensure participants have a voice in the research process, in part through breaking down the traditional power differential that exists between researcher and participant. PEI's collaborative approach also helps the researcher avoid overlooking or misunderstanding important points by allowing participants to drive the interview by using images they create. PEI is particularly well-suited for research that investigates trauma, disadvantage, and inequality and may even provide healing benefits for participants. Additionally, people sometimes can express experiences, especially painful experiences, more easily in nonverbal ways. PEI also has been shown to produce richer, more detailed recollections than interviews alone.[40]

Between December 2012 and July 2013, I conducted 99 interviews with 36 participants.[41] To recruit participants, I partnered with two recovery homes and one nonresidential program in Chicago that provide services to formerly incarcerated women. All 36 participants expressed an interest in taking photographs and received a camera at the end of our first interview, but only 32 participants completed a PEI. Women's ages ranged from 20 to 63 years old, with a mean age of 45.5 and a median age of 46.5. The vast majority of women (28) identified their race/ethnicity as Black or African American. Four women identified as White, two women identified as multiracial, and two women identified as Latina.[42] Thirty-one of the women were mothers, and none of the women with children under the age of 18 were living with them at the time of our interviews. Information related to women's social class indicated precarious living and financial situations in line with the structural challenges thoroughly documented in the literature on women's incarceration and reentry. All of the women indicated that their last incarceration was related to drug or alcohol use, even when the official charge was not drug related. For instance, women often were arrested for criminalized behaviors connected to their drug use, such as engaging in sex work in order to be able to access drugs.[43]

Each interview typically lasted between an hour and a half and two hours. I provided participants with a $20 gift card to the store of their choosing at the end of each interview session. Participants kept their cameras, which served as another form of compensation. Interviews were audio recorded and transcribed. I completed open coding and then focused coding, looking for linkages among the categories that had emerged.[44] Early on in the coding process, personal transformation emerged as a noteworthy theme. As I reread interview transcripts, I focused on specific ways women demonstrated their personal transformation. I also noted the tendency for women to contrast their current identities with their past identities. I came to understand the interview itself and women's photographs as sites of identity work.[45] Additionally, as I noticed similarities across women's personal transformation narratives, I began to connect their individual narratives to dominant discourses they encountered in jail and prison and across recovery homes and reentry programs. These discourses focused on faith and recovery from drug use. Over time, I came to understand these personal transformation narratives as working to oppose dehumanizing discourses and treatment women encountered throughout their criminalization processes, as well as racist controlling images of women of color that date back to the founding of this country.

OVERVIEW

In the chapters that follow, I examine the dehumanizing discourses criminalized women regularly encountered, the routine violence they survived, and the intense identity work they did to claim dignity and find joy, despite living within oppressive systems that continued to monitor and judge them. Recovering from criminalization is a lifelong process with no end point. I strive to center the voices of the women who participated in this research and present their experiences as they understood them, while developing my own critical analysis about the limiting discourses the state offered to women as ways out of the criminal legal system.[46]

Chapter 2 focuses on the dehumanizing nature of women's experiences of incarceration. Drawing on women's recollections of correctional officers' abuse, giving birth while incarcerated, and medical neglect in prison, I assess incarceration as gendered state violence. I also examine how the experience of incarceration attacked women at the level of identity, thus setting the stage for subsequent chapters that examine women's identity work. The chapter concludes with an initially confounding contradiction: despite painful recollections of incarceration, women often credited prison with saving their lives.

In chapter 3, I analyze the dominant discourse women encountered as they moved through the criminal legal system, what I term *the 12-Step logic*. Rooted in Alcoholics Anonymous and Narcotics Anonymous, the 12-Step logic is the fusing of faith- and abstinence-based discourses that instills a lifelong commitment to rehabilitating the self and embracing personal responsibility for one's criminalization, drug use, and recovery. I argue that this logic operates as an organizing force throughout incarceration and the postincarceration landscape, characterizing recovery and rehabilitation as lifelong interconnected moral and spiritual projects. I show how women engaged this logic in innovative ways to recast incarceration as a redemptive experience, while remaining critical of the dehumanizing treatment they endured.

Chapter 4 is the first of three chapters that analyzes how women's personal transformation processes are raced and gendered and how women work within the constraints of the *rehabilitated woman controlling image* to claim dignity and joy. This chapter focuses on the first two components of the rehabilitated woman controlling image: employment and appearance. I begin with these components, as they represent dimensions of independence. Employment held the promise that women would not have to depend on other people or institutions for their day-to-day survival. Women's self-described improved, healthy appearances communicated their recovery from drug use, in other words, that they no longer were dependent on drugs or alcohol. These dimensions of independence were foundational to all the identity work women did.

Chapter 5 assesses the next two components of the rehabilitated woman controlling image: domesticity and mothering. Through their photographs and reflections, women frequently discussed the importance of having their own space, whether that be a single room in a recovery home or their own apartment. Having their own space signaled their transition away from the vulnerability they faced when they were still actively using drugs and living in unstable arrangements. Women also connected their housing goals with rebuilding their relationships with their children. As such, women made an insightful connection between the structural and relational needs of housing. In reflecting on their relationships with their children, women also drew distinctions between the ways they felt they were not there for their children in the past, due to drug use and incarceration, and the ways they were present in their children's lives today.

Chapter 6 presents romantic relationships as the final component of the rehabilitated woman controlling image. Similar to the way women drew distinctions between their past and current relationships with their children, women contrasted their experiences of abuse in past romantic relationships with the healthy romantic relationships they either currently had or planned to have in the future. This chapter also presents women's reflections on their friendships with other criminalized women. These reflections reveal how, throughout their incarceration, women relied on other women to survive the daily stresses of prison life and do their time. Similarly, postrelease, women found a sense of community as they connected with other formerly incarcerated women and helped one another manage the challenges and setbacks they encountered. Women grew stronger in their own personal transformations as they did the work of recovery and reentry with supportive peers. I conclude the chapter by showing how women's critiques and moments of collective awareness—which in part emerged through their friendships with other criminalized women—challenged the individualistic focus on personal transformation and highlighted the need for broader social change.

In chapter 7, I summarize the main contributions of this study and provide suggestions for how to limit the harm the criminal legal system perpetuates in women's lives. The chapter asserts that our current system does not allow women the chance ever to move beyond the *criminal-addict* label and subsequently subjects women permanently to moral judgment and the threat of further criminalization. I argue that meaningful change requires abolitionist approaches that seek to shrink the carceral state and link formerly incarcerated women's personal transformation processes to organizing strategies for social transformation.

This book implores us to pay attention to what formerly incarcerated women want us to know about their journeys through the criminal legal system and their postincarceration experiences. The women with whom I have had the privilege to work on this project were complicated, strong, resilient, caring, determined, and funny. They were mothers, daughters, sisters, aunts, cousins, nieces, girlfriends, wives, and friends. They celebrated successes, such as earning GEDs and high school diplomas, completing drug treatment programs, and completing probation and parole. They found ways to keep moving forward after setbacks, such as relapsing, losing jobs, and being told to leave recovery homes. They survived multiple types of intersecting violence and employed creative strategies in their struggles to maintain sobriety, secure employment and housing, leave behind the criminal legal system for good, and ultimately turn their lives around. They had loud voices that they wanted people not just to hear, but also from which to learn. Scholars often write and talk about criminalized women in terms of numbers: incarceration rates, recidivism rates, the percentage who have experienced violence, and numbers who have lost their children. Through their words and photographs, the women I met while completing this project demand that we look beyond these statistics and take the time to deeply understand what it means for women to be entangled in the criminal legal system and how they work to survive that system.

2

"They Just Look at Us Like We Ain't Nobody and We Don't Have Rights"

The Violence of Incarceration

From the first time we met, Tinybig was eager to discuss her extensive experiences with the criminal legal system. At age 51, the Afro Native American Indian woman and mother of three adult children had been incarcerated five times and arrested more than 50 times. Drug use and poverty had kept her entangled in the system. When we met at Starting Again, a recovery home on Chicago's west side, Tinybig had been out of prison for just under two months, having served three and a half years for forgery. In addition to welcoming the opportunity to talk about her involvement with the criminal legal system, Tinybig was excited about the photography aspect of this project. She took photographs for two of our four interviews, going out of her way to capture the exact images she wanted to help tell her story. She even made a special trip to 26th Street and California Avenue in Chicago, the location of Cook County Jail and the George N. Leighton Criminal Courthouse, to take multiple photographs documenting different views of the expansive structure.[1]

Tinybig intended to take a particular photograph: the Bluebird bus that transports convicted women from Cook County Jail to one of Illinois's women's prisons. She missed the bus but took a series of photographs that elicited her reflections on how it felt to be detained at Cook County Jail. Her photograph of the intersection of 26th Street and Sacramento Avenue, showing the northwest corner of the complex, prompted Tinybig to recall what it was like to first arrive at the jail, being transported there from the police station where she had been held immediately following her arrest (figure 2). Looking at the photograph, Tinybig explained that on the other side of the building:

> It's a driveway . . . it's an openin' right there where the trucks or the paddy wagons . . . go in, but this building's in the back where you go in, and you go down under the

FIGURE 2. A spooky place (Photo credit: Tinybig).

ground, and then you come up through that back . . . Ooh! That's a spooky place . . .
It just has an atmosphere like somebody dead. And it makes you think . . . if you're
gonna be here for a while.

Arriving at Cook County Jail in this way was a pivotal moment. More often
than not, it marked the beginning of a long period of pretrial detention that
likely would end in imprisonment. In Tinybig's experience, receiving an I-Bond,
which would allow her to be released on her own recognizance without paying
any money to the court, was unlikely. Rather, bond often was set at an amount
she could not afford to pay, ensuring she would be detained without having been
convicted of anything. In other words, she would be detained for being poor.[2] In
the span of just hours, Tinybig transitioned from being free to being a detained
person with few if any rights.

Tinybig continued reflecting on the photograph and described the distinct
feeling associated with entering the jail via the driveway that leads beneath the
building in contrast to being taken into custody from the courtroom. She explained:

It's . . . just an eerie feeling . . . I've been to the court and got taken out of court and
had to spend a couple of weeks [in jail], but it didn't feel like it feels comin' in [via
the driveway], because it looks like, you know, like they said the pigs have been goin'
to slaughter, I'm gonna just affiliate it with that. It's like you're goin' to literally have

somethin' happen to you! And you are . . . And then the horrific aura . . . of going through the tunnels to get over to the different divisions that you end up in . . . [and to] receiving. Down under there, it is just, them tunnels . . . They need to change 'em.

Tinybig's vivid description was instructive in at least two noteworthy ways. First, her analogy "pigs . . . goin' to slaughter" communicated the dehumanizing nature of pretrial detention. Tinybig and the other detained people whom the police led down the ramp were less like people and more like "pigs" to be processed by a system that had no regard for their lives. She described the hopelessness and lack of control that accompanied arrest and pretrial detention. She only could brace herself for what would come based on the decisions and actions of people like police officers, correctional officers, prosecutors, and judges who, with the state's backing, now had complete control over her life.

Second, Tinybig's deliberate language communicated the violence of the criminalization process. Words like "spooky," "dead," "slaughter," "eerie," and "horrific" painted arrest, detention, and prosecution as terrifying events that exposed women to much more than simply a legal process. Her words resonated with those of ethnic studies scholar Dylan Rodríguez and English and American studies scholar Caleb Smith, who analyze incarceration as a type of social and civil death. Smith, for instance, describes prison as "a dungeon-tomb whose inmates are not subjects at all but human lives divested of subjectivity, of humanity itself, persisting as ghosts or monsters in a carceral living death."[3] The reflections of Tinybig and many of the women who participated in this project introduced a gendered emphasis to the analysis of incarceration as social or civil death. Criminalization was a life-altering, deeply traumatizing process that exacerbated the violence and abuse most women already had endured before encountering the police and entering Cook County Jail.

In this chapter, I examine how detention and incarceration attacked women at the level of identity.[4] Women's experiences resonated with the long history of scholarship that assesses the "pains of imprisonment" associated with the many deprivations of incarceration.[5] Their experiences also highlighted the relationship between violence and dehumanization. Violence—whether actions by individual correctional officers or the cumulative hostile environment created by policies and procedures—had more far-reaching effects than just attempting to control women's behavior and maintain the so-called security of the correctional institution. By foregrounding the gendered dynamics of what sociologist Erving Goffman referred to as the "mortification of self," I show how the gendered violence of incarceration stripped away women's sense of self, reducing them to nobodies.[6] This violence was justified by "controlling images" that paint women of color as dangerous threats to social order.[7] It also created an opening for state-supported rehabilitation discourses that promote personal transformation as the solution to incarceration, diverting attention from the structural inequalities that contribute to and become more firmly entrenched by incarceration.

THE GENDERED VIOLENCE OF INCARCERATION

In his classic book *Asylums: Essays on the Social Situation of Mental Patients and Other Inmates*, Goffman analyzed how "total institutions" not only imprison the body, but also systematically break down an individual's identity. Goffman defined a "total institution" as "a place of residence and work where a large number of like-situated individuals, cut off from the wider society for an appreciable period of time, together lead an enclosed, formally administered round of life."[8] Psychiatric hospitals, jails, prisons, and the military are quintessential examples of total institutions. Goffman developed the concept of "mortification of the self" to explain what happens to individuals as they become institutionalized. Upon admission, the person "begins a series of abasements, degradations, humiliations, and profanations of the self."[9] An incarcerated person, for instance, receives an inmate identification number that takes the place of their name, is stripped of their clothing and belongings, and receives a state-issued uniform to wear for the duration of their incarceration.[10] The total institution cuts individuals off from their lives, obligations, and relationships that exist outside of the institution and, with that, their sense of identity prior to containment.[11]

Importantly, this mortification process does not imply an abuse of power or unethical behavior on the part of staff members working in the total institution. Rather, the institution's routine procedures and environment target the individual's sense of self, replacing their previous autonomous identity with an identity subject to institutional control. Mortification is "the very premise of the American prison," "neither an accident nor an excess but a fundamental part of the institution's design."[12] Although incarcerated people adapt in myriad ways to the prison's controlling regime, that regime is designed to induce compliance to the new identity label and subsequent deprivations of liberty that criminalization imposes.[13] In short, mortification is a formidable technology of control.

Mortification has a distinctly American character that is intertwined with the Christian, colonialist, and racist origins of the penitentiary in the United States. Late 18th- and early 19th-century penal reformers conceived of the penitentiary as a more humane form of punishment, in contrast to pre-Enlightenment corporal and capital punishment practices. Reformers intended for the complete solitude of the penitentiary, coupled with hard labor and reading of the Bible, to promote deep introspection and remorse.[14] The incarcerated person would endure a "virtual death," shedding the criminal self and being reborn a moral, law-abiding citizen.[15] By and large, this narrative arc, in which mortification was a necessary prerequisite for redemption, was available only to White men. Smith notes, "as the era of the penitentiary's rise was also the era of Indian Removal and of the full-scale plantation, we might better understand these three as mutually constitutive institutions—sometimes opposed, sometimes overlapping—that represented the extremes of captivity and helped to determine the meaning of freedom in the antebellum period."[16] The penitentiary was a critical American institution through which White supremacy was established, and its evolution has helped preserve a racial social hierarchy across generations, particularly as the prison population shifted from majority White to majority people of color and correctional policy shifted from a goal of rehabilitation to containment. Race and colonization are only part of the mortification story, however.

The burgeoning feminist scholarship that has accompanied the steady rise in women's incarceration over the past several decades extensively documents how gender matters—from the pathways that lead to women's incarceration, to the distinct needs and vulnerabilities women face while incarcerated and after release, to an understanding of mortification as a gendered process of psychological and emotional violence.[17] The systematic, ongoing "erosion of self" that jails and prisons impose is strikingly similar to what domestic violence survivors experience in relationships.[18] Years of feminist activism and analysis have established that domestic violence is about power and control. Abusive partners rely on a variety of manipulative, threatening, and violent tactics to establish and maintain power over their partner. Abusive and controlling behavior can escalate to physical and sexual violence, and the ever-present threat of that violence makes the mental and emotional violence that much more effective. Survivors frequently explain that emotional and verbal abuse are just as damaging as, if not more damaging than, physical abuse, in part due to their long-term impact and the way they attack survivors' identities. As survivors become increasingly isolated and dependent upon their partners, their sense of self may begin to mirror the degrading ways their partners view and talk about them and make them feel they caused and deserved the abuse. For the approximately 80 percent of incarcerated women who are survivors of physical or sexual violence, the mortification process they encounter in prison likely feels familiar, as the conditions of imprisonment, particularly the isolation, lack of control, uncertainty, and ongoing threat of physical and sexual violence, parallel the dynamics of domestic violence.[19]

Mortification is just one type of gendered violence women experience while incarcerated. Many routine policies and procedures, such as those related to health care,[20] lack of programming, the coercive nature of available programming,[21] disciplinary measures,[22] contact with loved ones, and the overall conditions of confinement, neglect distinct issues women face and create unique hardships for incarcerated women. These negative consequences are particularly concerning since, in comparison to incarcerated men, incarcerated women have more health problems and more serious medical concerns and are more likely to enter prison with mental health issues or to develop them while incarcerated.[23] In place of therapy, women often receive psychotropic medications that do not address the underlying causes of their mental health issues, but rather make women easier to control for prison staff.[24] Furthermore, the conditions of imprisonment exacerbate existing issues and even cause mental health problems.[25] Indeed, it is questionable whether trauma-informed gender-responsive therapy can even be effective in such a harsh environment that replicates the dynamics of abuse many women endured prior to incarceration.[26]

Additionally, women have distinct health needs that typically are an afterthought or viewed as too costly in comparison to the services men need. Reproductive health care is particularly limited and can be a site of abuse.[27] When giving birth or receiving gynecological services, women may be coerced to undergo sterilization procedures, as was the case in California between 1997 and 2010.[28] Furthermore, doctors can use gynecological exams as an opportunity to sexually assault incarcerated women.[29] Even before the Supreme Court's ruling in *Dobbs v. Jackson Women's Health Organization*, which ended the constitutional right to abortion, accessing abortion services was notoriously difficult for incarcerated pregnant people, in part due to unclear policies and the refusal of prison staff.[30] Reproductive justice scholars and activists anticipate the *Dobbs* decision will severely worsen the availability and quality of reproductive health care available in jails and prisons, making a dire situation even more harmful and in some cases deadly.[31]

The treatment incarcerated women receive when going into labor and giving birth is no better than the so-called care they receive throughout their pregnancy. Incarcerated women routinely are shackled when transported to hospitals to give birth, despite hazards like tripping and falling that shackling causes. Some prison policies even require that women remain shackled to their hospital beds while giving birth. While the First Step Act of 2018 prevents shackling of incarcerated pregnant women in federal facilities, 23 states lack legislation that bans shackling of incarcerated pregnant women. Enforcement of this legislation is uneven, however, as incarcerated women are left to the mercy of prison staff who may or may not choose to follow the law. As reproductive justice scholar Rachel Roth summarizes, "Every dimension of reproductive justice is negatively affected by imprisonment—from access to abortion and basic medical care to maintain one's health and fertility to the ability to form and maintain relationships with one's children."[32]

Perhaps no practice more clearly replicates abusive dynamics than routine strip searches.[33] For the stated purpose of ensuring institutional security, correctional officers can force incarcerated women to submit to a strip search at any time. The practice is extremely degrading and inherently threatening. Journalist Meagan Flynn described the practice as it occurred at Lincoln Correctional Center, a women's prison in Illinois, in March 2011:

> [A] tactical unit armed with batons and shields stormed two women's housing units to round up about 200 handcuffed inmates and march them to a gymnasium. Once in the gym, they stood facing the wall for more than an hour, still unsure why, until the guards started taking groups of four to 10 into the adjoining bathroom and beauty shop. There, they were ordered to strip. Standing shoulder to shoulder, women on their periods were asked to remove their tampons and pads. Some stood bleeding on themselves or the floor. They were ordered to lift their breasts and hair, to cough

and squat, and then, finally, to bend over and spread open their vaginal and anal cavities. The bathroom had no doors and was visible from the gym, and the beauty shop's door was open too, allowing male guards to see the naked prisoners whenever they walked past, or as they deliberately stared at them from afar . . .[34]

goodness

It is difficult to fully comprehend the humiliation, fear, and vulnerability these women experienced. It is even more difficult to justify this practice. The correctional officers were not searching for contraband. There was no imminent threat of violence they were trying to prevent. This incident was a training practice for new cadets. It is difficult to interpret the incident as anything other than state-sanctioned sexual assault.[35]

Strip searches are but one type of sexual violence incarcerated women experience. Decades of research documents widespread sexual assault and harassment by correctional officers, the majority of whom are men.[36] Officers have access to women when they undress, shower, and use bathroom facilities, contributing to the ongoing threat of sexual violence even in the absence of explicit verbal and physical assaults. Officers may abuse their authority by demanding that women provide sexual favors in exchange for access to needed items and services, such as medical care, visits with family, and telephone privileges.[37] Importantly, even when women seem to go along with these requests or sexual advances, federal law stipulates "all sexual contact between prison staff and an inmate is abuse; 'consent' is an irrelevant concept when one person holds tremendous power over the other's life, including the power to reward or retaliate."[38] When women refuse these advances, they face retaliation such as loss of privileges, write-ups for alleged rule violations, and placement in solitary confinement, where they are even more isolated and thus more vulnerable to ongoing abuse.[39] The complete lack of recourse illuminates just how little control incarcerated women have over their own bodies and the pervasive threat of physical violence and sexual violence that structures women's prisons.[40] As prison abolition scholar-activists Angela Y. Davis and Cassandra Shaylor observe, "routine sexual abuse and harassment amount to a veritable climate of terror."[41]

Understanding incarceration as gendered violence situates jails and prisons within a larger framework of inequality and violence that structures the lives of socially marginalized women, particularly Black women and women of color who live in disadvantaged communities. "Women's prisons are located on a continuum of violence that extends from the official practices of the state to the spaces of intimate relationships."[42] Sociologist Beth E. Richie's violence matrix provides a useful theoretical framework to conceptualize this continuum of gender-based violence.[43] The matrix delineates three forms of violence—physical, sexual, and emotional—that occur across three contexts—intimate households, community, and state—and shows how these types and contexts of violence are interconnected. Richie examines multiple examples of state violence, including institutional responses that dismiss and blame women when they seek redress for interpersonal and community-based violence and public policies, like welfare reform, that withdraw support and limit women's autonomy. She shows how state violence exacerbates and justifies the vulnerability and abuse women experience in their homes and communities. Across contexts, gendered violence reflects an overarching discourse that dehumanizes socially marginalized women, particularly criminalized women.

JUSTIFYING STATE VIOLENCE

Reflecting on the gendered violence of incarceration raises the question of why such widespread abuse persists. One line of reasoning focuses on the understanding that incarcerated people give up a certain degree of their rights. Prison is not supposed to be fun or easy. People generally acknowledge that a host of deprivations will and even should accompany the deprivation of liberty that is the stated criminal sanction. Indeed, various "pains of imprisonment" are an unstated though expected part of the prison sentence. While important, this reasoning is incomplete. The gendered violence, particularly the sexual abuse, incarcerated women endure exceeds a degree of punishment even the most ardent tough-on-crime supporter could find reasonable. This violence taps into deeply embedded social-historical discourses that position some women as not real women and thus deserving of whatever violence they experience. These gendered discourses are structured by race and class. The feminine ideal is attainable to a select group of women who possess the social privileges of Whiteness, financial security, heterosexuality, and citizenship. Women who lack this social privilege are precluded access to this ideal and its associated benefits, such as support for mothering and protection from violence. These "Other" women provide the oppositional femininity against which White femininity is constructed.[44]

A variety of controlling images highlight the ways these "Other" women are not real women. As sociologist Patricia Hill Collins has theorized, controlling images are deeply engrained cultural tropes that mark women of color as inherently deviant and justify systems of inequality and oppression. Rooted in chattel slavery and colonization, controlling images define Black, Native American, and immigrant women of color as dirty, impure, hypersexual, and inherently rapeable. These controlling images provide "ideological justifications" for sexual violence against Black women and women of color and contribute to ongoing vulnerability to interpersonal and state violence, as well as to intrusive and punitive policies that paint marginalized women as threats to social stability.[45] These policies seek to regulate nearly every aspect of women of color's lives, including sexuality, mothering, morality, and work.[46]

The population of incarcerated women in the United States today consists largely of these "Other" women.[47] Based on their race, class, and criminalization, these women are dismissed as not real women. Beyond the rights they forfeit as a result of their convictions, controlling images of dangerous, deviant women deny their claims to basic human protections. The gendered violence of incarceration is neither an accident nor an anomaly produced by a few "bad apples" who abuse their authority. It is embedded in the structure of the prison and justified by the controlling images that divert attention away from the social conditions that funnel women into the criminal legal system and the jail and prison conditions that further traumatize women. The questions I take up for the remainder of this chapter are how do these racist gender ideologies shape criminalized women's detention and incarceration experiences and what impact does the gendered violence of incarceration have on women's identities.

There is an inherent risk in writing about women's violent experiences of incarceration, mainly the risk of reducing women to these violent acts. Rather than recognize women's full humanity, there can be a tendency to understand them primarily as victims or simply as points of evidence that illustrate a larger problem. The shocking and horrifying nature of this violence can reify it, creating distance between the reader and the women who experienced it, rather than a sense of connection. In short, there is the potential to dehumanize women in a similar way the prison dehumanizes.[48] There also is a risk in not confronting this violence, however, namely the risk of normalizing it to the point it becomes an unremarkable and thus acceptable part of imprisonment. There is a power in witnessing injustice and atrocities. Witnessing can foster connection and understanding, which are necessary precursors to push for social change that disrupts and uproots rather than simply softens the harsh edges of inherently dehumanizing systems.[49]

This book's remaining chapters focus on women's identity work. I devote this chapter to an unflinching examination of gendered violence, because it provides necessary context for understanding the full scope of what criminalization means for women and the subsequent identity work they undertake. As such, I foreground this violence before moving on to "motherhood, pleasure, friendship,"[50] joy, and resilience, topics that, as English language and literature scholar Megan Sweeney notes, too often remain at the analytic edges of scholarship regarding criminalized women. To recognize criminalized women's full humanity, we cannot turn away from the violence they experience. We also cannot allow that violence to define them. The examples shared here represent one part of women's complex lives and identities. I ask readers to keep these considerations in mind while reading this chapter.

HOSTILE ENVIRONMENTS

In total, women described jail and prison as hostile environments characterized by unsanitary conditions and a general lack of attention to women's well-being. Cook County Jail is particularly notorious for its abusive environment, as evidenced by multiple consent decrees and a string of class action lawsuits on behalf of people currently and formerly detained there.[51] In 2008, the United States Department of Justice's Civil Rights Division released findings from its 17-month investigation into Cook County Jail. Citing physical abuse by correctional officers, inadequate health care, medical neglect, withholding of mental health medication, and poor physical conditions, the report concluded "the jail had systematically violated the constitutional rights of inmates."[52] In November 2010, men and women who had been subjected to illegal strip searches at the jail won a $55 million settlement.[53] In February 2014, the MacArthur Justice Center at Northwestern University filed a proposed class action lawsuit alleging a culture of "sadistic violence and brutality" at Cook County Jail. The Center alleged that physical abuse by correctional officers was a significant factor contributing to the overall culture of violence, reflecting "systemic problems that have remained unchecked at the highest levels of Cook County government."[54] This well-documented history of pervasive and persistent abuse at Cook County Jail reflects an organizational logic in which intimidation and violence are common. As such, it was not surprising that women recalled similar experiences.

Given the inhumane conditions in Cook County Jail, women described a sense of desperation to get out of the facility. Some recalled how they agreed to plea deals just to get out, even when they did not fully understand the terms of the plea, felt they would get a better offer if they could just wait a little longer, or wanted to fight their cases. Stacey Williams, a 41-year-old African American woman, cited the overall horrible living conditions, as well as needing to end the limbo of being in jail, as reasons she accepted her plea. She explained, "I was ready to go to prison and get this over with. When you go to prison, you know, you got a out date. You know when you're goin' home. In the County, you're sittin' there waitin' on court dates after court dates. You don't want to deal with that."

Women typically described prison as a relatively better environment than jail, but they continued to endure dehumanizing treatment and living conditions once they reached prison. Moon, a 40-year-old African American woman, explained that people need therapy after they are released just to deal with the experience of incarceration. "I don't care how long you was [in], it's traumatic mentally, you know. Even though you make it back out sane, you still have like . . . this exterior or this . . . mask on, you know." Moon elaborated, "I felt like prison wasn't helpin' me. It don't better you. It doesn't. It makes you angry and resentful . . . Prison is like nobody cares . . . it's like a whole other world inside of a world. Nobody listens to you." Moon suggested prison was something she survived. She also focused on the dehumanizing impact of incarceration, highlighting loneliness, cold, hunger, and not being heard. Moon described a deep sense of alienation, like she was locked away in a completely different world, forgotten, and continuously reminded that nobody cared about her. Her concerns reflected basic physical, emotional, and psychological human needs. The cumulative denial of these basic needs amounted to trauma, leaving Moon disconnected not only from society, but also from herself. Prison changed her. In order to survive the trauma of incarceration, Moon put on an "exterior" or a "mask." Those outward changes reflected internal changes,

FIGURE 3. Bus ride to work (Photo credit: Chicken Wing).

what Moon referred to as mental trauma, that persisted even after "you make it back out." The mask was still on, and Moon needed time and support to heal from the trauma of incarceration.[55]

Chicken Wing, a 55-year-old Black woman, also used the language of survival and putting on a mask to describe the mental and emotional toll of spending 21 years in prison. Like Moon, she noted the impact of incarceration on her identity. This reflection was prompted by a photograph Chicken Wing took of a Chicago Transportation Authority (CTA) bus to represent her long ride to work (figure 3). Even though the "L" (shorthand for Chicago's elevated train system) would get her to work more quickly, she preferred the 90-minute bus ride because of how it made her feel. She explained, "I enjoy lookin' out the window at people. I just enjoy life . . . The long ride . . . Freedom. Can't take that. You can't buy that." She quickly clarified her comment, noting she still was adjusting:

> I'm learnin' how to talk to people, because I'm just gettin' out. I been had a guard up for 20 years . . . I had to keep a false flag up all the time, you know what I'm sayin'? I had to pretend all the time . . . I had to put a mask up. I couldn't be myself, you know, 'cause I don't want to get hurt . . . I keep people away from me. I keep a guard up at all time. And now I'm just . . . tryin' to let that guard go down, you know what I'm sayin'? I'm tryin' to trust people more. I'm tryin' to talk to people more gentler. You know what I'm sayin'? 'Cause . . . you got to survive in prison. You can't be no punk.

You know. You can't be cryin' and all that. You know, you got to hold them emotions inside, you know, you can't let that side of you show!

Like Moon, Chicken Wing adopted a hard exterior to survive prison's hostile, dehumanizing environment. Both women recognized those survival strategies did not serve them well back in society.[56] Perhaps even more importantly, both women indicated how these strategies changed who they were, such that part of their lives after prison included figuring out how to become the people they wanted to be. They invoked a symbolic-interactionist understanding of identity that posits the self only exists through social interaction and is structured by the different social settings people inhabit, as well as the different social roles people take on and off over the course of their lives.[57]

MEDICAL NEGLECT

Some women expressed gratitude for the health care services they received in prison and credited doctors with identifying health issues and providing treatment they likely would not have received otherwise. Alongside this gratitude, women also noted the poor quality and limited assistance these services sometimes offered.[58] Even when women could afford the five-dollar cost of a health care visit,[59] correctional officers could facilitate or hinder their ability to receive an appointment. Tinybig, for instance, said the health care she received in prison was "awesome," but "the procedure to get there is crazy as hell." She explained that submitting a request slip to see a doctor would first lead to an appointment with a nurse, who would determine if a doctor's appointment was necessary. Tinybig elaborated:

> You have to pay five dollars to see the nurse. And if that nurse don't think it's severe enough, you won't see no doctor. She'll give you some Tylenol and tell you, "OK, see if this'll work." That's five dollars. So if it don't go away, you gotta put in another request, see the nurse again, five more dollars. Now since it didn't go away and you came the first time maybe she'll sign you up to see the doctor. So you see, it's like a three-week process.

Tinybig gave voice to a widespread problem, as incarcerated people commonly are denied health care or subjected to long waits to see a doctor, in part due to suspicion they are faking their health concern. Incarcerated people often delay or forgo medical treatment due to costly fees they cannot afford. When they finally do access care, they frequently are denied treatment that addresses root causes in favor of treating symptoms, and they may have to undergo extreme medical interventions that could have been prevented had they received medical care sooner.[60]

Chunky, a 56-year-old Black woman who had been imprisoned nine times, recalled having to wait to receive treatment for a stomach ulcer because her supervisor in the kitchen claimed she was faking being sick to get out of work. Chunky recalled, "My stomach was tore up . . . I had felt like shit. I'm talkin' about felt like razor blades was in my stomach, my stomach hurt me so bad." By the time she saw a doctor, her "stool was completely black," and she spent three days in the prison infirmary. She explained that the private health care company with whom the state contracted to provide health care services for the Illinois Department of Corrections (IDOC) had to approve all medical tests and procedures. A provider told Chunky, "We can put you in for a test to see about your stomach, but you're gettin' ready to go home." The implication was that after her release, the state no longer would be responsible for Chunky's medical care, so it was not worth the state providing her with anything more than temporary care to address the immediate presenting issue. The prison doctor provided medication that ultimately resolved Chunky's stomach issue. Still, her experience indicated systemic problems with IDOC's health care. Like Tinybig, she made clear how incarcerated women lost precious time and money while navigating the prison health care bureaucracy and multiple gatekeepers, during which their health issues could worsen.

Chunky connected her experience of neglect to other women she knew who did not receive the care they needed while imprisoned and died shortly after their releases.[61] She explained, "A lot of those people do all that time, go on and die. Everybody that I know, just about, that went home died within a year or two." Chunky rattled off the names of three women with whom she had served time who died while incarcerated or shortly after their release and connected their deaths to inadequate health care. Recalling one of these women, she said, "She had cancer . . . They could've did more for her. I heard her on the phone one day, talkin' to her father, she told him 'You, you really need to get to the lawyer and take care of this. 'Cause this is gettin' outrageous.' And I'm quite sure that they got a [law] suit. 'Cause they didn't do nothin' for her. Nothin'. She had stomach cancer—they said it was a spot! And then it turned out to be somethin' else. You know, and they did nothin.'"

Sharon, a 44-year-old African American woman, also discussed the emotional toll of watching other women suffer from medical neglect. She recalled the death of a close friend:

> She always had asthma real bad . . . they said she died from an asthma attack. But what we heard [was] that she was tryin' to tell the officer that she wasn't feelin' well, and they just ignored her and just left the door, and when they came back to her door, she was dead. So, in prison they is so cruel to you. They just look at us like we ain't nobody and we don't have rights. And it's, it's sad to say when you get incarcerated how they treat you. Because we're human, too, we just made a mistake, and I'm pretty sure y'all made mistakes, too. So it's sad when especially with the sick people, they do them so wrong . . . If they would have listened to her I think she would've been still here . . . I think they thought she was faking, and when they came back to the door, she was dead.

Sharon linked her friend's death to a larger analysis of the dehumanizing nature of the prison system. She asserted her friend's and her own humanity despite knowing the criminal label marked her as less than human, leaving her and all of the women with whom she served time vulnerable to neglect and abuse. This undercurrent of vulnerability was a form of emotional violence that structured the incarceration experience and communicated the message to Sharon that she was "nobody." That message was reinforced with every death Sharon witnessed during her six incarcerations. As she recalled, "I saw so many deaths. A lot of people, so many people died when I was in prison."

Frequent deaths contributed to a culture of fear and concern. For instance, Sharon recalled many women dying from brain aneurysms. She frequently had headaches, which made her worry she also had an aneurysm: "I was scared because so many people was dyin' from that down there." Medical neglect is part of the "habitual violence" of prison that impacts more than the individual woman who is denied treatment.[62] "All women are subjected to [punishment] in an environment in which medical neglect is rampant. Many women are forced to watch other women deteriorate and sometimes die, and as a result must live in fear that they or someone they care about will be next."[63] Sharon's concern stemmed, in part, from a larger culture of dehumanization and disregard. Correctional officers had allowed her friend to die alone in her cell from an asthma attack; why should Sharon trust a prison doctor who tried to reassure her she did not need to worry about an aneurysm?

Tinybig shared a story that illustrated how even when women accessed medical treatment in prison, they had limited rights since they were "criminals" first and patients second. She focused on her powerlessness while recounting a problem she had with a correctional officer during her most recent incarceration. When I introduced the idea of "the state" at the beginning of our first interview, Tinybig interjected, "Let me talk about Illinois Department of Corrections, then," meaning "the people that have authorization over our lives when we're incarcerated." She described a time when an officer punished her by placing her in segregation after catching Tinybig "stealing" laundry detergent from the kitchen. After strip searching Tinybig and finding the detergent, the officer loudly explained she had suspected Tinybig of stealing because Tinybig requested sanitary napkins daily due to a medical condition.[64] Tinybig was furious and humiliated that her private medical information was shared publicly for anyone nearby to overhear. She explained:

> Why would you put my medical history out there like that? So that's what my grievance was about, for you to say in front of everybody about me askin' for pads every day. OK, granted I got caught stealin', I own that! I'll take that bad, 'cause that's mine. But there was nobody's business about me askin' you for pads every day, because of my medical history. It doesn't bother me that I have it, but it wasn't nobody else's business to know that I spot and bleed every day . . . She didn't have no reason to do that.

Tinybig did not object to the strip search, which was an expected and common degradation ritual. The lack of privacy and respect for her personal medical information, however, pushed that degradation to an excessive level. The officer violated a right Tinybig thought she still maintained.

Equally insulting to Tinybig was that no prison administrator acknowledged her frustration. Her concerns were dismissed, and it seemed like administrators did not even understand why she was upset. Tinybig filed three separate grievances against the officer for disclosing her medical history, in which she requested not to work under this officer's supervision again. Prison administrators denied each grievance. During our interview, Tinybig pulled out a folder containing paperwork related to the grievances. She read the response to the first one: "According to Food Supervisor [officer's name], your shakedown was a result of reasonable suspicion, which turned out to be true. Professionalism was maintained during and after this time. Also please be advised that offenders are unable to dictate the placement of staff." The response ignored her central request that the officer be reprimanded and instructed to "not discuss offender's medical history with others." Instead, the response reminded Tinybig of her status as an "offender" who was under the authority of prison staff and provided no rationale for how administrators determined the officer maintained "professionalism" during the "shakedown." Tinybig filed two more grievances to stress her point about the officer disclosing her medical information, but authorities dismissed both as "repeat grievances."

Tinybig realized the unfair treatment was just a part of her sentence she had to accept. She commented, "When I allowed myself to enter that institution, I opened myself up for the possibility of anything. And that's just what that is. Once we're inside that institution, even though there are laws, rules, rulebooks, regulations, all this stuff in order, everybody don't follow them." This realization recalled Tinybig's photograph (figure 2) of the underground entrance to Cook County Jail and the feeling of "pigs . . . goin' to slaughter." Just as she explained with the photograph, entering the correctional system signaled a dehumanizing transition where women were vulnerable to anything. The officer's behavior, coupled with the lack of response from prison administrators, reaffirmed this message that, as an "offender," there were certain rights Tinybig did not have and inappropriate behaviors by officers she just would have to accept. In fact, higher-ups would deem that treatment "professional," offering no recourse or check on officers' authority.

CORRECTIONAL OFFICERS' ABUSE

At times, correctional officers' treatment of women escalated to verbal harassment and threats, as well as physical violence. The Lioness, a 49-year-old African American woman, discussed a violent encounter she had with a woman correctional officer at Cook County Jail. In doing so, she provided a clear example of the intersections of gendered violence across the contexts of intimate households and the state.[65] Prior to her most recent incarceration, the Lioness had been arrested on a violation of probation charge for missing a court date. When she arrived at Cook

County Jail, she was going through withdrawal, which she described as "a state of mind of needing drugs. So I really wasn't in my best thinking." Within the first 24 hours of being at the jail, the Lioness got into an argument with another detained woman, and an officer intervened. The Lioness recalled, "I guess the guard, she was irritated, it was a holiday, and she didn't want to be there or whatever. And she kept cussin' me out . . . They're *very* mean at Cook County. I mean, seriously . . . they talk to you and calls us 'bitches' and 'whores,' I mean, serious. Well, anyway, she put this glove on, and she choked me, and I defended myself." When I pressed her for more specifics on the officer's behavior, the Lioness responded, "She choked me. That was enough. I mean, that was enough, you know, because I had been raped and brutally sodomized before, and so I was very on the defensive . . . I still have bad memories, things that happened that's not too pleasant, so of course I might react defensive at times." The Lioness could not recall exactly how she had defended herself. In addition to being in the midst of withdrawal, she explained, "it was just a heated time. I don't remember all that I did. But I fought her back." Once the officer subdued the Lioness, she handcuffed her in a chair, such that the Lioness was bent forward at the waist, with her hands cuffed beneath her knees, behind her calves. She estimated she remained this way, isolated in a holding cell, for about an hour and a half. During that time, other officers stopped by and "taunted" her, saying things like, "'If that had of been me, I would have beat you!' . . . I mean, it happens . . . you have people that's in high places, in authority, like Cook County Sheriffs that just have bad attitudes, you know, so. Yeah, they came in there and they was talkin' about . . . if it was them, what they would've did to me. They called me names."

The Lioness experienced layers of gendered violence in just this one assault and its immediate aftermath. Before physically laying hands on the Lioness, the officer used gendered, sexually violent insults (e.g., "bitch" and "whore") to establish her dominance and gain control of the moment. The officer then escalated from verbal to physical abuse that, regardless of the officer's intent, the Lioness experienced as sexually threatening. Given the Lioness's history of sexual violence, which began in her childhood and continued throughout adulthood, the officer's choking and physical restraint were distinct gendered forms of violence that recalled the multiple times the Lioness had been vulnerable to violence throughout her life. Although the officer was a woman, in contrast to the men who had been the perpetrators of the Lioness's past violence, the officer's actions reflected the jail's hypermasculine, violent organizational culture.[66] As an authority figure within that culture, she possessed the power to exert force over the Lioness in a way that evoked the powerlessness she experienced during past sexual assaults by men. The retraumatizing physical assault perpetrated by this officer linked the Lioness's current situation as a detained woman, with no recognized rights to safety and bodily autonomy and with severely curtailed power, to past assaults rooted in the same power dynamics.[67] Entering jail is a disorienting experience that many people experience as a crisis. Given that the Lioness had just arrived at jail, was going through withdrawal and not thinking clearly, and carried the memories of years of sexual violence in her mind and body, it is no wonder she defended herself against an officer who verbally and physically assaulted her.

The aftermath of the assault was equally troubling and evoked controlling images that paint Black women as animalistic.[68] Once restrained, the Lioness was held in a cage and put on display like an animal in a zoo. The officers who strolled by to get a look at the aggressive "inmate" who dared to fight back took on the role of spectators, complete with their voyeuristic looks and taunts. As a criminalized, drug-using, poor Black woman, the Lioness sat at the intersection of multiple systems of oppression. Yet, the officers viewed her as a threat that needed to be contained. The controlling image of the Sapphire, "Black women . . . conceived of as 'superwomen,' aggressive and prone to violence, requiring swift and forceful submission," loomed large, providing ideological justification for this harsh discipline.[69]

Like the long-lasting impact of gendered violence women experience in intimate households, the Lioness continued to deal with the consequences of defending herself against this officer. She was charged with aggravated battery and served two years in prison. As she explained, "So that was a bad decision I made, and I paid for it for two years." At the time of our interviews, she still was paying for that decision. The aggravated battery conviction meant the Lioness had another violent felony on her background, which subjected her to multiple collateral consequences.[70] For instance, the conviction already had prevented her from qualifying for a housing program. The rejection hit the Lioness particularly hard: "They said my background was unacceptable. You know, and when I first got it [the rejection notice], it was like they were sayin' I was unacceptable." The housing denial impacted the Lioness at the level of identity, as she perceived the rejection as a judgment of her character. She anticipated she never would be able to completely rid herself of the stigma associated with the violent felony conviction and explained, "It makes a statement that is not positive. It's negative. I'm always going to receive some negativity, some judgmental people." The Lioness would pay for defending herself against a violent correctional officer for the rest of her life. This outcome was particularly troubling considering the reason the Lioness had been in jail was for missing a court date, a minor, nonviolent violation of probation. In the violent context of the jail, she picked up a much more serious charge that permanently labeled her a "violent offender."[71]

Ann, a 47-year-old Caucasian woman, also discussed how correctional officers contributed to an overall hostile environment in Cook County Jail. She recalled how one officer repeatedly harassed her: "She always threatened she was gonna handcuff me to the gate and beat the shit outta me. And if I tried to run she'd get me for an escape." The officer would instruct Ann to take the garbage to an outside dumpster. Ann would refuse out of fear the officer was using the work assignment as an excuse to get her alone outside, where Ann would be particularly vulnerable out of sight from the other detained women. As Ann pointed out, if she tried to run, the officer could say she tried to escape, which could result in a prison sentence. The officer also tried to coax Ann onto elevators, saying Ann had to clean them as part of her work assignment. Again, Ann refused because "she had me scared, I wasn't goin' in that elevator with her."[72] Ann also worried that if she entered the elevator first, the officer would push the button so that Ann would be on the moving elevator alone, allowing the officer to allege Ann had tried to escape. In addition to these direct threats, officers also created an unsafe environment through their responses to women's interpersonal conflicts. As Ann explained, "A lot of fights break out, and the guards say they break it up quick, [but] they don't . . . if they like you, and you're in a fight, they'll protect you. But if . . . you're getting the best of the other one, they will back up and let you just dog walk that person. Beat 'em down bad before they break it up."

The officers' absolute power contributed to women's overall vulnerability, which mirrored the past violence women survived, largely at the hands of men partners and community members. The constant threat of violence and resulting worry and stress that came through in Ann's recollections were strikingly similar to the ways domestic violence survivors describe their home environments.[73] Regardless of the officers' gender, their actions within the bounds of the jail's organizational logic paralleled the gendered power dynamics women experienced in past abusive relationships and situations of community violence.

GIVING BIRTH WHILE INCARCERATED

Women's accounts of giving birth while incarcerated illustrated further dehumanizing treatment and resonated with scholarship that documents pregnancy as another site of punishment within the carceral system. In addition to inadequate prenatal care, common aspects of incarceration, such as diets that lack nutritional value, physical confinement, handcuffing, and shackling, jeopardize the well-being of both mother and unborn child.[74] Correctional officers typically are the first responders when incarcerated women suspect something is wrong with their pregnancy or go into labor, yet officers often downplay or ignore women's concerns altogether. Whether rooted in lack of appropriate medical training or lack of caring, this medical neglect results in miscarriages, stillbirths, and women giving birth alone inside their cells.[75]

Four women talked in detail about their experiences of giving birth while incarcerated, two of whom had been shackled during labor. In 1999, Illinois became the first state in the country to ban the shackling of women during labor, but officials have routinely violated the ban since its passage.[76] Corrine, a 63-year-old African American woman, recalled giving birth to her daughter while incarcerated at a women's prison in Illinois prior to 1999. By the time of our interviews, Corrine was in a very different place. Twelve years had passed since her last incarceration. She had since earned her master of social work degree and devoted her career to helping other women overcome the very same challenges she had faced, such as healing from trauma, ending drug use and entanglement with the criminal legal system, and reestablishing relationships with children. Each time I met with Corrine, I was struck by her deeply caring nature. She welcomed me into her home for each of our three interviews and made sure I was comfortable. She showed me family photo albums, and our conversations frequently returned to the topic of her family, particularly her love for her children and grandchildren. Her kindness and gentleness contrasted sharply with the hardships and outright violence she had experienced throughout her life.

Giving birth while shackled was one traumatic experience that still weighed heavily on Corrine. She recalled that although she had been transported from prison to a local hospital when she went into labor, she did not receive adequate medical care. "It was the first time I was forced to have . . . natural birth. Meaning that I was given nothing . . . No epidural, no pain medicine, no nothing," Corrine said. "And of course I was shackled . . . it was just one of the most horrific experiences. It liked to rip me. I felt like it just ripped me apart. I still have a tear that wasn't properly repaired in my vaginal area from that birth." In addition to the permanent physical damage she endured, Corrine also carried permanent mental and emotional scars that were caused by the hospital staff's dismissive treatment. She recalled, "I think I was seen as a prisoner, treated as a prisoner, treated as someone that did not have rights. Treated as someone [who] did not even deserve to be having a baby. This is how I felt giving that birth." When I asked who gave that message to her, Corrine referred to the nurses. She further explained she had been an "IV [intravenous] drug user" at the time, which she had felt was the "worst [kind] of an addict." Between the shackle on her ankle and the scars from her drug use, Corrine felt she was "degraded" in the nurses' eyes. She elaborated, "Well, I don't even know if the shackle, because that was a normal procedure back then, and I had had my first son as a juvenile in [a juvenile detention facility]. So that had been a pretty normal thing as for the shackle. I guess just . . . I'm thinkin' it was more so because of just the lack of empathy, the lack, I mean, it was just like I was a nobody."

Being shackled during childbirth was a normalized practice of physical and emotional state violence. The emotional and physical violence inflicted by hospital staff, however, was remarkable. Like Tinybig's acceptance of the strip search as routine, Corrine expected the shackle. Also like Tinybig, it was the excessive disregard for Corrine's rights and humanity that was so damaging, hurtful, and memorable. The hospital staff's treatment could not be justified, however weakly, as a required security measure. Their treatment felt targeted and personal, as it stripped away any remaining positive sense of self that Corrine possessed and denied any claim to motherhood. Corrine learned the same lesson Sharon articulated when recalling her friend's death after officers failed to respond to her pleas for medical assistance: incarcerated women were nobodies without any rights.

Corrine shared a deeper analysis about the intersection of criminalization, misogyny, and racism. When I asked Corrine if anything in particular about the nurses' or doctors' treatment stood out to her, she shared the following memory:

> *Corrine:* It's just this one little piece, Chez, I'll never forget because of the pain that I was enduring. I remember scooting almost up to the head of the bed. And I believe the head [of the baby] was already starting to come out. 'Cause like I can feel it like yesterday, and I remember scooting all the way to the head of the bed, and I remember them standing around doing absolutely nothing and telling me [Corrine uses a harsh, emotionless, monotone voice], "When you come down in the bed, we'll finish delivering this baby. You wanna come down and scoot in the bed so we can get this baby out?" I remember that voice right there . . .
>
> *CR:* It sounds like you weren't treated as a person, let alone a woman in labor.
>
> *Corrine:* No, you can feel the discrimination. You felt the prejudice, you felt the discrimination and all of that back then.
>
> *CR:* From being a prisoner or from more?
>
> *Corrine:* From being a prisoner and also I felt from being just Black. Yeah. I, 'cause, you know, I grew up, I'm a '50s baby, and I never lived in the South so my experience, I saw it on TV, and I never felt that I was impacted or affected by what happened to my generations or back then. And it took me as far as like pursuing my education and even looking back to feel what the impact of how all of that discrimination still affects me as a person today. Because back then I just kind of flowed through . . . I just never felt the impact of all of the racial biases and the prejudice and discrimination just didn't, it was like it happened to them but it did not apply to me. And it took me getting a little bit older to feel the impact and how I was discriminated to as a person, being a drug addict and being a felon. So now I've even added to my circumstances, so it was like I just felt entrapped with no way out for so long.

Corrine adeptly used an intersectional lens to situate her personal experience within a larger history of racism and gendered state violence. She recognized more than her prisoner identity shaped her interactions with the hospital staff. Her Blackness also did. Corrine exhibited what sociologist W. E. B. Du Bois called double-consciousness, the distinct experience Black Americans have of both knowing themselves and seeing themselves through the eyes of the oppressor.[77] As a Black woman shackled to a hospital bed, Corrine saw herself through the eyes of the nurses and doctors who made clear they viewed her as someone who "did not even deserve to be having a baby." In that moment, she understood she was perceived not as a mother, but as a nobody. Corrine was "entrapped" by the controlling images that have evolved from slavery through present day to deny Black women's legitimate claims to motherhood and justify the hospital's staff's inhumane treatment that lived on as a vivid memory 13 years later.[78]

Ranisha, a 34-year-old Black woman, gave birth to her youngest daughter while detained at Cook County Jail. She did so after the passage of Illinois's legislation that prohibits shackling of incarcerated women during labor. Although she had not been shackled, her experience paralleled Corrine's in notable ways, suggesting the limits of antishackling legislation despite its importance. Ranisha's experience began alone, locked in her jail cell in the medical unit:

> When I went into labor, the officer had left and went on a whole other unit. So my water bag busts, so I'm in the room panickin', beatin' on the door, the nurse don't have a key, and by the time I got downstairs blood is everywhere, and my water bag is busted. It was just, it was a mess . . . I panicked a lot. Because it was like . . . I didn't know if she [her daughter] was gonna come out right then, 'cause the pain was like that strong . . . So, then you had to wait for the ambulance to come to the jail. Then you have to wait for them to check you, and I'm like, "Why do you wanna stick your fingers in me if my water bag is bust?" So, I went through a lot.

The correctional officer's slow response and Ranisha's worry as she waited for medical attention are common experiences for incarcerated pregnant women.[79] Things did not improve when Ranisha reached the hospital. Like Corrine, she recalled the intense pain she experienced, as she initially was denied an epidural: "It was like I laid there in pain for like, almost three full hours. I had to start like actually knockin' stuff over . . . it was painful . . . by the time they gave it to me, it was like 20 minutes after that I had the baby."

Ranisha attributed the differential treatment she received from hospital staff with coming from Cook County Jail. She explained, "By us comin' from jail, they [hospital staff] treat us different. You know, the care is way different . . . if I would've been comin' from outside I wouldn't have to ask . . . 'Could you change my bed?' You know, 'cause I, like, bled all over everything. You know, I just had a baby." As further evidence, she described hospital staff forgetting to order a meal for her and ignoring her requests for sanitary pads. Their dismissive and discriminatory treatment let Ranisha know she was a criminal first and a mother second.

Hospital staff may have been hesitant to administer pain medication since both women's incarcerations were related to drug use.[80] Lynn, a 33-year-old Caucasian woman, had been detained at Cook County Jail for just a few days when she went into labor with her son. She disclosed to hospital staff she had used cocaine and heroin during her pregnancy. Lynn commented, "They wouldn't give me no epidural shot or nothing because of it. I didn't get no Tylenol or nothing. [She laughs, as if in disbelief.] They wouldn't give me no type of medication while I was in labor because they said they didn't want it to counteract with the drugs that I used in the street, but I'm like, you know that was two days ago." Lynn laughed, suggesting she knew better. She interpreted the excuse as a thin disguise for a more judgmental, punitive reason for denying her pain medication. Her Whiteness did not spare her from the harsh judgment that she was a failed mother, revealing the deep moral and cultural ideals embedded in U.S. ideologies about motherhood.[81] Layers of stigma and discrimination regarding gender, criminality, drug use, and race converged to create particularly painful and dehumanizing birthing experiences for Ranisha, Corrine, and Lynn.

Like all women who give birth while incarcerated, Ranisha, Corrine, and Lynn also had to deal with the difficult experience of being separated from their newborn children just hours after giving birth. Lynn recalled how restricted her time with her newborn son was while they remained in the hospital together:

> Lynn: They treated me like dog crap up in there. I didn't get to see my son until the next day. I guess, you know, 'cause he was born with drugs in his system . . . and plus I was incarcerated I guess they felt like I didn't care. You know, like, I wanted to see my son. They didn't bring him to me till like 17 hours later, and I was handcuffed to the bed, and I had to feed him and change him while I was handcuffed to the bed, and, you know, I had to use the, the port-a-pot right next to, I couldn't use the regular bathroom. I couldn't walk to the bathroom 'cause I was chained to the bed, and, I'd have to be, I was supervised with my son at all times. I couldn't have no private time with him. You know, I had to use the bathroom in front of male officers, 'cause I was, they had a officer sittin' with me the, the whole time . . .
>
> CR: Like while you actually gave birth?
>
> Lynn: Yeah. While I gave birth. While I was in labor. While I was in recovery. I was only in the hospital for two days. Then they took me right back [to jail].

When I asked Lynn how this intensive monitoring made her feel, she replied, "violated." Even before her physical separation from her son, hospital staff and the correctional officer made sure Lynn knew she was not trusted as a mother. Her criminal and drug user statuses superseded any claims to motherhood, thereby opening her up to degrading—and even illegal—treatment the staff deemed justified.[82]

Ranisha returned to jail within 24 hours of giving birth to her daughter, whom the Department of Children and Family Services took into custody and placed in a foster home. She described holding her newborn daughter for the first time: "Actually I had like detached myself because I knew that I was going back to jail. So I really didn't wanna, when I went to the nursery before I left, I remember seeing her laying there and I'm like, you know, 'This is a bunch of bullshit.' And, you know, having to go back to jail and just sit around and look, and you know, mind wandering, and it's crazy." Lynn also described the anguish of returning to jail without her newborn son: "I was just like in disbelief . . . I felt like I like lost a part of me . . . 'cause and I wasn't pregnant anymore. I felt I was still . . . but I wasn't. And that's just like all that occupied my mind was like, I have a baby at the hospital, and I'm here. I'm locked up. I can't do nothin'. My mom won't accept no collect calls from me. What am I gonna do?"

Ranisha and Lynn gave voice to the overwhelming set of hardships thousands of incarcerated women face after going through the painful ordeal of giving birth. Women routinely are separated from their newborns and must return to jail or prison within just 24 to 72 hours of giving birth. Upon return, women generally do not receive appropriate postpartum care, including mental health care to help cope with the abrupt separation from their newborn.[83] That separation can have a devastating emotional impact on women and their children. The stress and worry of not knowing who is caring for her newborn or the quality of care her baby is receiving compound the pain of separation. If an incarcerated woman does not have someone who can care for her newborn, Child Protective Services will take the baby into custody, as Ranisha experienced. In these cases, women may never regain custody of their children, thanks to legislation such as the Adoption and Safe Families Act (ASFA) that allows the state to begin the process of terminating parental rights when a child has been in foster care for 15 of the prior 22 months.[84] When an incarcerated woman retains her parental rights through release, the requirements she faces as part of the reunification plan can be unattainable, particularly given common postincarceration challenges, such as finding housing and employment.[85]

The reflections of participants who gave birth while incarcerated revealed childbirth was a site of gendered violence, where the state inflicted physical and emotional pain on women. Rather than treat women as mothers who deserved support throughout labor and time to bond with their newborns, doctors, nurses, and correctional officers continuously reminded women in explicit and subtle ways that they, above all else, were "criminals" and drug users who had forfeited any claim to motherhood. The swift separation from their children solidified that message. Women returned to prison and jail grieving their children and wondering how well they would be cared for, when they would see them again, and, in some cases, where their children ultimately would be placed.

CONCLUSION

Through specific incidents of violence, general neglect, and the pervasive hostility of jail and prison environments, women repeatedly received the message that they were "nobodies" without any rights. Incarceration stripped women not only of their freedom, but also of their identity.[86] By the end of my interviews, I had heard numerous stories illustrating how gendered violence was embedded in the institution of incarceration.[87] Therefore, I initially was surprised by a parallel theme that emerged across interviews, as woman after woman credited prison with saving her life. Specifically, they described arrest and incarceration as God's way of saving them. Although this type of religious redemption narrative, where prison is identified as a necessary turning point that leads to a better life, is well documented in the literature,[88] the juxtaposition of women's recollections of the gendered violence of incarceration with their assertions that prison saved them was striking.

Consider the Lioness's experience of being restrained by the correctional officer in a manner that recalled a previous sexual assault. She concluded her story on a note of critical self-reflection and even gratitude. Referring to the incident and subsequent aggravated battery conviction, she explained, "today I can say it was a foolish thing that happened, but it saved my life, because since I've been . . . incarcerated, I lost a lot of people. People died, and I probably would've still been active in my addiction. I could've, it was a possibility that I might've died. So I look at the bad and think of it as good, because God saved me and gave me a chance. And today I'm a better person." The Lioness conceptualized the violent jail encounter as an unfortunate but necessary turning point in her life, one made possible by God's saving grace.

But how could violence that dehumanizes women, reducing them to "nobodies," also lead to salvation? How was the civil and social death ideology—an ideology that holds mortification as a necessary precursor to redemption and is as old as the penitentiary itself—still alive and well in women's jails and prisons more than 200 years later? Furthermore, given the gendered nature of mortification, how was redemption also a gendered experience? In the next chapter, I examine how women drew upon available drug recovery discourses, specifically the 12 Steps of Alcoholics Anonymous and Narcotics Anonymous, to resolve this tension between their critiques of the gendered violence of incarceration and their gratitude that God had saved their lives by placing them in such a dehumanizing, hostile environment.

3

"You Cannot Fight No Addiction without God First"

The Permanent Moral Judgment of the Criminal-Addict Label

Denise and I sat down for our first interview on a snowy Friday evening at Growing Stronger, the recovery home where she had resided for almost two years. The 45-year-old Black mother of five had a warm, engaging demeanor. Over the month or so leading up to our interview, we had chatted numerous times while I was at Growing Stronger for scheduled interviews. Denise would be hanging out near the front desk or in the living room, swapping stories and laughing with staff and residents. Without fail, she would tease me when I arrived, stating matter-of-factly, "You're here for me, right?" fully knowing I was there to meet with someone else. It was hard to believe this cheerful, confident woman who was a central part of the Growing Stronger community had spent the past 20 years struggling with drug use and caught up in the criminal legal system. Over the course of our three interviews, Denise made clear just how much her life had changed and she had grown since her last arrest nearly three years ago. Her public defender had been confident Denise could beat the case, but it dragged on month after month, and Denise was eager to get out of Cook County Jail. She eventually pleaded guilty to possession with intent to deliver, even though it meant having a third felony conviction on her record. A judge sentenced Denise to two and a half years of intense probation, which required her to meet weekly with her probation officer, "drop" weekly (provide a urine sample for drug screening), and attend a monthly court date so a judge could monitor her progress. After Denise relapsed and had a "dirty drop" (a positive drug screening), she had to complete a residential drug treatment program, after which she moved into Growing Stronger.

At her monthly court dates, Denise repeatedly asked the judge to downgrade her to regular probation, which would have significantly reduced the surveillance she faced. Judge Hopkins refused each request. While these denials made Denise "boiling mad," by the end of her probation, she was grateful for the judge's strict approach. Denise recalled the day she successfully completed her probation. By that time, Judge Hopkins had transferred to another courtroom, so Denise had to seek her out to share the good news. Denise explained how she entered the judge's new courtroom and asked the sheriff's officer stationed in the seating area if she could speak with the judge. Judge Hopkins welcomed her into the main courtroom. Denise continued:

> So I went in there and I stood in front of her and I said, "Judge Hopkins . . . I'm here today because I completed my probation . . . So it's terminated satisfactory . . . And I want to tell you that I thought that you was really bein' hard on me . . . and I was really angry, but once things . . . start comin' into place, I realized that you cared more about my future than I did . . . I know you probably have never had a person come back and thank you . . . but I made it my business to thank you because I am truly grateful. God worked through you to help me." And she came . . . out of her seat, and she said, "You gonna make me mess up my mascara." And she started cryin', and she hugged me. And the state's attorney and everybody started clappin'. And she said, "Denise, I'm so proud of you. Stay on the right path." And I said, "I will."

While the specific details of this touching moment were unique, Denise's story shared several components with the narratives other women told about their paths into and out of prison.

Denise explained her journey of personal transformation, from resentment and anger about her sentence to acceptance of the drug treatment she had to complete and the surveillance measures she experienced. Additionally, Denise grew to understand Judge Hopkins's tough love approach as God's work. Denise drew on her faith to make sense of what she initially thought was Judge Hopkins's unfair treatment, and she came to believe the judge was hard on her because she cared for her. Beyond just completing her probation, Denise publicly verbalized her changed character and earned the state's recognition of her rehabilitated identity, as evidenced by the state's attorney's applause and the judge's hug, tears, and praise.

Although Denise successfully completed her probation, she was not finished with her project of personal transformation or with proving her commitment to her new identity. Judge Hopkins reminded her as much with her encouraging though cautionary words, "Stay on the right path." With her response, "I will," Denise pledged to continue this ongoing work. Indeed, she was eager to greet Judge Hopkins several months later when the judge visited Growing Stronger. Denise described their reunion:

I went upstairs [to my room]. I got all nice, and . . . when she came, I said, "Judge Hopkins! . . . I'm workin' now." I said I was in school. I said, "I am just on a whole new different path . . . Because I remember you used to always tell me, 'I'm doin' this for your *good*.' And I didn't see it. I was just so angry and resentful . . . But knowin' that somebody really do care about your future . . . you gotta tell 'em thank you." I said, "And I love you! You know, I love you." And she was like, "I'm just proud of you." And it's like every time I heard that she comin', I make sure I be in this house, because [*pause*] I look back where I was and where I'm at today. Man, that lady was Heaven sent.

Each visit Judge Hopkins made to Growing Stronger provided Denise with an opportunity to demonstrate and receive validation of the vigilant work she was doing to maintain her new self. Looking nice, holding employment, attending school, and maintaining her good standing at Growing Stronger provided evidence Denise was staying on the right path. Denise did not need Judge Hopkins's approval in any legal sense. She no longer was under correctional supervision and did not need to worry about the judge revoking her probation. Judge Hopkins's continued approval provided something more meaningful to Denise about her ongoing personal transformation process. It also served as a reminder that while Denise solely was responsible for the work of her personal transformation, it was possible because of God's support. God worked through Judge Hopkins to help Denise.

Like Denise, woman after woman shared their personal transformation processes with me and identified noncriminality, sobriety, spirituality, and morality as the building blocks of these processes. Women were not just fighting to stay out of prison; they also were fighting to prove to themselves and others they were good people who were abiding by God's plan for their lives. These personal transformation narratives revealed how women's experiences with the criminal legal system encompassed much more than punishment for breaking the law. As they became caught up in the system, women engaged identity projects to show just how far they had come in leaving behind their past *criminal-addict* identities.[1] Identity is not just a personal feeling or sense of self. As symbolic interactionists explain, identity is an accomplishment people create through their interactions with other people and institutions.[2] Poststructural theorists examine how subjectivities are constituted through available discourses and state interventions into people's lives.[3] Identity does not just exist; it is created and recreated over time and through different power relations. As women moved through the criminal legal system, they interacted with people, institutions, and ideologies that shaped their sense of self. This relationship was not unilateral, however; women did not passively or even fully internalize the discourses offered by people working within the criminal legal system and its related social service network.[4] Rather, women actively engaged available discourses about recovery from drug use and leaving behind the criminal lifestyle as they crafted *rehabilitated* identities.[5] Their personal transformation processes reflected an assemblage of discourses women refashioned to suit their needs.

The next three chapters focus on women's identity work, particularly the creative ways they negotiated available raced and gendered discourses about criminality, addiction, and dependency in order to claim dignity and find joy. To contextualize that identity work, this chapter examines the dominant discourse women encountered as they moved through the criminal legal system, what I refer to as *the 12-Step logic*. I first explain what the 12-Step logic is and how it operates as an organizing force throughout incarceration and the postincarceration landscape that characterizes recovery and rehabilitation as lifelong interconnected moral and spiritual projects. This logic impacted criminalized women's identity work, providing an organizing narrative through which women made sense of their criminalization and rehabilitation and imagined new possibilities for their lives. I then argue that, following release, women's task was not to stay out of prison or to reintegrate into society, but rather to manage rehabilitated identities under omnipresent surveillance and moral judgment. Resuming drug use or breaking the law did not just introduce the risk of returning to prison. The stakes were much higher, as these behaviors also represented straying from God's path and returning to an immoral identity.[6]

While I critique the 12-Step logic for encouraging an individualistic, depoliticized understanding of the causes of women's imprisonment and the challenges they faced after release, I show how women engaged this logic in innovative ways that allowed them to access resources and support and to recast incarceration as a redemptive experience, while remaining critical of the dehumanizing treatment they endured. As such, the 12-Step logic resolved the tension introduced at the end of the preceding chapter between women's critique of the gendered violence of incarceration and their reframing of criminalization as God's intervention to save their lives.

THE 12-STEP LOGIC

Every woman who participated in this project spent time in jail or prison on charges stemming from their drug or alcohol use either explicitly (e.g., intent to distribute) or implicitly (e.g., retail theft to secure the means to access drugs). As they moved through the criminal legal system, the linking of criminality and addiction intensified. Through jail and prison programming, court-mandated drug treatment, probation and parole conditions, and recovery home programming, women regularly learned that in order to end their entanglement with the criminal legal system, they had to end their drug and alcohol use. Abstinence was easier said than done, however. According to the 12-Step model, which is the dominant addiction framework used throughout the criminal legal system, drug and alcohol issues stem from a problem with the self.[7] Incarceration not only reduced women's identities to that of *criminal* (or a *nobody*), as the previous chapter showed. It affixed *addict* to that identity, thereby relegating women to the distinct interconnected, socially degraded category of *criminal-addict*.[8] Exiting the revolving door of the criminal legal system required women to engage in a lifelong project of personal transformation.[9] Specifically, women had to end their drug use and establish a rehabilitated identity that would replace their *criminal-addict* identity.[10] This focus on creating a new self is a common objective of recovery programs that cater to criminalized low-income and poor women of color.[11] Throughout their incarceration and postincarceration experiences, women encountered the 12-Step logic as *the* mechanism to do just that.

⊛ The 12-Step logic is the fusing of faith- and abstinence-based discourses that instills a lifelong commitment to rehabilitating the self and embracing personal responsibility for one's criminalization, drug use, and recovery. Rooted in Alcoholics Anonymous (AA) and Narcotics Anonymous (NA), the 12-Step logic extends well beyond 12-Step meetings and is deeply embedded throughout the correctional system and U.S. culture.[12] As sociologists Susan Sered and Maureen Norton-Hawk point out, "the Twelve Step model so permeates the entire U.S. correctional-therapeutic system that it is not possible to untangle its impact."[13] Twelve-Step meetings typically are the only drug treatment available in prisons, and regular attendance at 12-Step meetings often is a requirement of parole.[14] Even drug rehabilitation programs that claim to use a trauma-informed or gender-responsive framework draw heavily on the 12-Step logic and often require participants to attend weekly 12-Step meetings. Program staff and participants regularly use 12-Step terminology in formal and informal conversations to explain the causes of women's drug use and incarceration, as well as the cognitive and behavioral changes women must make in order to turn their lives around.[15] Indeed, women seamlessly wove 12-Step ideas and lingo throughout our interviews as they reflected on their lives and plans for the future, and I constantly overheard this language when I was at recovery homes or their events.

The 12-Step model established its dominant position within the U.S. correctional system despite a lack of rigorous scientific research documenting its effectiveness.[16] Research on the impact of AA and NA participation is notoriously difficult given the anonymous nature of membership.[17] The limited research that does exist suggests participation in 12-Step meetings has no demonstrable impact on sobriety.[18] Furthermore, resuming alcohol or drug use is viewed as a failure on the part of the individual, not the 12-Step model. According to 12-Step proponents, people relapse because *they* are not working the program hard enough, not because the program is inadequate.[19] As cultural and literary historian Trysh Travis concludes, "the question of whether, how, and to what degree 12-Step approaches to addiction are effective remains largely unresolved."[20] Yet, this model saturates the criminal legal system, which forces millions of people under correctional supervision to participate in 12-Step programming.

There are several practical and ideological explanations for why the 12-Step model has become so embedded throughout the U.S. correctional system. Practically, 12-Step programs are relatively inexpensive. The model explicitly rejects professionalism and is rooted in self-help and peer support.[21] Members, not licensed drug treatment specialists, facilitate 12-Step meetings, where people share their personal stories of drug use and recovery. The idea is that 12-Step meetings and groups will connect people to a welcoming community that helps them understand their drug and alcohol use and provides collective strength and resolve in managing their ongoing commitment to sobriety.[22] In this decentralized, peer-support model, no one is paid for the work they do as meeting facilitators or group officers.[23] Twelve-Step meetings essentially are a free service jails and prisons can offer by allowing members to come in and run meetings for those who are incarcerated. When state and local money runs out for contracted programming, 12-Step meetings can continue.[24]

The ideological reasons for the 12-Step model's dominance are perhaps even more noteworthy than the practical reasons. Institutionally, the model aligns with shifts in correctional policy and prison management. In a swift backlash to the progressive gains of the 1960s and 1970s, including those won by a robust prisoner rights movement, U.S. correctional policy took a punitive turn, explicitly abandoning rehabilitation as a goal. Decreased state and federal funding for rehabilitative prison programs was accompanied by an increase in Christian volunteers, materials, and programming.[25] In tracing the rise of faith-based prison ministries and programming during the buildup of mass incarceration, religion and gender studies scholar Tanya Erzen explains, "the corps of free labor drawn from conservative, nondenominational, faith-based groups has filled the void created by budget cuts, stepping in to do the work of the state."[26] In her research on incarcerated women's reading practices, English language and literature scholar Megan Sweeney notes a shift in the types of available books in prison libraries. Books offering more critical and radical analyses were replaced with those offering a Christian framing of self-improvement. This shift facilitated a shrinking of narratives available to women, from which they draw to make sense of their lives, selves, and futures.[27] Twelve-Step programming fit right in with this larger trend of increased religious programming and depoliticized prison education.[28]

Beyond prison, the 12-Step model is deeply embedded throughout U.S. society, as its approach resonates with U.S. cultural ideals of individualism, personal responsibility, and morality.[29] While these ideals are endemic to U.S. society,[30] they have taken on added significance in the current neoliberal era, with particularly damaging consequences for socially marginalized groups.[31] One of neoliberalism's hallmarks is its locating of the cause and regulation of social problems within the individual. Scholars refer to this process as "responsibilization."[32] This move absolves the state of responsibility for social problems, framing structural issues like poverty, racism, and patriarchy as peripheral concerns and excuses people cite

blames ppl for their problems instead of acknowledging outside circumstances

to avoid dealing with their personal inadequacies, and subjects individuals to invasive technologies of governance.[33] Following Foucault, these technologies make up the individual as a certain type of person and then induce a particular way of being to create a self-regulating subject. In this way, the state's power is not only repressive, but also productive, as it creates subjectivities. In other words, identity is a technology of governance.[34] In the case of criminalized women, the 12-Step logic is a particular technology of governance that promotes a distinct rehabilitated identity. It subjects women to lifelong performances of morality, spirituality, sobriety, and noncriminality and intersects with race, gender, and class to relegate women to a permanent degraded social status.

As the 12 Steps show, a sober lifestyle encompasses much more than abstinence from alcohol and drugs; it requires a full transformation of one's self.[35] This requirement follows from the 12-Step model's "hybrid"[36] definition of addiction as a "disease or illness . . . [that is] spiritual, mental, and physical."[37] In practice, the medical nature of disease takes a backseat. Managing addiction is less about treating a medical illness and more about morally and spiritually reforming the addict's identity. The 12-Step model is less concerned with identifying the cause of addiction than it is with prescribing rigid guidelines—famously known as the 12 Steps—one must follow to live a sober lifestyle.[38] The 12 Steps are:

1. We admitted we were powerless over alcohol—that our lives had become unmanageable.
2. Came to believe that a Power greater than ourselves could restore us to sanity.
3. Made a decision to turn our will and our lives over to the care of God *as we understood Him.*
4. Made a searching and fearless moral inventory of ourselves.
5. Admitted to God, to ourselves, and to another human being the exact nature of our wrongs.
6. Were entirely ready to have God remove all these defects of character.
7. Humbly asked Him to remove our short-comings.
8. Made a list of all persons we had harmed, and became willing to make amends to them all.
9. Made direct amends to such people wherever possible, except when to do so would injure them or others.
10. Continued to take personal inventory and when we were wrong promptly admitted it.
11. Sought through prayer and meditation to improve our conscious contact with God *as we understood Him,* praying only for knowledge of His will for us and the power to carry that out.
12. Having had a spiritual awakening as the result of these steps, we tried to carry this message to alcoholics, and to practice these principles in all our affairs.[39]

The first three steps stress a lack of willpower and control, situating the cause of the problem squarely in the addict's weak self. In addition to denying the legitimacy of social factors that contribute to substance abuse, this focus is particularly concerning when applied to women survivors of domestic violence and sexual assault. Gender-based violence is a consequence of patriarchy and is rooted in a power imbalance and lack of control. It can be particularly retraumatizing for women to survive interpersonal, community, and state violence, only to encounter a recovery discourse that denies the impact of that violence and again positions women as powerless.[40] Regardless, adoption of the 12-Steps lifestyle necessitates taking on a weak identity and admitting that while one is not personally strong enough to overcome addiction, they are personally responsible for being an addict. Importantly, that weak identity is a permanent identity, not a temporary one through which a person progresses on their way to being recovered.

While the first three steps establish a particular identity, the next nine steps establish a particular way of being. They stress how lifelong commitment to moral and spiritual reform will empower the addict to regulate the weak self. Twelve-Step proponents stress that references to "a Power greater than ourselves" and "God" do not necessarily refer to a Christian God or even a religious being, but a wealth of research traces AA's roots to the Oxford Group, an early 20th-century fundamentalist religious organization.[41] Undeniably, the focus on moral and spiritual reform remains, which resonates with the neoconservative ideology that has gained political influence and strength throughout U.S. culture since the 1970s.[42] The addict is not just weak, but also immoral and bereft spiritually. Recovery is a project of reforming one's morality and achieving a "spiritual awakening" that must be maintained by deepening one's relationship, through prayer and meditation, with a higher power and accepting that higher power's will as one's own. Step 4 makes clear "[t]he notion that people with addictions suffer from a failure of morality to be indexed and removed is fundamental to Alcoholics Anonymous."[43]

A final noteworthy tenet of the 12 Steps is that recovery is a lifelong project. The addict is never recovered. At best, they are recovering. The 12 Steps do not offer a cure to addiction. Instead, they prescribe a new identity and lifestyle one must commit to in perpetuity for the program to work.[44] The recovering addict undergoes "a radical transformation of personal identity that signals a conversion and commitment to a new way of life;" this transformation and commitment make the recovering alcoholic an outsider to society, as their behaviors and values now contrast with the "larger society that continues to sanction the cultural and interactional use of alcohol on a regular basis."[45] For this reason, Travis refers to recovery as a "subculture" since the "term accurately captures the sense of distance from the mainstream shared by many recovering."[46] Being an outsider subjects one to stigma.[47] Stigma takes on added significance when the 12 Steps are applied in a criminal legal context, as the *criminal-addict* inhabits a double-outsider status and experiences the intensified judgment, discrimination, and social marginalization that follow. That outsider status intersects with multiple oppressions criminalized women already experience based on multiple parts of their identity, such as race, class, gender, and sexuality.

The 12-Step model's merging of personal responsibility, immorality, and lack of spiritualty as the core of addiction is the key to its social and cultural dominance today. The model bridges two dominant political ideologies in the United States: neoliberalism, with its promotion of personal responsibility, and neoconservatism, with its promotion of morality and religion, thus making it a powerful governing technology for criminalized people, who overwhelmingly are people of color from socially marginalized and economically disadvantaged communities. The completely embedded nature of the 12-Step model throughout the criminal legal system merges recovery and punishment, creating the distinct subject position of *criminal-addict*. The criminal-addict is not only punished for breaking the law; she is judged as immoral and lacking spirituality and subjected to interventions that will reform both deficits. Regulating the criminal-addict is not a project of creating law-abiding citizens, but rather certain types of subjects who can maintain their freedom through demonstrating their ongoing moral and spiritual rehabilitation. In sum, the 12-Step logic is a distinct governing technology that integrates regulation of the self (the state's productive power) with regulation of the body (the state's repressive power) through surveillance and confinement. If the criminal-addict fails to self-regulate, the state will step in, in a more explicitly coercive way, regulating once again through the violence of incarceration.[48] Through its expansive and invasive reach, the 12-Step logic structures the lives and identities of criminalized women.

A MORAL AND SPIRITUAL TRANSFORMATION

The 12-Step logic provides a narrative structure adherents can use to contrast their recovering identity with their addict identity. As people work the 12 Steps, they chart ways they are different from who they were when they were actively using. The personal improvements they make, such as repaired relationships with loved ones or a sense of inner peace, become markers of their recovery. As they clean up the "wreckage of their pasts," a common phrase used throughout 12-Step programming, they become new people and establish a physical, moral, and spiritual distance from their disordered selves and the chaotic lives they previously lived. Overwhelmingly, the stories women shared about their lives and involvement with the criminal legal system followed this narrative structure, emphasizing personal transformation. Throughout our interviews and with their photographs, women contrasted their past *criminal-addict* selves with the *rehabilitated* identities they were working to achieve and maintain, strongly echoing the moral and spiritual dictates of the 12-Step logic.[49] Nyla was among the women who did so most clearly.

I sat down with Nyla, a petite 42-year-old Black mother of six, for our first interview on a December afternoon in one of the Chicago Public Library's South Side branches. Just as when we had first met a few weeks prior at one of my recruitment sites, I was taken in by Nyla's humble demeanor, cheerful smile, and joyful laugh. Within the first five minutes of our interview, she began sharing multiple experiences of police sexual harassment and assault, including being forced to engage in sexual activities with officers to avoid arrest. As a Black woman living in public housing who engaged in sex work to support her heroin use, Nyla described continuous targeting and harassment by the police. There was a sense she could be arrested just for stepping outside her front door.

While Nyla critiqued the police, she also critiqued herself. At the time of our first interview, she had been out of prison for about four months and was living in a faith-based recovery home and regularly attending NA meetings, which was a requirement of the home. Nyla welcomed the religious focus, as she viewed strengthening her relationship with God as a critical part of her recovery process. She had struggled for years to stop using heroin. Each time she stopped and felt like she had turned her life around, something undermined her progress. Nyla described a two-to-three-year period of relative calm prior to her last arrest and incarceration, during which she sought drug treatment and stopped using. She eventually began a relationship with a man who became severely physically violent. His frequent attacks caused Nyla to fear for her life and prompted her to resume using heroin. It was not long before police profiled and arrested her, sweeping her back into the criminal legal system.

Nyla centered her own morality and spirituality in her analysis of this cycle of domestic violence, drug use, and criminalization. She recalled how she felt during the months she spent awaiting trial, six of them in Cook County Jail before a friend bonded her out. While quietly crying, Nyla said:

> It was very scary to be in a place where I'm right back in that dark hopeless state of mind and body. Right? After havin' been taken out of it . . . because God began to do some things in me, unlike other times, because I sat still long enough to allow Him to work on me and get a relationship with Him. Only for me to return to that lifestyle, and even when I returned to it, I remember that first week how everything in me said, "You are playing with the devil." *rationalized her arrest as falling to the devil*

Nyla continued, describing the horrific abuse she survived at the hands of her boyfriend and sinking deeper into "the lifestyle" of drug use and sex work over the year and a half leading up to her last arrest:

Nyla: While I'm sitting in this type of lifestyle, considerin' where I had come from and where God had brought me to, and then I picked back up again, and this was a result. All this was playin' itself out. So now I'm findin' myself sitting in it . . . And now I'm going dark, light, light, dark. Do you understand what I'm sayin'?

CR: What do you mean, what do you mean about that?

Nyla: Meanin' I know how it feels to be on the light side versus bein' on the dark. The dark I'm familiar with, meanin' the sexual immorality, the activity, the doin' everything that God would have me not do. The dark side. And yet know what it feels like to be in the light.

CR: And what does that feel like to be in the light?

Nyla: Meanin' I'm bein' obedient. I'm doin' all the right things for the right reasons. I'm helpin' others. I'm helpin' myself. I'm bein' a mother to my children . . . I have first and foremost a relationship with my Father. And I'm protected. I'm covered. Unlike on the other side, you know, anything goes. Because I've put myself out there, and I'm not, I don't feel like I'm under my Father's, the umbrella of His protection because I'm doin' everything outside of what He would have me do.

For Nyla, using heroin did not just mean she had relapsed or broken the law. As she understood it, her behaviors represented a moral and spiritual failing. She held herself responsible for stepping out from under the "protection" of God's "umbrella." Her explanation of turning away from God invoked the 12-Step logic. Nyla explained that when she had turned her life over to God, she lived "on the light side" and was "obedient." In addition to following the law, she was living in a moral and spiritual way that aligned with God's plan for her. Resuming her heroin use meant she exerted her will over God's will, as she did "everything that God would have [her] not do." While she had come to know God's will for her, the first part of Step 11, she lacked the "power to carry that out."[50] Of course, domestic violence and incarceration were experiences Nyla wanted to avoid, but in this recollection, she struggled just as much, if not more, with the moral and spiritual implications of falling back into this lifestyle, what she referred to as "the dark side" and "playing with the devil." Furthermore, she assessed her weak self as the cause of that fall, explaining she was not strong enough to stay on God's path.

ENCOUNTERING THE 12-STEP LOGIC

One interpretation of Nyla's reflections could wholly center the influence of faith and perhaps even link that influence to the important role the Black Church has played in providing protection against the onslaught of racist violence that characterizes Black life in the United States.[51] I argue that interpretation is incomplete for the women who participated in this study, however. I root that argument in the language women used and the explanations they offered about their recovery processes. Religion and spirituality alone cannot fully explain the identity work criminalized women engaged. The merging of 12-Step programs with religion and spirituality in the carceral context created a distinct redemptive/punitive hybrid logic that structured women's identity work. Only an interpretation that centers this unique mix of influences can provide a full understanding of Nyla's reflection. Neither faith, nor recovery, nor carceral discourses alone can unpack the complex web within which women's identity work occurred. Paying attention to women's stories about where and from whom they encountered lessons about recovery and rehabilitation brought the 12-Step logic into focus.

FIGURE 4. 12-Step meeting directory
(Photo credit: Tinybig).

FIGURE 5. Religious books
(Photo credit: Tinybig).

During our PEI, Tinybig, the woman whose photographs of an intersection near Cook County Jail open chapter 2, shared two photographs that symbolized the moral and spiritual underpinnings of the 12-Step logic.[52] We had been discussing some of the differences between 12-Step programs, such as AA versus NA. Tinybig concluded, "When it all boils down to it, the basic things about any A [i.e., Anonymous program] stems from the 12-Step program and the literature that goes along with it, because when you break it down it all reverts back to the Bible." She then flipped through her photographs to find two she had in mind: one of a 12-Step meeting directory (figure 4) and one of religious books, specifically *The Life Recovery Bible*, the Holy Bible, and an "Our Daily Bread" booklet (figure 5). Placing the photographs side-by-side, she explained:

This is how come I put these two on there . . . it's a format that some kind of way goes hand in hand . . . I admitted there was problems with my addiction, that my life had become a mess, but when once I got the manageability right, I still gotta admit that I'm powerless. And without a God of my understanding, I'm gonna remain powerless. Whereas now I have some deliverance that I see, I'ma keep on top, I'm goin' to stand tall, I'ma sit back . . . and came to believe that a power greater than myself could restore me to sanity . . . all it is, is having had the spiritual awakening as a result of these steps. It all reverts back to the Bible to me.

For Tinybig, her recovery and faith were one in the same. In order to turn her life around, she had to have a "spiritual awakening," and the 12 Steps provided her with a structure to nurture that awakening and subsequently her sobriety. She ticked off the core tenets of the 12 Steps, in the process accepting her weak identity and trusting God would give her the strength to return order to her life. *The Life Recovery Bible*, for instance, connected each of the 12 Steps to corresponding Scriptures. As explained in a promotional video for the book, "Its personal notes, themes, and helps will walk you through the 12-Step program, as it integrates what God has to say specific to what you are facing. Each and every day, it will point you back to your Creator, who alone is the source of recovery and capable of bringing new hope and healing."[53] Like Nyla, Tinybig understood ending her drug use and criminalization required nothing less than her complete moral and spiritual transformation, and she must remain vigilant in continuing that transformation.

Xenia, a 41-year-old Puerto Rican woman, who had briefly stayed at Starting Again but had moved out by the time of our first interview, spoke about her own recovery work in ways that closely echoed Tinybig's reflections. While incarcerated, Xenia participated in an intensive drug treatment program she described as "a 12-Step program based on a God of an understanding. And they'll teach you biblical with treatment . . . And they also have a 12-Step Bible, recovery Bible. It's called *12-Step Recovery Bible*. And, it's a regular Bible, but it also speaks to you in an addict's point of view." I asked Xenia for an example of how the recovery Bible used an addict's point of view. She explained:

> They'll break it down. First it'll talk about the Bible, then it'll break it down in what terms [an addict can understand]. And then it'll say in an addict's point of view, like me being the addict . . . I don't know how to explain it . . . All I can tell you is it speaks as saying, "Me, as the addict." The addict, if they talked about Abraham having a baby and, or like when you trust in faith, us, as in addicts, we don't have faith because, and then it breaks it down . . . When they talk about faith or love—it has love, it has faith, and it has other stuff in there broken down into an addict's point of view. And then they have Scriptures you can read up on it.

While Xenia struggled to precisely explain the recovery Bible, the point she stressed was addicts are different from everyone else. They are so different, in fact, they cannot understand the Bible, a text widely regarded as universal and applying to all people. The prison's drug treatment program had taught Xenia new insights about her drug use. One insight she named was "powerlessness," meaning "knowing when you're just powerless over certain situations, you know? Meaning, I'm powerless over this. I have no control over that. You know, and having accepting it. You know, 'cause at first I just would challenge it. You know, now I just let go and let God. You gotta learn how to let go and let God. That's what it taught me: to believe in a higher power greater than yourself."

That lesson about the co-constitutive nature of morality, spirituality, noncriminality, and sobriety is the core of the 12-Step logic, and it pervades jails, prisons, and the postincarceration landscape. Whether women internalized that logic and regardless of if they would have embraced it on their own, it is noteworthy that encountering this logic as part of their criminalization was inescapable. Treatment interventions that centered the 12-Step model and a Christian God were standard fare across incarceration and postincarceration programs. Consider Susan, a 59-year-old Black woman, who estimated she had been arrested more than 50 times for various behaviors, such as shoplifting, associated with her ongoing heroin use. It had been just under a year since she had been released from jail when we sat down for our interview at Women Helping Women's storefront office on Chicago's southeast side. Susan explained she had served her most recent sentence, about four months for a probation violation charge, in Cook County Jail's Division 17, a drug treatment unit for women. She recalled, "That's where I learned . . . that you cannot fight no addiction without God first." Susan described how she thrived in the program and gained an understanding that had eluded her previously. "I wanted to know how to stay clean," she said. "They told me that I had to pray about it and go to meetings, you know, take a few suggestions, and, you know, call somebody, you know. And that was a sure way of staying clean."

Susan's recollection mapped on to Tinybig's photos. In Division 17, Susan learned that prayer and attending 12-Step meetings, both of which would help her reestablish her relationship with God, were the keys to turning her life around. These lessons resonated with Susan's religious upbringing and aligned with the beliefs and values of her "very professional and religious family." But Susan did not identify her family or her personal beliefs as catalysts for embracing recovery and understanding the work it entails. Court-mandated drug treatment within the confines of Cook County Jail was the catalyst.

Women frequently recalled how they began to understand the relationship among spirituality, sobriety, morality, and noncriminality—in other words, the 12-Step logic—during their time in jail or prison. Their experiences with reentry programs, specifically recovery homes, reinforced that understanding. While Tinybig acquired *The Life Recovery Bible* in prison, she received her copy of the Holy Bible upon arriving at Starting Again from the director's "box of Bibles." Growing Stronger and Starting Again were explicitly faith-based recovery homes. They accepted any woman regardless of religious beliefs, but an explicit embrace of Christian beliefs undergirded programming and events (e.g., family gatherings, graduations, barbecues), even beyond the required participation in 12-Step meetings. Throughout interviews, women shared their experiences staying at a variety of recovery homes over the years. Every recovery home women discussed were faith-based programs that required 12-Step meeting attendance, with many offering 12-Step meetings on-site.

New Life, a Black 30-year-old mother of two had been out of prison for a little over four months when I met her at Growing Stronger. While she had since settled into the Growing Stronger community, she recalled having struggled early in her stay with the program's rigid schedule and requirements. New Life had preferred to spend most of her time away from the home, but Growing Stronger staff wanted her to participate fully in the daily groups and spend more time in the house. This tension almost prompted New Life to move out of Growing Stronger about a month after she arrived. She recalled a weekend when, without explanation, the staff revoked all residents' weekend passes, preventing her from staying out overnight as she had planned. New Life decided to pack her bags and move out. As she waited for a family member to pick her up, the on-duty staff member phoned Pastor Geraldine, one of the administrators who oversaw the house, at home and told her New Life was preparing to leave. Pastor Geraldine came back to the recovery home to try to change New Life's mind. When she asked New Life what was going on, New Life replied:

> "I'm fittin' to go, because, you know, I don't get my weekend pass, I didn't do anything." She [Pastor Geraldine] said, "Stop right there. It's much more than just a weekend pass. Just say you don't wanna be here." I say, "It's not that." She said, "Yes it is. You know how bad the devil wants you back?" And it was like, when she said that, it was like, "Oh my God!" Cuz if I leave here, what is my plans? You know, I mean, seriously what is gonna be my plans? To get back in contact with the same old people. And she was just breaking it down to me, and I was like, "Wow."

Pastor Geraldine presented New Life's decision as a choice between staying with God's plan or succumbing to the devil's wishes. In the process, she reframed New Life's concern about an arbitrary rule change that limited her freedom as an excuse to go back not just to her old ways, but also to a lifestyle that the devil wanted for her. Within this framework, New Life recognized her impulse to leave as a moral and spiritual decision between good and evil. To borrow Nyla's language, leaving Growing Stronger meant being out from under the umbrella of God's protection. New Life explained that had she moved out that night, she likely would have resumed selling and using drugs, or, as Nyla and Pastor Geraldine put it, playing with the devil. Pastor Geraldine had told New Life that her decision was not really about the weekend pass; rather "It's you battling with yourself because you really want that freedom, but you know the consequence of that."[54]

While neither New Life nor Pastor Geraldine explicitly cited the 12 Steps during this encounter, the 12-Step logic undergirded their interaction. In addition to the clear moral and spiritual overtones, New Life referenced the common 12-Step admonition to avoid the "people, places, and things" associated with one's past alcohol and drug use. Additionally, Pastor Geraldine invoked New Life's weak self by warning her that she was not yet ready to handle the freedom of living outside of Growing Stronger; New Life still needed the program's structure to impose the regulation she could not yet provide for herself. Recalling the story in our interview, New Life agreed with Pastor Geraldine's assessment and explained that, at the time, leaving Growing Stronger would have meant a return to her past lifestyle: "Like, if I can sell drugs without being incarcerated, I'm serious! And without

FIGURE 6. Starting Again exterior (Photo credit: Red).

FIGURE 7. Climbing the ladder (Photo credit: Red).

having the conscience that I have now, I would do it . . . If I could smoke weed without worrying about getting dropped out of nowhere, I probably would do it. You know, but I'm more grown up now." Her final comment here was instructive: New Life clarified she was stronger today. She had grown up and had a different conscience. She felt confident she could handle the freedom today, but on the night she had contemplated leaving, she would not have been able. As the pseudonym she chose for this project suggests, she was a new person, one who was moral, spiritual, law-abiding, and sober.

Red, a 41-year-old Puerto Rican woman who had been living at Starting Again for about five months since her release from prison, captured the recovery home's interconnected focus on faith and recovery perfectly with two photographs. Although the images were dark and hard to decipher, Red made her intention behind them clear. She explained her photograph of Starting Again's exterior (figure 6) showed how the building "looks like a castle. So it reveals a second chance in life to be honest with you . . . and just thinking of a castle just reminds me of God . . . like His mother, she's the queen, and it just reminds me of just a castle. It just looks like a castle." Turning to her photograph of a staircase inside Starting Again, Red said it showed "Climbing the ladder, like 12 Steps, 'cause this is a place, you know, that provides 12-Step routines and helps you through them. So that's our ladder . . . 12 Steps of recovery" (figure 7). Like Tinybig, Red visually represented the two cornerstones of her postincarceration process: faith and the 12 Steps. God was so central to Red's experience at Starting Again that the building, itself, embodied His presence. Similarly, the 12 Steps provided such an all-encompassing structure and were such a part of Starting Again's programming that Red saw reminders of them in the physical layout of the building. These two photographs represented the organizing principles of her life.

Red also explicitly connected her faith and the 12 Steps to her personal transformation process. As she flipped through her pile of photographs, she shared a summative reflection about Starting Again: "This is what this is about, right? Us recovering, us changing from bad to good. God giving us a chance in life instead of keepin' us in prison or keepin' us sick, addicted to the wrong thing. So the pictures that I took of Starting Again would be like the entry. And then these NA pictures, it's documenting the information of what, you know, some things you have to do to get ahead in life."[55] Like Nyla's fight to go from dark to light, Red was working to change from bad to good. Red had not had an easy life. For years, she had struggled with domestic violence, mental illness, her mother's death, losing her children to Child Protective Services, drug use, and incarceration. Also like Nyla, for Red, these very real issues that largely were outside of her control took a backseat to her personal responsibility to become a good person by following the 12 Steps and allowing God to do His work. Red embraced the 12-Step logic, with all of its lessons about morality, spirituality, criminality, and sobriety. The moral transformation from good to bad was interdependent with the transformation from addicted to sober, criminal to noncriminal, and distant from God to close to Him.

The 12-Step logic puts the authority of the state behind faith-based recovery, creating a merging of church and state that powerfully prescribes how women should understand their very sense of self—as moral, worthy, redeemable, or not. That message coming from either institution alone would be quite authoritative. To have that message imposed by both institutions is concerning, at best, and potentially oppressive, at worst, in ways with which carceral studies scholarship has not fully grappled.[56]

PERMANENT OUTSIDERS

The all-encompassing transformation of identity the 12-Step logic requires means, following release, women's task was not solely to stay out of prison or reintegrate into society. The postincarceration process required women to manage rehabilitated identities that aligned with the moral and spiritual dictates of the 12-Step logic under omnipresent surveillance and moral judgment. While recovery homes and reentry programs offered much-needed support and affirmation, they also extended the dominant 12-Step logic into women's lives and closely monitored women's adherence to it. Between parole conditions and recovery home rules, women had to meet a host of requirements that far exceeded simply being lawful, such as attending 12-Step meetings and at times more intensive drug treatment programming; participating in individual and group therapy; completing a variety of mandated classes, such as parenting and life skills; following program rules like adhering to a curfew, completing daily chores, and participating in program meetings and activities that centered faith and the 12 Steps; embracing prayer as a recovery practice and in some cases even attending church; and becoming fluent in the 12-Step lingo. Indeed, there was a distinct culture—language, beliefs, and ways of being—that structured the postincarceration landscape.

The expansiveness of this culture is significant. Sociologists like Jill A. McCorkel, Lynne A. Haney, and Allison McKim also have critically analyzed the invasive reach of gender-responsive drug treatment programs that subject criminalized women to intense surveillance as part of an effort to remake the self.[57] While these scholars have conducted extensive ethnographies of specific programs, my research approach allows me to show how the identity transformation dynamics that are so prevalent in criminalized women's lives are not confined to individual sites or even to particular drug treatment models. I focus on the network of programs and overarching discourses that work inside and outside prisons to create a far-reaching carceral web that zeroes in on criminalized women's selves.

Even when women adapted to that distinct culture, the postincarceration process never was complete, because the personal transformation process never was complete. In the context of the 12-Step logic, linking criminality and addiction meant that just as women were always recovering, never recovered, women were always rehabilitating, never rehabilitated. There was no endpoint to the postincarceration process. There was no marker that denoted when one was rehabilitated or no longer viewed with suspicion of criminality.[58] McCorkel's incisive analysis in *Breaking Women: Gender, Race, and the New Politics of Imprisonment* deeply informs my argument here.[59] Based on her ethnographic research of a drug treatment program in a women's prison, McCorkel examined how women experienced and responded to routine institutional practices that sought to break down their sense of self. Rooted in a habilitation model of drug treatment, the private program taught women their diseased selves were the cause of all their problems and that creating and managing a new self was a lifelong process. Women's responses to the program's harsh treatment practices varied, but a noteworthy portion accepted and internalized the program's assessment of their diseased selves and moral blameworthiness. Borrowing the phrase more skeptical program participants used to describe these women, McCorkel referred to this process of surrendering to the program as "rentin' out your head."[60]

Building upon McCorkel's analysis in *Breaking Women*, I conceive of postincarceration as a permanent liminal state. Women existed "betwixt and between" mainstream society and prison in a distinct marginalized space constituted by the intersection of criminalization, racism, patriarchy, and class.[61] Thus, even as women "succeeded" at reentry, they remained set apart from society as they faced distinct expectations and social norms that connected their moral worth to their sobriety and, by extension, to their "noncriminality." In addition to the well-documented, pervasive collateral consequences and legal discrimination based on felony conviction, women encountered a distinct, closely regulated recovery lifestyle postrelease.

SURVEILLANCE

While almost every women spoke positively about the support and resources they received at the recovery homes where they lived, they also explained how surveillance was a trade-off they accepted in exchange for that support. That surveillance took explicit and subtle forms, which at times created a sense of instability and reminded women the recovery home's support could be withdrawn at any time. It included the objective enforcement of rules—like maintaining sobriety and participating in mandated programming—and the subjective assessment of women's rehabilitation.

Parole officers and recovery home staff explicitly monitored women's abstinence from drugs and alcohol through mandating 12-Step meeting attendance and random urinalysis. Even for women who were in compliance, these surveillance technologies caused significant stress. During our PEI, Red shared a photograph of her NA meeting attendance sheet.[62] One of Starting Again's program rules required residents to attend a minimum number of 12-Step meetings each month. Attending these meetings also was a condition of Red's parole. By attending meetings, she fulfilled two requirements. If she missed a meeting, though, she faced double consequences, such as termination from Starting Again and revocation of parole. Red had no trouble meeting the 12-Step attendance requirement, but she struggled to provide proof of her attendance. On three occasions, she had lost her NA sign-in sheet, which Starting Again's director required residents to submit weekly. Red faithfully carried the sheet to every meeting, noting the date and location and securing the signature of the person chairing the meeting. But when she misplaced the sheet, she had no documentation of her compliance with Starting Again's rule and this parole condition. When she lost her sheet, Red sought out the meeting chairperson, hoped they remembered her face, and had them re-sign her sheet. Red commented, "I always got saved. I always saved my life. But if the person, like, doesn't want to do it or all of a sudden that person's not chairing anymore . . . she [Starting Again's director] could take us out for it, too . . . Because you never know what people are fed up with."

The phrases "saved my life" and "could take us out" revealed how much Red needed Starting Again and how much she valued the support and sense of community she had found there. She equated losing her spot in the home with death. The statement was not hyperbolic. Red carefully was working to put her life back together. Without stable housing, she easily could end up back in prison. Even if

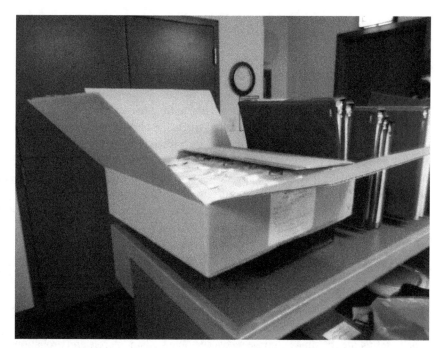

FIGURE 8. Drop cups at the recovery home (Photo credit: Jean Grey).

Starting Again's director gave her a pass on the documentation, Red still would have to convince her parole officer not to impose further restrictions or even move to revoke her parole, which could send her back to prison.

In addition to mandating 12-Step meeting attendance, recovery homes monitored women's abstinence from drugs through the more invasive practice of random drug tests. Jean Grey,[63] an African American woman who was about one year into serving a five-year probation sentence at the time of our interviews, drew my attention to the impact of this surveillance technology during our PEI. At 20 years old, she by far was the youngest woman who participated in this project and who was residing at Growing Stronger. In addition to her age, Jean was distinct from many of the women at Growing Stronger because she had never been to prison and did not identify as having a drug problem. She still had to adapt to the 12-Step logic, however, and submit to the recovery home's random drug tests. She documented this practice with her photograph of a box of "drop cups" on the counter at Growing Stronger (figure 8).[64] She explained the photograph:

> These are the drop cups. Like randomly, you know, they'll just be sittin' out there on the desk, and, you know, word'll pass that we're being dropped today. And . . . it's like if I've made it this far into the recovery process, why do you have to drop me? Like, do you not trust me? Well, you know, I guess not 'cause you have to drop me . . . I don't really like that, because I don't identify with being an addict, but it's one of the

stipulations to stay here, so . . . I don't like how it looks. I don't like how they present it. I don't like how it makes me feel.

Jean described the invasive mechanics of going through the drug test, including drinking a bunch of water, avoiding going to the bathroom so she would be able to drop when it was time, urinating into the cup, waiting for 15 minutes after a staff member put the test strip into the urine, pulling the strip together with the staff member to reveal the results, pouring the urine out of the cup, and finally throwing the cup in the garbage. But what she returned to was how the process and even just seeing the cups on the counter made her feel: "It just makes me feel real untrustworthy. Like, it makes me feel like I'm not working on anything, like, especially 'cause it's random . . . I just don't like it. It makes me not feel good."

The cups were not only a way to monitor and enforce the recovery home's rules. They assessed the women's character. Even a negative urinalysis result, which affirmed women's recovery work, required women to participate in a paternalistic process shrouded in suspicion. As Jean explained, the cups reminded her that other people, particularly people who held a significant amount of power over her life, viewed her as untrustworthy and that she must be able to prove her commitment to her rehabilitation and recovery at a moment's notice. Like Red's signed NA meeting attendance sheet, Jean's clean test result communicated her recovering/rehabilitating identity in a language recovery home staff and parole and probation officers recognized as legitimate.

Recovery home staff also monitored women's recovery and subsequent rehabilitation in more subjective ways, such as by paying attention to signs of so-called risky behavior that suggested women had not embraced the 12-Step logic. Abstaining from drugs and alcohol alone was not a sufficient indication of recovery. As sociologist Norman K. Denzin explains, people who abstain without also committing to the complete transformation of identity the 12 Steps demand are viewed by AA members as likely to relapse because they "did not make the commitments and side bets into AA that would have anchored the recovering self in the AA way of life."[65] Any sign that women were not fully invested in the recovery home's programming could be considered risky. Not spending enough time in the home was a telltale sign, as I learned one day sitting in Growing Stronger's front room, waiting for a participant to return home for our scheduled interview. While I waited, Iris, a 49-year-old White mother of two, returned home from another long day of submitting job applications. I knew from my prior interview with Iris that she was desperate to secure a job so she could move into her own apartment. Only then would she be able to see her children, who lived in another state with her ex-husband. Iris held a bachelor's degree, and prior to her troubles with alcohol and DUI convictions, she had enjoyed a solidly middle-class lifestyle with her family. She was confident she could attain that level of financial stability once again. While Iris was deeply grateful for the support Growing Stronger provided, many of its programs did not apply to her. The education programs were geared toward people with lower levels of education than Iris, and the vocational programs could not offer much to assist her reentry into the accounting profession. Iris knew it was up to her to make the progress she needed to make. It was unlikely Growing Stronger would be able to connect her with the type of job or housing that met her needs.

Iris looked distressed as she signed the residents' logbook to indicate her arrival time back at the house. She explained to the staff member working at the front desk that she would be unable to go out the next day to continue to look for employment because she did not have enough money to purchase another bus card. Pastor Geraldine overheard Iris and sternly told her she needed to "sit still" and "let God do His work." She admonished Iris for "moving too fast" and running all over the city, when what she really needed to do was focus on working on herself. The message was clear; Pastor Geraldine had drawn a connection between Iris's absence from the house and her unsuccessful job search. Presumably, if Iris would spend more time at the recovery home participating in its groups and activities, God would help her strengthen her inner self and thus be more successful in her employment search. By taking matters into her own hands and setting her own agenda, Iris was not giving her will over to God or accepting her weak identity and powerlessness. She was not waiting to be restored to sanity by a power greater than herself.

What the 12-Step logic demanded of Iris clashed with the structural reality of her life, particularly the need to have her own stable apartment in order to meet the criteria of her custody agreement that would allow visitation with her children.[66] While the 12-Step logic required her to slow down, Iris felt an urgent need to move forward. Despite her sobriety, Iris failed to demonstrate her internalization of the 12-Step logic. Fully participating in Growing Stronger's programming and being an active part of the Growing Stronger community communicated women's serious commitment to turning their lives around, as opposed to just going through the motions or relying on the recovery home as just a place to stay. As such, Pastor Geraldine read Iris's recovery as superficial and anticipated Iris was setting herself up for another relapse and subsequent run-in with the criminal legal system

Chicken Wing, the 55-year-old Black woman who enjoyed taking the bus to her new job, shared how staff members' subjective assessments of one's character seemingly could come out of nowhere. In the six months or so since she had been released from prison, she already had secured part-time employment, had become deeply involved with a church she identified as providing her with critical support and community, and was in a romantic relationship she described as the healthiest and most fulfilling of her life. Throughout our interviews, she exuded confidence and joy, laughing frequently and speaking bluntly about her past, present circumstances, and future plans. Having served more than 20 years in prison, she seemed determined to fully enjoy this second part of her life and not take anything for granted. Nevertheless, she still faced challenges at Growing Stronger, typically as the result of conflicts with roommates or staff. She reflected on one particularly significant disagreement with a staff member who, when a two-person room became available, did not ask Chicken Wing if she was interested in moving from her three-person room to the newly available room. This oversight was consequential, since the only way to move into a single room was to first progress from a three-person to a two-person room. Chicken Wing elaborated:

> When the two-man came open she [the staff member] never asked me. But she said she heard I didn't want a two-man because they was too small. But I told her, I said, "But you never *asked* me." And then I said, "Well, forget it then. I'm movin' anyway, so leave me where I'm at." I got cocky cuz I was *pissed*. You know what I'm sayin'? I was mad because I felt that she overlooked me.

The disagreement took on added significance when Chicken Wing's parole officer revoked her movement for the upcoming weekend and New Year's Day because of it. Chicken Wing had not even been aware recovery home staff could or would share such information, but they had, and her parole officer responded by punishing Chicken Wing for being "cocky." Chicken Wing had not violated a condition of her parole or even a house rule. But the staff member and parole officer did not like her attitude, which was enough to warrant a punishment that cut deep. Chicken Wing explained, "It affected me bad. I cried. I cried like a baby. I was hurt. This is my first New Year. You took it from me."

It is noteworthy how Chicken Wing's assertiveness contrasted with the humble, powerless identity prescribed by the 12-Step logic and with racist, sexist, and classist respectability politics.[67] As a poor, criminalized Black woman, Chicken Wing was supposed to perform subordination. Voicing displeasure and asserting her impending independence ("I'm movin' anyway") were read as insubordination and "cockiness," which were antithetical to the rehabilitating/recovering identity she must embody. Chicken Wing explained that while she still disagreed with her punishment, she learned an important lesson about how she must present herself: "I should've kept my mouth shut. And that's why I say, I've got to learn how to keep my mouth shut. I've got to learn how to talk to people. So I was wrong. But I didn't feel that you should go tell my parole officer that. And then she take my movement for the weekend. And then took my movement New Year's Day. I couldn't go nowhere. Snatched it." Regardless that she was abstaining from drugs, not breaking the law, following her parole conditions and the recovery home's rules, working, engaged in a church, and attending 12-Step meetings, if she did not present herself accordingly, her parole officer would treat her like a criminal. Chicken Wing reflected:

> Anything negative is right up her [the parole officer's] alley to take your . . . movement from you, to make you feel like you ain't nothin'. I did twenty years. Give me a break. You know what I'm sayin'? I work. You would think they'd be encouraging you more instead of like the system is designed for them to send you back. And she told me, "If you go out of the house, I'm gonna violate you. I'm gonna put a warrant out

on you." Like I stole somethin'. Like I did a crime or somethin'. Like I did, like I tested dirty. You know. I just said somethin' out of my mouth!

Chicken Wing's parole officer could ignore all of her markers of rehabilitation and recovery in favor of surveilling her speech and attitude in ways that effectively returned Chicken Wing to her past *criminal-addict* self. Her parole officer made her feel like she was nothing, a nobody, which was exactly how Chicken Wing described feeling about herself at the time she was arrested more than 20 years ago. Despite all she had accomplished, the parole officer's punishment made her feel as she had before she became a changed person, the new Chicken Wing that she was today. Working in concert, the recovery home staff and the parole officer guided Chicken Wing not just toward sobriety and noncriminality, but also toward a particular way of being.

NEVER REHABILITATED, ALWAYS REHABILITATING

Perhaps the most significant consequence of the 12-Step logic is that the surveillance and judgment women described enduring after their release never quite ended. They might become less explicit and overtly intrusive over time, especially as women moved into their own residences and accumulated a track record of sobriety and noninvolvement with the criminal legal system. Once Chicken Wing completed her parole, for instance, she would not have to worry about losing her movement over a weekend or holiday. Once Red moved out of Starting Again, she would not have to fear losing her housing if she lost her 12-Step meeting attendance sheet. In fact, she would not even have to carry around the sheet and secure signatures from meeting chairs. She would be able to simply attend meetings for herself, without needing to prove attendance to anyone. Even so, the work of personal transformation—of maintaining and demonstrating a rehabilitating/recovering identity—and some degree of surveillance never ended. As Cathy, a 52-year-old White mother whose life had been upended by DUI charges related to alcohol, commented, "You've got to remember, once you've crossed the line and become addicted to this, it's always inside of you, and it can be woken up at any time." Cathy returned to this point throughout our interview, later adding, "You're labeled for the rest of your life." Ms. Fields, a 47-year-old Black Afro-American woman, similarly reflected on the permanence of addiction and never-ending work of recovery:

> Ms. Fields: You have to work the steps for the rest of your life. You know, once you do 12, then you can start all over. You know.
> CR: Back at one?
> Ms. Fields: Yeah, back at one. 'Cause see, 'cause every year, you know, like I might have a resentment about you ... maybe I felt like you didn't help me with my homework good enough or somethin' ... I'm just hypothetically

speaking. And so then I have to, I have to do a 4th Step on that. And so then, you know, every time, you can't let them things sit in you . . . So, I want to at least work the first 12, you know. And I'm willin' to just keep workin' them over and over, 'cause one thing I know [is] that AA'll be a part of my life until I die.

Cathy and Ms. Fields made clear they never would be recovered, even if they established a lengthy amount of clean time. The risk of waking up the addiction that permanently resides within them always was present. As Ms. Fields explained, she must diligently monitor herself for signs that her addiction was waking and proactively work to contain it.

The reawakening of addiction was interconnected with vulnerability to recriminalization. Resuming drug or alcohol use did not just signal a return to one's addict identity, but to one's *criminal-addict* identity. Whereas drug treatment specialists routinely note relapse is a common part of the recovery process, formerly incarcerated women did not have the luxury to relapse.[68] That luxury typically was reserved for more privileged groups for whom criminalization, drug use, and recovery are not intricately intertwined.[69] When the women who participated in this project relapsed, they encountered severe consequences, such as terminated stays at recovery homes and revocation of probation or parole. The permanence of the criminal-addict label played out in women's lives in significant ways, particularly when past criminal records impacted new criminal court cases and limited women's chances of avoiding additional prison sentences.

Olivia, a 49-year-old Afro-American woman who had served three prison sentences and was detained numerous times in jail, spoke powerfully about this impact, likening the practice of judges and state's attorneys taking defendants' backgrounds into consideration when determining guilt and sentencing to "double jeopardy." She explained, "Instead of your case carryin' one to three [years], they're gonna upgrade it to three to six [years]. That means you're lookin' back in my background, and in a way I feel like that's double jeopardy, 'cause I did the time for that, and you're gonna bring it up again . . . You bringin' up my old case. You tryin' me again off of that case. I don't think that's fair." Olivia's past cases and prison time were albatrosses from which she never could escape. A new charge erased whatever rehabilitative progress she had made and amplified the impact of her old case. She effectively was punished again for her past behaviors and for her new case.

Corrine, a 63-year-old African American woman who had been incarcerated eight times and whose experience giving birth while incarcerated was discussed in the previous chapter, shared a strikingly similar assessment of this type of double jeopardy. Prior to her last incarceration, she had sought drug treatment on her own while she was out of jail, awaiting sentencing for a shoplifting charge. At the time of her sentencing date in court, she had completed nearly six weeks of outpatient treatment. Two counselors from the program accompanied Corrine to court and vouched for her progress, legitimizing her claim that she actively was working to turn her life around. Corrine hoped the judge would realize yet another prison sentence was unnecessary, since she already was getting the help she needed to address the root cause of her troubles with the law. The judge praised Corrine's initiative but did not spare her another trip to prison. With her voice cracking and holding back tears, Corrine recalled the judge's exact response: "She said, 'I would never be able to face society or my constituents,' as she kind of put it, 'if I were . . . to let you back out on the streets today. And I hereby sentence you to four to ten [years]. And I hope that when you're done that you still continue on your path.'"

The judge acknowledged Corrine already was on the right path. She made no pretense the prison sentence was about rehabilitation. Rather, she was clear the sentence was a purely punitive act to benefit her constituents and assuage her own concerns about public backlash. The judge did not address how another prison sentence would sever Corrine's relationship with a helpful treatment program and separate her from her young daughter or how these two losses would derail Corrine from the positive path she was following. Further, the judge reminded Corrine that, in the eyes of the court, she was a *criminal-addict* above all else. Corrine explained, "So here's a judge telling me that I was such a menace to society and that she would never be able to face society if she gave me a chance. And here I was goin' to prison for thirty-seven dollars." Corrine's recognized criminality precluded any acknowledgment of her identity as a woman in recovery or as a mother.

Like Corrine, Ann Williams was a Black mother who struggled with drug use throughout her adult life and never received mercy from the judges or prosecutors she faced. At age 44, she already had served four prison sentences, her most recent one following a conviction for retail theft. Throughout our interviews, Ann drew connections among her drug use, homelessness, and ongoing entanglement with the criminal legal system. She shared a nascent critique of the system's reliance on punishment over rehabilitation when recalling how, while being processed for her last arrest, she already knew she would have to return to prison yet again. Unlike Corrine, Ann had no hope of leniency. She explained, "Now some people have, they go to the County [Cook County Jail], they get treatment and all that. I never got none of that. Treatment, probation, none of that, I went straight to prison." "Every time?" I clarified. "Every time," Ann responded. "I never got treatment. I did detoxes in my life when I was out on the street, but I never did treatment . . . And now that I look back on it, I felt like I should've maybe . . . that that's what I should've got a share of. I mean . . . even if then if I wasn't ready, I felt like I should've got treatment."

Rose, who took the alley photograph that opens this book, shared a story that echoed Ann Williams's experience. Following her first stay at Growing Stronger, Rose had moved into her own apartment, secured a job, and enjoyed a brief period of relative stability. When her boyfriend cheated on her, that stability ended. She began using drugs again and eventually lost her job and apartment. Rose commented, "I gave up. It's like I gave up on life." With her being unhoused and actively using, it was just a matter of time before she was arrested again. A police officer stopped Rose and two of her friends one night after she had been unable to secure a spot at an overnight homeless shelter. Rose was holding a couple of bags of crack. The officer arrested and detained her for possession of a controlled substance. When she eventually met with a public defender (PD), he explained the state's offer: if Rose pleaded guilty, she would receive a sentence of 18 months in prison. Rose recalled, "I guess this PD . . . had already seen my file, so, when he came out and talked to me, he was like, 'This is what they offerin' you. Probation is not an option.'" Rose made the connection between her background, which included two prior incarcerations, and the state's refusal to offer probation and treatment. Because of her permanent *criminal-addict* identity, the consequence for Rose's relapse was a severe form of punishment, not treatment.

Corrine, Ann Williams, and Rose would have welcomed treatment. Like the other women in this study, however, the permanence of the *criminal-addict* identity kept them stuck in a cycle of trauma, poverty, relapse, and punishment. The benefits of Whiteness, financial means, and lack of a criminal record converge for some to construct relapse as a painful but useful turning point that can trigger more intensive treatment and support to overcome recurring drug use. Those benefits eluded women like Corrine, Ann, and Rose, as the criminal legal system effectively criminalized recovery for women living on the margins of society. Before the court, they were nothing more than *criminal-addicts*. The permanence of that identity shaped each encounter with the criminal legal system, leading to what seemed like a predetermined outcome.

FINDING DIGNITY THROUGH THE 12-STEP LOGIC

The 12-Step logic was the dominant framework women encountered as they moved through the criminal legal system and postincarceration landscape. Its ubiquitous presence bridged larger political and cultural discourses, particularly neoliberalism and neoconservativism, and distilled them into a specific, enforceable framework that structured criminalized women's lives indefinitely. The logic encouraged an individualistic, depoliticized understanding of the causes of women's imprisonment and the challenges they faced after release, locating responsibility squarely within the individual and casting aside structural forces as mere excuses drugusing women made to detract focus from their weak selves and shirk the real work of personal rehabilitation. Yet, women engaged this logic in innovative ways that allowed them to claim dignity and recast incarceration as a redemptive experience, while remaining critical of the dehumanizing treatment they endured.

Recall Denise's recollection of her evolving relationship with Judge Hopkins. At the end of her probation, Denise told Judge Hopkins, "God worked through you to help me." Multiple women similarly explained how God worked through the criminal legal system to directly reach and save them. Referring to the period prior to her last arrest when she was homeless and using drugs again, Rose said, "I really felt like I wanted to die . . . but, I also knew that, that ain't how God sees everything. You know. It's not up to me to say that I want to die, so. And I walked around like that, feelin' like that, for a while." Rose asked God to help her; she explained how He did:

> *Rose:* Well, actually it was the police. It was the police because . . . I got arrested for these certain amount of bags that I had on me. And . . . if it was [not] for them, you know, who knows where I'd be today . . . I think that God sent them, you know, for that to happen. All the time that I was tellin' Him that I was tired, you know, didn't have nowhere to go, I didn't want to live my life like this, so, He just put me in a situation and a place to think about all of it. You know.
>
> *CR:* And where was that?
>
> *Rose:* Prison. Prison. From the County [jail] to the prison . . . by the grace of God, He gave me these amount of months, you know, to think about it. And I thought about it strongly . . . I thought about it real, real strongly after I got in jail and a couple of weeks went by and stuff, and I started gettin' my strength.

Faye, a 46-year-old Black woman, described a similar process of growing tired and asking God for help: "You get tired of that pain . . . Tired of goin' to jail . . . Tired of people tellin' you what to do, what you can't do, and how to eat and all that. Tired of being homeless and, you know, all that. Out there, you get tired of that. Nuh-uh. I'm through, I'm done. God help me." Like Rose, Faye believed God answered her call for help through arrest: "I looked in the mirror and said, 'God help me.' And that night I was in jail."

Ann Williams recalled the same progression of growing tired of using drugs and "tired [of] the pain. The things that I did in my life, the pain . . . bein' homeless with my kids, by myself, sleepin' on the train, sleepin' under Wacker Drive." She continued, "I said, 'Man, there's gotta be a better way.' 'Cause I felt like I wanted to die." After her last arrest, she "felt like I was rescued . . . God saved me from myself, because the stuff that I was doin' out there, you know, and to me that's why I said I felt like I was rescued 'cause it, I got another chance." Nyla also had come to understand her last arrest as God's work to save her. She explained that on the night of her last arrest, the police had not had any legal cause to stop and search her. She was in an area with high drug activity and felt the police were simply trying to meet a quota when they targeted her. In hindsight, she said, "When I look at it, it was actually God doin' for me what I couldn't do for myself, because I was really out there really bad."

Nyla, Ann Williams, Faye, Rose, Denise, and many more women reached a point where they were desperate for their lives to change but felt powerless to make that change happen. At what they described as their weakest and most vulnerable moments, God did what they felt they were not able to do themselves. God saved them by acting through the criminal legal system—specifically judges, police, and correctional officers—to physically remove them from dangerous environments and lifestyles. Yet, a noteworthy tension existed between the women's reframing of their arrests and subsequent incarceration and their critiques of the system. Nyla knew the police legally should not have stopped and searched her. Ann Williams wondered if she perhaps did *not* need to go to prison and might have benefited from treatment. Still, they reframed these unjust encounters with the system as God quite literally saving them from death.

This redemptive arc, in which God saves women's lives through incarceration, is familiar. Indeed, the language women used in interviews with me was almost interchangeable with quotes shared by scholars Megan Sweeney, Lora Bex Lempert, and Rachel Ellis in their research with incarcerated women.[70] A distinct quality of the narratives women shared with me was the completely intertwined nature of drug recovery and religious discourses, as encapsulated in the 12-Step logic. Faith *and* recovery were required for redemption. Women's identity narratives did not just "shift from 'flawed' to 'faithful,'" as Ellis found, but from flawed to faithful and sober.[71] Denise's account of her initial resistance and then growing acceptance of the court's mandated drug treatment in jail and harsh probation restrictions again provides an illustrative example. Drawing heavily on the 12-Step logic, Denise explained how she now viewed her recovery work as a partnership with God. He would keep her sober, as long as she did her part:

> I know that I didn't have no control [over my drug use] at all. And I still don't have none. I still don't have no control . . . It's a daily reprieve. I always ask God to keep me sober, help me. Yeah, because I can't do it without Him, and He told me, "As long as you trust that I will keep you sober, I'm gonna keep you sober. As long as you don't go back and do what you was doin', because then you're takin' your will back. I can't keep you sober if you're steady runnin' in the crack house." You know what I'm sayin'? So . . . I got work to do, too.

Denise's partnership with God followed the first three of the 12 Steps: admitting powerlessness and turning her will and life over to God. It also required that she change her behavior and avoid the "people, places, and things" associated with her past drug use. Like Denise, women embraced the 12-Step logic, rooting their recovery in their relationships with God. In doing so, they took up the 12-Step logic to make sense of the unfairness and violence they had endured, casting it as a necessary prerequisite for the dignity now made possible through the lifelong work of recovery and rehabilitation.[72]

The 12-Step logic demanded women divert their focus away from the very real structural factors that lead to their criminalization and accept personal responsibility for the many forms of violence—interpersonal, institutional, and structural—they survived. Despite this rigid framework and restrictions, women took up the 12-Step logic in such a way that they found joy in the never-ending personal transformation work. Julia, a 51-year-old African American woman who had been

FIGURE 9. Certificates (Photo credit: Julia).

incarcerated nine times, used a photograph for our PEI to share evidence of her personal transformation process (figure 9).[73] The photograph showed a number of personally meaningful items she kept on the windowsill next to her bed at Growing Stronger, including framed certificates of completion for a drug treatment program, self-improvement class, and nutrition program; memorabilia from a large AA convening; a figurine of Mary holding baby Jesus; and a "spiritual warfare prayer" a drug treatment counselor had given to her. The objects were a physical manifestation of the 12-Step logic.

Julia explained the "spiritual warfare prayer" is "a prayer you pray every day to like clear your way for that day. Any type of spirit that's not right, ask God to remove that spirit from around you . . . 'cause that's not how you want to be, you don't want to be a part of that. 'Cause those the type of spirits that can keep you in depression. Or can get you in trouble. Or how you said things out your mouth that's gonna get you in trouble." In the self-improvement class, Julia learned "self-improvement is changing your thinking pattern, your behavior pattern, but you have to get to the core of the situation to find out. It's like doin' inventory. You have to dig deep in yourself to find out what these defects of character you have are doin' to you, how they damagin' you, how can you improve 'em." She planned to add to her windowsill a certificate for a "mortification program" she completed, where the instructor taught "deliverance through recovery. It's like puttin' the AA, NA with the Bible. Because that's where the AA originated from, the Bible." Julia expressed admiration for the instructor, who drew on his own recovery process to teach the 12 Steps, "but then he could tell you about the Word of God because . . . he was brought up with the Word . . . so he combined everything together and he made all things possible."

Building upon the religious imagery, Julia described her windowsill as "a shrine. It's a reminder of the achievements that I made and that it could be more if I keep goin'. And I'm proud of it." At the time she took the photograph, Julia was relatively early in her recovery, with less than a year of clean time. She was not employed, had not earned her high school diploma, and did not have her own apartment—all accomplishments she later achieved. Julia knew she had a long road ahead of her, yet she was able to feel pride in how far she already had come and a commitment to continuing her personal transformation. The certificates testified to Julia's recovering identity and provided a reminder of her self-worth, dignity, and deservingness of a better life than she previously experienced while unhoused, using drugs, and regularly surviving gender-based violence. Her particular engagement of the 12-Step logic unlocked that joy and dignity.

Like Julia, many women indicated how they used the 12-Step logic to achieve a delicate balance between accepting personal responsibility and demanding more. Taken together, their recollections showed the immense pain and overwhelming hopelessness that emerged from the intersection of drug use and structural violence. For these women, the alternative to incarceration was death, either as a result of drug use or the routine violence they faced. Their limited life chances reflected the social reality of living in disadvantaged communities in the U.S. "prison nation."[74] In the wake of disinvestment from public institutions and social welfare programs, jails and prisons have stepped in to fill the gaps.[75] As a result, women are caught up in a hostile system that demands not only that they stop using drugs and breaking the law, but also that they accept their subordinated position within a larger social system. While they can be critical of racism, sexism, poverty, and the violence and discrimination the criminal legal system perpetrates, they ultimately must accept personal responsibility for their situations and embrace the 12-Step logic, with its perpetual surveillance and moral judgment, as the only viable way to survive in such a hostile world.

Despite this oppressive circumstance, women found ways to work within the 12-Step logic to claim self-worth and advance legitimate critiques. Women embraced the religious disposition of the 12-Step logic, in particular, to take ownership of their recovery, without justifying the criminal legal system's violent and unfair treatment. They used the logic to resolve the tension among violence, personal responsibility, and critique of systems and individuals who repeatedly failed and outright harmed them. Although the system judged and punished them for their drug use and mandated that they get "clean," it was God who offered a way for them to save their lives. While the state labeled women as *criminal-addicts*, women used the 12-Step logic to contest this stigmatized identity. In doing so, women subverted the underlying judgments and affirmation of the criminal legal system that are embedded in the 12-Step logic.

CONCLUSION

As Mariana Valverde explains, recovery programs rooted in the 12 Steps hinge on the concept of freedom: people are "addicts" because they lack the willpower to control their substance use.[76] Freedom from addiction requires strengthening one's will. For criminalized women, the relationship between freedom and will took on added significance. Willpower was necessary not only to be free from addiction, but also from incarceration and the overarching violence of the criminal legal system. Women embraced the 12-Step logic to have the best chance of achieving some semblance of freedom. Personal responsibility did not justify or excuse the violence they endured throughout the criminalization process or the trauma that so often led to their drug use. The 12-Step logic's focus on personal responsibility offered a way for women to claim control, albeit limited, over their lives, while the logic's religious nature offered an opportunity, albeit rigid, for women to feel worthy of love, salvation, respect, and a chance at a more peaceful, fulfilling life.

My goal is not to critique 12-Step programs or people's engagement of 12-Step discourses. Countless people, including many women who participated in this study, credit 12-Step programs with saving their lives, and it is important to honor those experiences. What I am critiquing, however, are the venues and institutions through which criminalized women engaged the 12-Step discourse.[77] In the context of criminalization, the 12 Steps become something other than a helpful, voluntary program that can provide an opportunity to connect with a supportive community. They become what I have termed the 12-Step logic, an organizing discourse that totally structures women's lives and creates a particular type of self—specifically a moral and spiritual self that, if constantly tended to, might keep women out of the clutches of the carceral system, though the threat of criminalization remains ever present. The 12-Step logic provides the discourse the state uses in tandem with punitive laws and policies that promote social exclusion.

Throughout the next three chapters, I examine women's identity work, particularly how they engaged the 12-Step logic to create *rehabilitated* identities in contrast to past *criminal-addict* identities. Foregrounding women's gendered markers of rehabilitation, I show how redemption, much like mortification, was a gendered experience.

4

"I Feel Good about Myself Now"

Recovering Identity through Employment and Appearance

Ella and I were in a celebratory mood when we sat down for our third interview at Growing Stronger. Along with Sister Mary, one of the staff at Growing Stronger, I had accompanied Ella the previous day to court for her scheduled hearing to have her criminal record sealed. Ella had been eagerly awaiting this day. In our previous interviews, she had explained in detail the steps she had taken over the past eight months to navigate the record sealing process. She had begun our PEI with a photograph of her rap sheet, which she had retrieved from the Chicago Police Department's headquarters. The pro bono attorneys who staffed the expungement help desk at the Daley Center needed to see Ella's complete police record in order to advise her on the record sealing process. The first page of the rap sheet included Ella's mug shot from one of her earliest arrests (figure 10).[1] Looking at the photo, Ella explained:

> Wow. Yeah. I know physically I look different. Mentally I was different, too. I was much smaller. Right now, I'm in a size 20. Right there, I was in a size 3. So it's a big difference. I don't think I look what you would say happy here, which most people don't goin' to jail. But I'm just sayin' sometimes you can tell if a person have an inner peace . . . people say I have a kind spirit, and a lot of people tell me it's like I have an aura about me, that I come off nice. I'm sure I still have that, but you can see, at least I can, the trauma and stuff in my face, in my eyes. I don't look happy. And it's not just from goin' to jail. My spirit was damaged in a lot of areas, and I used to try to cover that up with drugs instead of dealin' with it.

Ella's reflection resonated with the personal transformation theme that emerged across interviews, as women contrasted their past *criminal-addict* identities with their *rehabilitated* identities, and acknowledged the deep healing work required

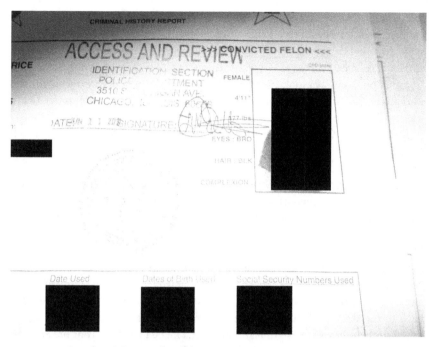

FIGURE 10. Rap sheet (Photo credit: Ella).

for women to move forward from the violence that characterized many of their lives prior to and during incarceration. Ella's reflection added nuance to how this transformation process occurred. Specifically, her focus on her appearance and what it revealed about her internal state drew attention to the markers of recovery women used to distinguish their past and current selves.

Walking into court for her hearing to have her record sealed, the 46-year-old African American mother of five could not have looked more different from how she appeared in the mug shot. Her braided hair was neatly styled into a bun. Her skin had a healthy glow. Her eyes were vibrant. Her face frequently broke into an easy, genuine smile. All together, these features communicated a warm, open, caring personality that made Ella one of the most respected and trusted staff members among the Growing Stronger residents whom I interviewed. When the court clerk called Ella's name, Sister Mary and I accompanied her to the front of the courtroom. We stood with Ella before the judge, one of us on either side, as he quickly flipped through the stack of paperwork that included certificates of program completion and letters of support written by various people who had been part of Ella's rehabilitation process over the past seven years since her release from prison. Ella had worked diligently for nearly a year assembling the collection of documents she hoped would attest to her good character. The judge seemed more interested in hearing from Sister Mary and me, whom Ella introduced as her boss and her friend, respectively. He asked each of us to say a few words. Sister Mary spoke first and described Ella as one of Growing Stronger's stars and an excellent employee. Ella had stayed at Growing Stronger as a resident following her release from prison. Now, as a staff member, she supported newly released women who were in the beginning stages of their recovery and postincarceration processes. It was undeniable that Ella had come a long way.

Sister Mary mentioned the more detailed letter she had written that was included in the stack of documents before the judge. The legal aid attorney who was assisting Ella interjected to note the stack of certificates Ella had provided. The judge said documentation was good, but sometimes the "personal touch" was more important. He then asked me if I wanted to say anything. I did my best to hide my surprise. The judge had no idea who I was and certainly did not know I had only known Ella for about two months. I knew in this context, however, that my Whiteness and middle-class appearance were more compelling than the nature and length of my relationship with Ella. I said I echoed what Sister Mary had shared and added that Ella was an amazing woman who had overcome a lot and was determined to keep going. The judge nodded. He turned his attention back to the stack of documents Ella had provided and asked her some cursory questions before posing a significant one: What helped you turn your life around? Ella clearly and confidently explained that a well-known local drug treatment program for women, Growing Stronger, and God were the key factors that allowed her to change her life. The judge smiled with satisfaction and granted Ella's request to seal her criminal record.

On the drive back to Growing Stronger, we reflected on what had just happened. Ella commented she was happy Sister Mary and I had been in the courtroom with her, because the judge had wanted to hear from us.[2] Sister Mary asked Ella how she wanted to celebrate. Ella replied that she could not drink and she was working on her diet, so maybe with a smoothie. When we arrived back at Growing Stronger, staff and residents shared in Ella's good news. Sister Mary had someone take a photograph of the three of us that later was displayed on the "Accomplishments" bulletin board. Ella seemed genuinely happy and proud, smiling, laughing, and answering questions from residents and staff about the process. One coworker asked whether she could have her own record sealed even though she had a battery charge. In her characteristic honest and encouraging way, Ella replied that it was hard but not impossible to seal a record with a battery charge. The celebration continued the next day, when Sister Mary brought flowers and a congratulations sign for Ella, as well as ingredients to make smoothies.

To begin our third interview, I asked Ella if she had any reflections about what had happened at court the previous day. She said she "still was on cloud nine, elated about the whole situation." She quickly added that she had read over the paperwork the court provided and had a better understanding about the difference between sealing and expunging one's record. Since her record was sealed, not expunged, it remained in the system and could still create limitations in certain situations. She gave the examples of trying to get a job working with children or in a hospital. In both situations, a potential employer could still access her record. Ella wanted to become a social worker and work with youth, so she was going to have to pursue expungement. Additionally, she had three cases on her record that, due to their classification, did not qualify for sealing. Those cases thus remained visible to anyone who had the ability to complete a background check, such as a landlord or potential employer. Ella explained she would have to seek clemency from the governor in order to have those cases removed. Yesterday's court hearing was a win, but it was not an end point. Ella had more work to do. Even after explaining these limitations, Ella asserted, "Man, I feel good."

Ella's mug shot photo, experience in court, and reflections on both revealed the tension that existed between her agency and the judgment she continued to face. Despite the persistent influence of her past criminalization and drug use, Ella found joy in demonstrating her rehabilitated identity. She was "elated" knowing the judge recognized her as a new woman. Her neat, clean appearance communicated her sobriety, and her employment communicated her stability. On paper and in person, Ella did not just look like someone who had stayed out of trouble with the law for the past seven years; she looked like a strong woman who was thriving. In this context, Ella's appearance and employment worked as gendered markers of her rehabilitation. The image captured in the mug shot of a gaunt, dull, disheveled, sad figure swimming in a wrinkled T-shirt several sizes too big—and all of the racist, sexist stereotypes it evoked—might as well have been a different woman.

In this chapter and the next two, I examine women's personal transformation as a gendered and racialized process. Within the context of the interlocking stigmas associated with criminalization, drug use, and race, women drew upon gendered markers of recovery across five areas in their daily lives: appearance, employment, domesticity, mothering, and relationships.[3] Although normative femininity was not an available social status, the women who participated in this project used femininity creatively and adeptly to demonstrate their ongoing rehabilitation and claim dignity in the face of intersecting oppressions and ongoing judgment. Women's identity shifts represented a balance between independence and nurturing others and were grounded in sobriety and faith. As Ella summarized for the judge, drug treatment, God, and Growing Stronger—a faith-based recovery home that focused on both—helped her become the woman she is today. I also show how these identity shifts emerged in relationship to racist controlling images of Black femininity and explain how women's identity work reflected a new controlling image that has emerged in the era of mass incarceration: *the rehabilitated woman.*

The rehabilitated woman image refers to a formerly incarcerated woman, most likely a woman of color, who has successfully transitioned from prison to the community. It entails a healthy physical appearance, legitimate employment, stable housing, being there for one's children, and, if involved in a romantic relationship, it is one that is mutually beneficial and free from abuse. Demonstrating this new identity required fluency in the 12-Step logic, with its focus on the intertwined relationship between faith and sobriety and lifelong commitment to personal transformation. Despite this rigid framework, women experienced joy and were motivated by the pleasure they felt as they became the women, mothers, lovers, and friends they wanted to be. The story of personal transformation encompassed much more than judgment, uncertainty, and fear.[4] Still, there were drawbacks to the rehabilitated woman image. As discussed in chapter 2, controlling images are racist, dehumanizing tropes, such as the "welfare queen" and "crack ho," that reduce women of color to stereotypes and provide ideological justification for punitive policies and structural arrangements that perpetuate social inequality.[5] Like all controlling images, the rehabilitated woman image ultimately justified inequality by ignoring structural factors that contributed to women's criminalization in favor of blaming individual women as inherently deviant and responsible for their personal troubles and for society's ills.

Through working the 12 Steps, deepening her faith, and staying out of trouble with the law, the rehabilitated woman showed it was possible to make it on the outside. This success was important. Staying out of prison and building a stable life free from drug use and gendered violence were undeniably positive developments for the women in this study. Yet, this success also reinforced the personal responsibility rhetoric and moral judgment inherent in the 12-Step logic. It supported responsibilization processes that hold individuals solely responsible for the consequences of decades of systematic disinvestment and marginalization. Similar to how the "welfare queen" controlling image provided ideological justification for welfare reform, the rehabilitated woman controlling image provided ideological justification for lifelong surveillance and normalized the degraded social status criminalized women occupy in a society where they never can fully overcome the moral judgment that follows them long beyond the end of their formal sentence. Thus, criminalized women faced a lifelong double bind: succeed and inadvertently provide validation for an oppressive system, or fail and be swallowed up by that system.

This chapter focuses on the first two components of women's identity work: employment and appearance, both of which were rooted in deep-seated ideologies about gender and race. I begin with employment and appearance because they represent dimensions of independence. Dependence is a contentious, multilayered term in feminist and carceral studies. It is instilled with gendered, racial, and moral meanings. In their influential article "A Genealogy of Dependency: Tracing a Keyword of the U.S. Welfare State," Nancy Fraser and Linda Gordon explain the historical shifts in the political, economic, sociolegal, and moral/psychological meanings of the term. They conclude the meaning of *dependency* has shifted from a description of social relations to a description of "inherent character traits

of individuals or groups" and today "designate[s] . . . an anomalous, highly stigmatized status of deviant and incompetent individuals."[6] With this new meaning,
"postindustrial culture has called up a new personification of dependency: the
black, unmarried, teenaged, welfare-dependent mother . . . a powerful ideological
trope that simultaneously organizes diffuse cultural anxieties."[7]

Dependence is a pervasive discourse that organizes criminalized women's lives
and structures the criminal legal system. Sociologist Jill A. McCorkel examines
how the carceral state today frames dependency as the source of women's criminality in a way that differs from its assessment of men. In this framing, men's criminality reflects a reasonable effort to gain money or respect and is a threat to public
safety. Women's criminality, on the other hand, reflects a deep internal problem,
like lack of self-respect, self-esteem, and self-empowerment, and is a threat to
social mores.[8] As sociologist Susan Sered summarizes, "If men . . . are punished
for being too aggressive, women are berated for being victims."[9] Dependence not
only suggests an inability to take care of oneself. It also suggests a disordered self,
still lacking in self-respect, self-esteem, and self-empowerment, and therefore still
susceptible to criminality. As such, the punitive and rehabilitative interventions
women experienced throughout the criminal legal system took on a moral tone.

As dimensions of independence, appearance and employment were foundational to all the identity work women did and therefore to women's overall personal
transformation processes. Women's self-described improved, healthy appearances
communicated their recovery from drug use, in other words, that they no longer were dependent on drugs or alcohol and therefore were "clean." Employment
held the promise that women would not have to depend on other people or institutions for their day-to-day survival. With each component of the rehabilitated
woman controlling image (appearance, employment, domesticity, mothering, and
relationships), I highlight the tensions between women's past and current identities, the vulnerability associated with their past identities, and the joy women
experienced in performing rehabilitation.

To do so, I build upon two frameworks: Julie Harris and Karen McElrath's
clean/dirty dichotomy and Kelly Moore's fear/joy spectrum.[10] Harris and McElrath explain how abstinence-based models, like the 12 Steps, construct recovery
as an all or nothing identity project and impose a strict "'clean/dirty' dichotomy"
that effectively erases additional, "incremental" identities by recognizing only
two subject positions: "clean" or "dirty."[11] Relapse wipes away days, months, and
even years of living a clean life, returning people to a dirty identity. Moore argues
that neoliberalism demands the continual production and improvement of the
self, with fear and uncertainty constituting one set of motivators for change and
pleasure, excitement, and fun constituting another. Focusing on exercise regi-
mens, Moore examines how women face social expectations to show enjoyment of
their self-improvement—a gendered emotion work that accompanies the physical
work of producing a "healthy" and "fit" body. Taking pleasure in this never-ending

TABLE 1 Criminalized Women's Identity Work

	Criminal-addict identity		Rehabilitated identity
Social status	Dependence	←————————→	Independence
Feeling	Fear	←————————→	Joy
Recovery status	Dirty	←————————→	Clean
Controlling image	Welfare queen Crack ho	←————————→	Rehabilitated woman

production and "enjoy[ing] being between the now and the future state" is a gendered component of neoliberal embodiment.[12] I bring together these two frameworks to show how criminalized women feel fear *and* joy as they used gendered markers of rehabilitation to navigate the clean/dirty dichotomy and, in the process, manage the controlling image of the rehabilitated woman.

Table 1 summarizes the social context and lived experience of women's identity work. Women were constrained by dominant discourses (e.g., dependency, the 12 Steps, and controlling images) and also creatively engaged these discourses to claim dignity and affirm their rehabilitation. Identity work occurred on a spectrum, as women made progress and experienced setbacks in their rehabilitation processes, yet the institutions and people who had control over their lives typically recognized women as fitting in one of two categories at any given moment: either clean or dirty, crude designations that reduced women's complex experiences and identities to simplistic labels.

Below, I first provide contextualizing points on sociological understandings of identity; controlling images that denigrate women of color, specifically Black women; and the criminal legal system's work to contain and produce racialized gendered subjects. This context illuminates the layers of marginalization with which criminalized women contended and the available discourses upon which women drew to construct new, credible identities.

CONSTRUCTING IDENTITY

In the symbolic-interaction tradition, the self is an inherently social product. Individuals do not possess a core, innate identity; rather, one's identity only exists through social interactions.[13] Social theorist George Herbert Mead theorized the self as being formulated and reformulated through the ongoing negotiation of one's sense of who they are in relationship to the self that is mirrored back to them by others.[14] Sociologist Erving Goffman analyzed social interactions as a stage upon which individuals perform different roles, using tools such as dress, body language, and facial expressions to manage others' impressions and create an authentic performance that is received as credible.[15] Social discourses guide these performances and how they are received. For instance, behaviors are interpreted differently based on the race, class, gender, and sexuality of the person performing that behavior. In short, the self is an interactional accomplishment that is deeply social and structured by social hierarchies. As political theorist Barbara Cruikshank argues, "the self is . . . not personal but the product of power relations."[16]

Understanding the social-historical context and available discourses within which identity work occurs is immensely important. The symbolic-interaction tradition has produced significant insights about the social construction of gender. Gender scholars Candace West and Don Zimmerman famously coined the phrase "doing gender" to examine how gender is an achieved status and interactional accomplishment. As people receive positive reinforcement for socially conventional performances of femininity and masculinity, and negative sanctions for performances that transgress gender norms, the very definition of gender is reproduced.[17] Yet, gender performances never are solely about gender, as they always are structured by additional intersecting systems of inequality.

Feminist critical race scholars examine how race and class shape the construction of multiple, unequal femininities. Patricia Hill Collins, for instance, examines how "controlling images of Black womanhood" discursively work to close off attainment of hegemonic (i.e., White) femininity to Black women and uphold the structures of patriarchy, White supremacy, and capitalism.[18] The feminine ideal of the virtuous woman who selflessly cares for others and defers to the authority of men, who in turn will provide her with the security and protection she not only needs but deserves, is attainable to a select group of women who possess the social privileges of Whiteness, financial security, heterosexuality, and citizenship.[19] Women who lack this social privilege are precluded access to the true womanhood ideal and its associated benefits, such as support for mothering and protection from violence. While all women experience gender-based oppression, the nature of that oppression is shaped by race, class, sexuality, nationhood, and additional social locations; gender-based oppression serves additional projects that differentially benefit and harm women.

THE CRIMINAL LEGAL SYSTEM
AND FEMININE SUBJECTS

Criminalized women face judgment and stigma for the double violation of the law and feminine norms.[20] The state's interventions in criminalized women's lives, whether explicitly punitive or supposedly therapeutic, always have aimed to enforce compliance with both the law and gender norms.[21] Women's economic class and racial identities structure these interventions. Women's reformatories of the late 19th and early 20th centuries used isolation, education, and surveillance to prepare middle-class women to be devoted mothers and wives and working-class and poor women to work as domestic servants, thereby restoring "fallen women" to respectable social positions.[22] Notably, Black women largely were not sentenced to reformatories and were housed in men's penitentiaries, based on the assumption they were not real women and could not benefit from interventions to restore femininity. During the era of convict leasing in the South, White women largely were spared placement in convict labor camps, based on the belief they were too fragile for the intense labor and punishment that were common in these camps.[23] Black women, however, were sentenced to these camps, forced to do the same work, and subjected to the same physical punishments as men. Black women additionally were responsible for the domestic labor that kept the camp functioning and were subjected to sexual violence, which historian Sarah Haley refers to as the "double burden of both labor and violence."[24] Labeling Black women as inherently nongender normative provided ideological justification for the torturous racist and sexual violence Black women routinely experienced under convict leasing and reaffirmed normative femininity as White.[25]

Criminalized women today regularly encounter a particular type of gendered governance that targets their emotions, desires, and morality.[26] The tasks the criminal legal system imposes on women include getting in touch with and learning to contain their emotions;[27] controlling "dangerous desires" that lead to unhealthy lifestyle and relationship choices;[28] creating strong selves to replace "diseased and incomplete selves" that are the source of their troubles;[29] and building up their sense of empowerment and independence so that they can make better decisions about their lives.[30] As sociologist Kelly Hannah-Moffat summarizes, "By attending programmes such as parenting, life skills, substance abuse, anger management and vocational classes [incarcerated] women are expected to conform to a series of normative standards."[31]

Three common threads run through these well-documented interventions to reform criminalized women. The first is the neoliberal logic of personal responsibility, which absolves the state of responsibility for social welfare and reframes social problems caused by structural inequality as individual problems to be overcome through personal change.[32] The second is the interwoven thread of dependency, which, as noted above, puts a gendered spin on personal responsibility. Women's imprisonment encompasses more than the loss of liberty; it is a state project to regulate and reformulate women's selves. The third is the unrelenting relationship between punishment and racist gender ideology that remains alive and well in the U.S. criminal legal system today.[33] These interventions are deeply rooted in controlling images about women of color's dependence, lack of discipline, and promiscuity. These "enduring legacies"[34] continue to mark women of color as always already deviant and dangerous.[35]

As with all controlling images, the rehabilitated woman controlling image is inherently racialized, even though White women also are harmed by criminalization and struggle with postincarceration challenges. Similar to the "crack ho" or "welfare queen" controlling images, the rehabilitated woman controlling image is rooted in White supremacy and reflects the interconnected nature of the social constructions of both race and gender. The women who participated in this study recognized the relationship between race, gender, and criminalization. As I discuss further in chapter 6, several Black participants critiqued racial inequality in the criminal legal system and throughout society. Only 4 of the 36 participants identified as White. Two of these four White women shared some version of a fish out of water story while reflecting on their own experiences of criminalization. Cathy Hill, for instance, struggled with losing some of the benefits of Whiteness and her middle-class background. Using explicitly racist terms, she repeatedly commented on how she was not like the other women caught up in the criminal legal system, suggesting she was not supposed to be part of this system. When Iris first called me to express her interest in participating in the project, she made a point to clarify her story was a bit different from most of the other stories I likely was hearing. She offered this clarification to ensure I still wanted to interview her, almost as if she did not want to mislead me. These reflections shaped and affirmed my conceptualization of the rehabilitated woman as a controlling image.

Considering how criminalization works within the context of controlling images reveals that criminalized women of color face judgment as more than just "doubly deviant," as race already marks a violation of normative femininity. Criminalized women of color, thus, face a distinctly gendered stigma related to the *criminal-addict* status and to race. In addition to the "dirty," "impure" controlling images poor women and women of color encounter on the basis of race and class, criminalized women encounter the further "dirty," "impure" label of "criminal" and often "addict." Indeed, 12-Step discourses label people who are still using as "dirty" and people in recovery as "clean," and urinalysis results that show the presence of drugs commonly are referred to as "dirty drops." For the women in this study, perhaps no controlling image was more prevalent than that of the "crack ho," as it exists at the nexus of race, gender, poverty, drug use, and criminalization. The image connotes a promiscuous, immoral, manipulative poor Black woman who is so overcome by her dependence on drugs that she cannot be trusted to take care of herself or her children, maintain a home or job, or even follow the law.[36] Along with its masculine counterpart "the gangbanger," the racist, gendered controlling image of the "crack ho" provided ideological justification for the policies and practices that gave rise to the current era of mass incarceration.[37] These overarching systems and discourses constitute the social context within which formerly incarcerated women did the work of personal transformation.

REHABILITATING THE SELF

Incarceration breaks down the self.[38] As such, rebuilding the self is a central part of postincarceration life.[39] That rebuilding often entails a cognitive transformation process in which people make sense of their past behavior and envision a future rehabilitated self.[40] Formerly incarcerated people who are "making good" frequently draw distinctions between their past, current, and future selves, highlighting the work they are doing to facilitate this change.[41] Claiming a rehabilitated identity entails showing just how distant one's current identity is from one's past "criminal" identity. Simply believing in one's own personal transformation, however, is insufficient. Creating a rehabilitated self is a process of constantly negotiating how one feels about their personal transformation process, how others respond to this process, and institutional recognition or rejection of it. Additionally, structural constraints that suggest rehabilitation is not possible—such as continual denial of employment, housing, and other supports—can derail one's identity work.[42]

Criminalized women worked to craft rehabilitated selves against the intersecting stigmas and vulnerability associated with criminalization, drug use, poverty, race, and gender. Acknowledging this social-historical context raises a number of questions about criminalized women's understandings of their own identities—past, present, and future. How do criminalized women claim a sense of self in the face of institutions that read them as never rehabilitated but, at best, as working to maintain their rehabilitation? Against a backdrop of stigmatizing discourses that are so deeply gendered, how do criminalized women use gender—implicitly and explicitly—in their narratives of personal transformation?

For the remainder of this chapter, I show how criminalized women traded in a currency the state recognized, specifically feminine appearance and employment. The rehabilitated woman controlling image presumes a particular idea of femininity. I cannot point to a specific vehicle through which this idea of femininity reached the women who participated in this study. Because I did not conduct ethnographic research, I did not observe support groups or other interactions where recovery home or program staff explicitly taught or subtly encouraged a particular type of femininity. It is likely women pulled from a variety of formal and informal sources—such as popular culture, books, classes, groups, counseling, drug treatment programs, family members, and peers—to develop their notion of what it meant to accomplish femininity. The gendered governance literature meticulously documents how carceral programs explicitly push a particular idea of what it means to be a reformed woman. I presume the organizations with which women in my research interacted operated in similar ways, in part because of this extensive literature, but even more so because the components of gendered rehabilitation that make up the core of my analysis were so prominent across the interviews I conducted. It is noteworthy that the women who participated in this study were engaged in a variety of postincarceration and drug treatment programs. While there was overlap in program participation, women were not always engaged in the same programs. This diversity of program participation suggests just how pervasive this idea of femininity was.

Additionally, as the remaining chapters show, there was room for variation within the rehabilitated woman controlling image. Women did not have to approximate White beauty standards to demonstrate rehabilitation through their appearance, for instance. Nor did they have to partner with a man to show rehabilitation through relationships. There was not even one acceptable way to mother. The key way women accomplished femininity was through drawing a stark contrast between their past *criminal-addict* selves and their current *rehabilitated* selves. As long as this general contrast existed, the specifics could vary.

Still, there are questions regarding how much variation or departure from conventional notions of femininity, particularly regarding sexuality, would be acceptable in the eyes of program staff and actors within the criminal legal system. Only two women, Lynn and Faye, talked about being in a same-sex relationship, and they happened to be partnered with each other. As I note in chapter 6, Lynn reported confronting homophobia at multiple recovery homes and being kicked out of one when she and Faye were caught engaging in sexual activity in the home. In one of our interviews, New Life was critical of some of the church services offered in prison for being explicitly homophobic, with preachers condemning homosexuality as a sin. As such, there is evidence heterosexuality was a presumed part of women's rehabilitated identities on the part of at least some service providers. What is noteworthy for my analysis, though, is how women rejected such rigid and discriminatory constructions of sexuality, retaining a positive sense of self despite others' judgment. Additionally, none of the participants in this study identified as transgender or nonbinary. Future research should investigate how criminalized LGBTQ+ people accomplish rehabilitated identities and what those efforts reveal about the coconstitutive nature of gender, sexuality, and criminalization.

Criminalized women worked within, challenged, and adapted available discourses, primarily the 12-Step logic, to craft rehabilitated identities. It was not so much that prison programs and recovery homes laid out a precise discourse of what a good woman was; rather, the 12-Step logic made clear what she was not, which informed the oppositional nature of the identity work women engaged. I am critical of these discourses because they were so rigid, subjected women to invasive moral judgment and extensive surveillance, largely ignored the structural oppression and violence that have deeply harmed criminalized women, and reduced these social issues to individual problems. In this way, I join a long line of feminist scholars who critique the carceral state for focusing on individual-level responses to structural issues that legitimize punitive interventions, the harm these interventions cause, and the social inequality they deepen.[43]

In order to truly listen to the women who participated in this project and honor their lived experiences, I also examine how these discourses provided hooks women could engage to create more fulfilling lives and feel good about themselves. The paradox of the rehabilitated woman controlling image is that it made it possible for women to carve out a space of personal protection, growth, and joy—an undeniably positive outcome—while also reaffirming the overarching discourses that structured women's lives, including those that cause severe harm. This tension reflects a fundamental social truth embedded in all controlling images: women subject to these images are not, in the eyes of society, real women. They exist outside the bounds of what is recognized as normative and fully human. Criminalized women were not passive subjects, however. They played with the rehabilitated woman controlling image to resolve (or at least manage) the tension between structural arrangements and ideological discourses that denied their humanity, and their intense commitment to personal transformation and living in ways that brought dignity and joy.[44]

APPEARANCE: EMBODIED FEMININITY

Women often included pictures of themselves in the PEIs.[45] Discussing these photographs, women reflected on how they viewed themselves, how they suspected others viewed them, and how their physical appearances communicated a great deal about their personal transformation processes. Incarceration is an embodied experience that causes long-lasting changes to one's body, dispositions, and sense of self.[46] Formerly incarcerated people contend with these embodied changes as they navigate postincarceration experiences. For the women who participated in this project, improved physical appearances were signs of moving forward not only from incarceration, but also from drug use and histories of abuse.[47] As women's appearances more closely approximated normative standards of femininity, they demonstrated and felt they were achieving rehabilitation. Sociologist Edward Flores found in his research with gang-involved men that "embodied masculine practices and performances facilitated recovery, as the body symbolically and concretely represented the struggle between gang life and recovery."[48] Similarly, women in this project described how *feminine* practices and performances reflected their personal transformations from *criminal-addicts* to *rehabilitated women*. Cultivating a healthy feminine appearance was a pleasurable experience that created distance from the fear and risks associated with past identities.

Multiple women referenced weight gain and changes in their complexions as evidence of improved health and abstinence from drugs. Carmel, a 44-year-old Black woman, recalled a time during her past drug use when she had looked so unhealthy that she would not visit her long-time partner while he was in jail. She explained, "I was so ashamed, I didn't even wanna look at myself! You know, I had lost so much weight, you know, 82 pounds, and cocaine has got me just this black. You know, 'No, I'm not comin' to let you see me.' You know. And my auntie, she would tell me that, you know, 'God, you lookin' bad' . . . You know, I didn't comb my hair or anything. She, 'Girl, you look terrible, Carmel.'" Others' interpretations of Carmel's weight and complexion mirrored back to her a vision of herself as an "addict." The shame that reflection evoked compelled Carmel to limit contact with loved ones. Conversely, women's new appearances were testaments to their "clean" identities.[49]

Simply having control over their appearances signified progress. Prison is a "defeminizing" experience; rules that limit or prohibit personal expression through dress, makeup, and hairstyles strip women of their individuality and traditional markers of femininity.[50] Recovery homes often provided women with special salon and spa days, which helped women reclaim their femininity and distance themselves from their experiences in prison and on the streets. Nyla, a 42-year-old Black woman, reflected on this transformation when discussing a photograph of herself following one of these "beauty days." For Nyla, the photograph revealed more than just a transformation in her physical appearance. It also revealed her recovery from drug use. She had sent the photograph to her incarcerated son so he could see the physical evidence of her recovery, specifically her weight gain. In an earlier letter, her son had told her that he forgave her for being absent, explaining, "I never could hate you. It was just that I hated to see what the drugs were doin' to you and how skinny and pale in the face you were." When sending the photograph to her son, Nyla wrote to him, "You can laugh, because I know I have gained some weight." She explained that for her children "to see me just healthy, you know, that means a lot." Nyla's weight gain and darker complexion were positive changes that reflected her good health and communicated her fitness as a mother.

Nyla took pleasure in displaying her femininity in ways that reaffirmed her rehabilitated identity. The physical markers of her recovery reminded her that she was becoming the woman she wanted to be. She explained she had been "amazed" by her appearance following the beauty day. Wearing her hair down and fashionably styled rather than in a ponytail as she typically did was a fun way to demonstrate how far away she was from prison. She knew she had to remain vigilant in her identity work, though. The beauty day photograph prompted Nyla to recall what she referred to as a "before picture" that showed how she looked when she was in "that lifestyle." Nyla hung the "before picture" on the wall in her room at the recovery home. It offered motivation and reassurance that no matter how bad things seemed today, "it's just not all that bad. It's . . . getting better." It also was a reminder of the *criminal-addict* identity she was working to leave behind. Nyla recalled first seeing the "before picture" when a friend sent it to her while she was incarcerated. "It simply said to me that my soul was hurting. I was so tired. It, my soul was just cryin' out . . . I actually cried when I saw that picture . . . I looked at that picture, and I could feel the pain."

The similarities between Nyla's description of her "before photo" and Ella's reflection on her mug shot were striking. Both women went far beyond noting their criminalized status or drug use and zeroed in on the way trauma and violence impacted their identities, specifically the hurting of Nyla's soul and the damage of Ella's spirit. The pleasure Nyla felt in her new appearance existed in tension with her fear of returning to her past self that was documented in the "before picture," the self that looked like a woman who was dependent on drugs and an unfit mother. Recall the lightness and darkness imagery Nyla used to contrast periods of her life when she was under the protection of God's umbrella with periods when she was doing what the devil would have her do. The healthy, bright image she was able to share with her son reflected alignment of her faith, recovery,

FIGURE 11. Chicago police (Photo credit: Chicken Wing).

and gendered identity. Her changed appearance reflected her commitment to the deep internal moral and spiritual identity work the rehabilitated woman controlling image demanded.

The way others reacted to women's physical appearances provided a gauge of how well they performed the rehabilitated woman identity. Chicken Wing, a 55-year-old Black woman, took a photograph of a police officer (figure 11)[51] and explained what it showed: "I don't have to be scared of the police no more . . . I can go up and ask them, 'Can I take your picture?' You know, I don't look like a crackhead. I don't look like I'm fittin' to rob nobody. I can go in stores now. I feel good about myself now." Chicken Wing's friendly exchange with the officer when she obtained his permission to take his photograph revealed a dramatic change not only in how she felt about herself, but also in how the officer viewed her. She had explained to him she wanted to take his picture because she was making a documentary about criminals. He had responded, "But I'm the good guy, right?" Chicken Wing had replied, "Yes, you are."

She clearly had fun with this exchange, even joking with the officer. This interaction was possible because of his assessment of her as a fellow person on the right side of the law, which stemmed from her appearance. She no longer looked like a "crackhead," which she described as "breasts . . . sunk in. Your neck's sunk in. You're lookin' like a *wreck*. Like I was 20 years ago. I looked bad. I looked like I was *dead*. I just didn't have the dirt poured on me." Chicken Wing had not just looked unhealthy, she had looked decidedly unfeminine: too skinny, sunken-in breasts, disheveled, an overall inattentiveness to her appearance, which broadcasted a "dirty" identity. Chicken Wing's healthier and more put-together appearance directly repudiated the "crack ho" controlling image and helped her draw a strict boundary between her current self and her past self.

Ella shared a similar experience when describing the process of acquiring her rap sheet from the Chicago Police Department's headquarters. The officer who assisted her was surprised to learn Ella was picking up her own rap sheet. She recalled their exchange: "He was like, 'And who is this for?' I was like, 'For me.' He said, 'OK. But who is the *person*?' I said, 'Me!' He was like, 'For real?' I was like, 'Yeah.' So . . . I guess he was surprised . . . it's like you didn't believe that it could be me that was in trouble. Yeah, I been in trouble [*laughing*], you know. Maybe I don't have that look, so I felt good." Ella no longer had "that look" of the *criminal-addict*, which completely changed the tone of her interaction with this officer. When she returned a few days later to pick up her records, the same officer assisted her and informed her there was a three-dollar fee. Ella did not have any money with her, so the officer waived the fee. Ella decided to ask him for "one more favor . . . He said, 'What do you want now?' I say, 'Can I have some of them peppermints?' [*laughing*] He was like, 'Here, girl. Go on!' [*laughing*] So it was funny, but he was real nice . . . I think people look at you different, and people don't mind helpin' people if you're willin' to help yourself, you know."

Like Chicken Wing's exchange with the officer, Ella's interaction with this officer took on a playful tone and represented a complete break with her past experiences with police. She contrasted her friendly exchange while picking up her records with past arrests, noting some police officers "feel that you're the scum of the earth, or they treat you real bad because you did something that might not meet their standards." She explained a time when she was arrested for possession of a small amount of cocaine, and six squad cars encircled her:

> You would think I shot the president. I didn't do nothin'. I just had some drugs on me. You know. And they jump out the car and like five or six of 'em tryin' to grab little, ol' me! Little, ol' me! It don't take six of y'all to grab me! I didn't run. I didn't try to run. I didn't try to resist. Well, when they start twistin' my arm, yeah, I tried to get my arm. 'Cause why you twistin' my arm? You know. And they like, "You better stay still! I'll break this MF and all!" I'm like, I say, "It seem like you tryin' to anyway!" You know. "You ain't got to do all that!"

While critiquing these officers' abusive treatment, Ella also recognized her efforts to change her self were a necessary prerequisite for the changed response she now received from police officers. She explained, "First you have to seek that help, and when you do, it is people that are willing to help and want to help, you know. And I think they look at you different knowing that, OK, you made a mistake, or you did wrong, but now you're trying to correct it. Oh, you want to do better. And it's OK. We're human, we do that, you know." Ella's assertion "we're human" was critically important. When her appearance looked as it did in her mug shot, she was recognized and treated as less than human. Her new appearance reclaimed her humanity and demanded a basic level of respect that should have been a baseline for all interactions, but routinely was absent from criminalized women's lives.

FIGURE 12. Personal hygiene items (Photo credit: the Lioness).

Taking control of one's appearance was a way for women to communicate personal transformation and to accomplish femininity. The Lioness, a 49-year-old African American woman, also took pride in her new appearance, sharing a photograph of her personal hygiene items to illustrate how important it was that she took care of herself (figure 12). The photograph showed how the Lioness was different from the woman she used to be, when she would stay out overnight getting high at unfamiliar places and would be without any personal hygiene items in the morning. She recalled a specific incident when she had stolen soap, toothpaste, and deodorant from a store. The man working behind the counter confronted her outside. She explained:

> He said, "Hey!" And I turned around, and I was fittin' to run. He said, "I'ma let you have that!" He said, "But a real woman would keep," you know . . . he was sayin' things that made me feel bad as a woman . . . he was sayin' things that . . . I should be ashamed of myself . . . he made me feel so bad as a woman that I could not keep my personals and keep my hygiene up. I mean he was just tellin' me that I need to keep myself clean and my hygiene up, I shouldn't have to steal, I should have money to buy it, I mean he made me feel *so bad*. So from that day, I vowed that I would never, ever, *ever* be without hygiene products. And I am *not*. Never ever.

The store worker did not judge the Lioness for breaking the law but shamed her for failing to behave like a "real woman."

Prisons institutionally perpetuate this shame through routinely denying women sufficient access to needed items like toilet paper and sanitary napkins. Forcing women to ask officers for these items not only "infantilizes women," it constrains their ability to manage basic hygiene needs, with dehumanizing and defeminizing consequences.[52] It also connects the institutional violence incarcerated women endure to the longstanding historical reality that "black women's bodies did not belong to themselves."[53] The pervasive gendered violence throughout criminalized women's lives—interpersonal violence, community violence, and institutional violence, specifically at the hands of police and the entirety of the incarceration experience—continues that legacy and robs women of control of their own bodies. For the Lioness, drug use also robbed her of control. Taking care of her personal hygiene and appearance was a way to claim control and demonstrate her rehabilitated identity. She added that she now made sure to have three of every personal hygiene item she might need to ensure she never ran out. She commented, "Because a woman is supposed to always be clean, and fresh, and smelling good."

In this context, the Lioness's use of the word *clean* took on multiple meanings. It obviously referenced her hygiene and physical cleanliness, but at a deeper level, it also referenced her recovery from drug use. Aside from looking nice and approximating normative feminine beauty standards, the Lioness rejected dependence on drugs and tried to decrease her vulnerability to gendered violence, such as another assault by a correctional officer.[54] In doing so, she claimed power and dignity by asserting ownership of her body. As with Nyla, the Lioness's appearance reflected deep internal work and growing independence from drugs, abusive men, and violent institutions.

Just as drug use, violence, and trauma were embodied, so was recovery in women's weight gain, complexions, and overall improved appearances that approximated feminine norms. Women repeatedly noted their clean, healthy appearances as signs of recovery from drug use and criminalized activity. To underscore this point, they contrasted their current appearances with vivid descriptions of how they looked when they were "in their addictions" and "in the streets." In the past, women's appearances were evidence of their drug use and "criminality" (i.e., their "dirtiness") and reflected ways they were not living up to their roles as respectable women and mothers. Rehabilitating their feminine appearances provided a way to demonstrate the deeper changes they were making in their lives and to gain recognition for these transformations.[55] In contrast to the shame they previously felt regarding their appearances, women took pleasure in their new performances of femininity and distinguishing their past and current selves. Employment provided another way to mark this distinction.

EMPLOYMENT: THE MARK OF RESPONSIBILITY

Work is a key component of identity, particularly for formerly incarcerated people, as the ability to hold a job communicates self-discipline, moral redemption, and the transformation from *criminal* to contributing member of society.[56] As has been documented with men, sociologist Tara Opsal shows that formerly incarcerated women "saw work as an opportunity to create new identities and new lives that contrasted from those they inhabited prior to incarceration."[57] Yet, it would be a mistake to equate the meaning of work in formerly incarcerated men's and women's lives. Work is a gendered institution, as are prison and reentry.[58] As sociologist Susila Gurusami shows, the state's monitoring of formerly incarcerated women's employment connects to a long history of carceral and welfare work mandates that seek to reform and regulate Black women's presumed laziness and immorality and make them "legible" as an exploited source of labor under capitalism.[59] It follows that work not only is a site of gendered regulation, but also of gendered identity construction.

Although employment runs counter to traditional femininity scripts, it is a fundamental component of the rehabilitated woman controlling image. In her research with women on parole, Opsal found that "none of these women relied solely on traditional gender roles as they crafted their replacement selves."[60] This finding reflects the reality that normative femininity is out of reach for most criminalized women. Few formerly incarcerated women possess the myriad social privileges necessary to achieve the true womanhood ideal, regardless of whether that ideal is attractive. As poor women and women of color (primarily Black women) with criminal records living in the neoliberal era of postwelfare reform, the women who participated in this project could not rely on the state to provide financial assistance.[61] They also could not rely on partners to provide for them financially. Those who were involved in romantic relationships were partnered with men, and in one case a woman, who had their own criminal backgrounds. These partners faced intersecting discriminations based on their criminal records and race, which constrained their access to employment.[62] In short, romantic relationships did not offer financial security or an avenue out of poverty.[63] Employment thus provided critical material assistance.

For women who had stopped using drugs, appearance was the most immediately attainable gendered marker of rehabilitation. Employment, on the other hand, was a more aspirational component of the rehabilitated woman controlling image. Of the 36 women who participated in this project, only one-third (12 women) were employed at the time of the interviews, and only 5 of these employed women (less than 14 percent of all participants) held full-time jobs. Yet, almost all of the women identified employment as a goal and a necessary part of their rehabilitation processes.

This disconnect between formerly incarcerated people's desire to work and the ability to secure stable employment is well documented. Despite employment being a common requirement of parole, employer bias, criminal background check policies, and laws that bar occupational licenses for people with convictions systematically exclude formerly incarcerated people from employment.[64] It is no wonder that in 2008 formerly incarcerated people had an unemployment rate over 27 percent, almost five times higher than the general population's unemployment rate.[65] As with all parts of the criminal legal system, race and gender matter. Formerly incarcerated women experienced higher unemployment rates than formerly incarcerated men across all racial categories. Women of color, particularly Black women, fared worst. In 2008, the unemployment rate was 40 percent for formerly incarcerated Black women, 39 percent for formerly incarcerated Latinx women, and 23 percent for formerly incarcerated White women. As Lucious Couloute and Daniel Kopf conclude, "both race and gender shape the economic stability of criminalized people."[66] In addition to their criminal records, many women had limited work histories and had been out of the workforce for extended stretches while using drugs and while incarcerated.[67] Plus, women struggled to find employment that was not temporary, seasonal, or part-time and that was accessible by public transportation. Race, gender, poverty, drug use, and criminalization intersected to create a formidable barrier between formerly incarcerated women and mainstream society, with especially deleterious effects for women of color.

Women's reflections on employment indicated securing a job was about much more than just securing an income. A secure financial income would help women take care of their personal appearances, obtain stable housing, provide for their children, and protect against the vulnerabilities—both material and ideological—associated with dependence on drugs, institutions, and other people. As such, employment was a key component of women's identity work.[68] It helped women contest the controlling images of the "crack ho" and "welfare queen" and showed they were becoming productive members of society. Work was a way for criminalized women to show they were worthy of integration into society, although integration would be partial, relegating women to the margins. In a postincarceration landscape structured by surveillance, moral judgment, and control, the rehabilitated woman is a working woman.

At the most basic level, employment was necessary for women to have any chance of moving forward from the transitory period many found themselves in during the months after their release from prison. In this way, securing a job provided peace of mind and reassurance that things would get better. Nyla, for instance, explained her recent hiring at Dunkin' Donuts meant "a door open . . . I'm relieved of some of the questions. How will I do this? How will I do that? It kind of opens the door to and gives me leeway to do these things now as far as financially. Even from, like health care, like a good example is my teeth. You know, stuff like that. Little stuff. From day to day my personal items that I need . . . Bein' able to support my son in his incarceration. And just bein' able to pay my way. And somethin' is better than nothing." The part-time job alone would not provide enough to be financially independent, but it provided Nyla with reassurance she was moving in the right direction. Notably, she connected employment to her appearance, health, and relationship with her son and in doing so suggested how appearance and employment were two foundational components of the rehabilitated woman identity. Overcoming her dependence on drugs and incrementally establishing her financial independence allowed her to take care of herself and her son. The connection between material and relational needs came into focus. Nyla also highlighted that achieving the rehabilitated woman identity was a work in progress. The part-time job at Dunkin' Donuts would not allow her to rent her own apartment yet, but it signified she would be able to do so one day, perhaps even soon. In the meantime, it also allowed her to feel good about herself and proud of her progress—feelings that were unreachably distant when she was out from under the protection of God's umbrella.

Moon, a 40-year-old African American woman, made an explicit connection between employment and independence when reflecting on the progress she had made during the approximately three months she had been living at Growing Stronger. She had completed an intensive outpatient drug treatment program and was attending an adult high school program with the goal of earning her diploma. Not having a job was holding her back, however. Moon commented, "I desperately need a job . . . that's my only thing now, is I need a job." Once she had a job, she would be able to move out of Growing Stronger and start the next phase of her life. Moon continued:

> I wanna work. I don't want a handout . . . bein' here can be a blessing as well as a curse, because, if I get so complacent whereas I just don't gotta worry about no bills, I can stay at Growing Stronger. They don't have no time limit on how long you can be there . . . it'll make you lacksy daisy, you know. I don't wanna be lacksy daisy . . . Then once I get a job I can start saving my money and be independent . . . I definitely need housing, but in order to maintain housing, I need a job first, you know, so, and I'm in school that I may get a better job instead of just a job. You know, but for right now I'd be happy with just a job, you know, because I don't have the income, and that's a door that definitely needs to be opened for myself, and I want to do whatever it takes in order to make that happen so that . . . I'll still be able to be independent . . . on my own and pay rent, even if all I can do is just pay rent and insurance on myself, I'd be pleased with that, you know.

Like Nyla, Moon talked about employment as a "door" that, once opened, would propel her forward past the barrier of financial dependence that had paused her progress. Without steady employment, Moon would remain dependent on others, whether that was social service programs or other people. That financial dependence hindered her ability to truly achieve a rehabilitated identity.

While Moon made an explicit connection among employment, housing, and independence, she also alluded to the deeper personal meaning employment held. Moon made clear dependence was not a neutral description of a social relation but rather a reflection of her moral character.[69] She expressed fear of becoming "lacksy daisy," a character trait that suggested a lack of will or determination on her part.[70] Having a job would communicate she was not taking a "handout," lazy, or content with living in transitional housing programs. Employment would ward off the specter of the "welfare queen" and communicate her rehabilitation, which necessitated not only a desire to have "a better life," but also the ability to achieve one.

Employment was a marker of personal transformation that women referenced as part of establishing a boundary with their past lifestyles.[71] Although she was not employed at the time of our interviews, the Lioness discussed how becoming employed would not only show she was a "responsible" person and "a productive part of society," but would also change the way others viewed her. She explained, "When you [are] . . . a working person, people tend to look at you different. When I say, 'Oh, I gotta go to work,' or, 'I'm on my way to work,' people . . . would never look at me and say, 'Oh she's an ex-offender.' See it's a big difference. They look at you with respect. I'm more respected when I'm a working person." The Lioness noted the pride she felt when others recognized her as a responsible, productive person. These affirming views contrasted with her recollection of the corner store worker who had shamed her for not being a "real woman."

These markedly different social interactions produced two very different selves. Caught between her past identity and aspirational identity, the Lioness relied on more attainable gendered markers of rehabilitation, such as appearance, while striving toward employment. She anticipated how employment would increase the pleasure associated with performing the rehabilitated woman identity and offer further protection from the judgment and uncertainty she faced in her past "dirty" identity. The Lioness added that once she had a job, she would be able to pay back a debt she owed to a professional school. Paying this debt was important "because then . . . I will be clean . . . I won't be owin' nobody. You know, it's just . . . a sense of responsibility." Her use of the word *clean* again was important. Her debt was a reminder of her past involvement with drugs and incarceration. Erasing the debt would mark her as a responsible person and help her have a fresh start. Employment was a critical part of being able to attain a "clean" identity unencumbered by past mistakes.

Chicken Wing also discussed the importance of having a job. She took a photograph of her place of employment, a church where she prepared food, cleaned, and assisted with additional day-to-day tasks (figure 13). More important than the income it provided, the part-time job was a sign of the new person she had become. She commented, "I never had a *job* before. This is my first job. I'm 55 years old! My first job." She added she had "money in the bank" for the first time in her life and recently obtained a credit card, which showed "that I'm a productive citizen now . . . It just feels so good. And my sons are so proud of me. Least when I die . . . they can't say their mother died a crackhead." Chicken Wing expressed pride in her job and took pleasure in the markers of success it made possible. As

FIGURE 13. "My first job" (Photo credit: Chicken Wing).

she did when discussing her photograph of the police officer, Chicken Wing again invoked the controlling image of the "crackhead" and explained how she actively contested it. Further, she linked her repudiation of that image to her relationship with her four adult children, who had ranged from toddlers to teenagers when she was incarcerated 21 years earlier. Her sons' pride, which she in part attributed to her employment, helped Chicken Wing accomplish not just a new "clean" and "rehabilitated" identity, but also a new identity as a mother.

Chicken Wing's attention to her credit card was echoed by Ms. Fields, a 47-year-old Black Afro-American woman, and Denise, the 45-year-old Black woman who had worked so hard to earn Judge Hopkins's approval. Without prompting, all three discussed how obtaining a credit or debit card was a milestone that represented becoming part of society. Ms. Fields even took a photo of the Chase bank branch where she had opened a bank account after obtaining her first job postincarceration (figure 14). She talked at length about how happy she was to have a debit card: "I just felt like I was a part of something . . . I had some money, [and] I hadn't had money in 14 years, you know, unless I was stealin' or beggin' my mother . . . Everywhere I went, everybody, you know, my sponsor would swipe, my sister, everybody swiped. So I don't know if it was just the prestige or I just wanted to swipe . . . I just wanted to feel like I was a part of gettin' better, I guess." Swiping her debit card was a pleasurable act for Ms. Fields. Each swipe showed she was

FIGURE 14. Debit card (Photo credit: Ms. Fields).

a responsible person whom the bank trusted and that she was capable of taking care of herself in dignified and legal ways. With each swipe, she performed independence, countering her past dependence on drugs, theft, and family members to get by. She also affirmed her connection to people she admired and strengthened the boundary between the respectable woman she identified as today and the untrustworthy woman she viewed herself as being in the past. The public act of swiping her debit card and the sense of prestige it afforded were part of creating a rehabilitated identity as a capable, independent woman. Securing legitimate work made being a debit cardholder possible and was a cornerstone of Ms. Fields's identity work.

Denise also discussed the importance of being able to open her first bank account after she came to the recovery home and started working. Like Ms. Fields, she used her debit card with pride: "That makes me feel special, like when I . . . [am] going to the stores with the ladies [from the recovery home] sometimes and they'll put cash on there. And, baby, I'll just bust out with that card and they . . . give me the look, but they [were] probably saying the same thing that I was saying. 'Man, I wish that was me.' But see, a lot of us in our addiction, we . . . took from banks and . . . wrote bad [checks], so you can't get [an] account [now]. So the only way they can go it is [to] pay in cash." Bank accounts, credit cards, and debit cards were status markers that distinguished women from others who were not as far along in their recovery and postincarceration processes. The accounts and cards were signs of respectability that represented their rehabilitated, "clean" identities. Swiping a debit card thus became a fun feminine performance of respectability and responsibility that publicly distanced women from the controlling images of "crack ho" and "welfare queen."

Denise underscored this point by recounting a story from when she had first arrived at Growing Stronger. She explained that without a legitimate job, she had returned to sex work. She reasoned, "Well, you know, being an addict and didn't have an income, it's quite expected that you was prostituting or whatever to get money." Again, Denise linked employment with her sense of self and showed how the rehabilitated woman identity exists in a constant tension with her past. She described sex work as "humiliating, you know . . . being with people I didn't wanna be with just so I can get some money," and associated that work with her *criminal-addict* identity. For Denise, employment, even when it paid minimum wage and was temporary, guarded against going down the wrong path back to her past identity. She suggested that not having legitimate work could lead back to dependence—on work she found to be humiliating, on men, on drugs—and the associated fear, uncertainty, and risk of criminalization.[72]

Legitimate work allowed Denise to keep money in the bank and protect multiple components of her "clean" identity. For instance, she recalled that her daughter recently had called her from jail, requesting help with posting bail. Denise responded by going directly to the bank:

> I took out $250 and I went to the police station and I got my daughter . . . And I was so happy that I could do that. 'Cause she was saying she called her daddy and he was like, "I ain't got no money." But he worked, made good money. Told her he ain't got no money . . . And I was able to get my daughter outta jail. That meant so much to me. And it was like I knew that was gonna happen one day. I said, "Denise, you sittin' up here savin' this money, but watch, one of your kids gonna need you, and you gonna wind up, you know." And I was okay with that, too.

Employment allowed her to maintain a bank account and respond to her daughter as the type of mother she wanted to be. Like Chicken Wing, Denise connected her employment to her identity as a mother on whom her children could confidently rely. Her growing independence—rooted in her employment and sobriety—made this new type of caretaking possible.

Again, given that two-thirds of the women who participated in this project were unemployed at the time of our interviews, it is important to consider how employment is an aspirational component of the rehabilitated woman controlling image and how elusive stable, full-time employment remained. During the course of our interviews, Stacey Williams, a 41-year-old African American woman, and Tinybig, the 51-year-old Afro Native American Indian woman who described arriving at jail as "pigs . . . goin' to slaughter," began doing telemarketing work with a company

FIGURE 15. Two-hour commute to work each way (Photo credit: Stacey Williams).

in a far western suburb. While they needed the money and the work experience, both ultimately left their positions after several weeks due to the long commute and inconsistent pay. Stacey took a photograph of the Chicago red line L station, which was just one leg of her two-hour commute each way to her job (figure 15). She commented that her days lasted "12 hours, including from me getting up at four in the morning to get out there . . . But I'm only working eight hours a day. But it's just too much." Because she had not yet made any sales, she had not earned any commission. Thus, her earnings totaled only about $400 every two weeks. Stacey explained how desperately she needed the money. Her sister, who took care of Stacey's two daughters, was ill and needed Stacey's help. Thus, she felt a great deal of pressure to secure a stable income so she and her sister could pool their resources and rent an apartment. The costs associated with the telemarketing job simply were too great, however, so Stacey continued to look for more stable employment that would allow her to fulfill her caretaker role for her sister and children.

Stacey's reflection on her work underscored Chicken Wing's and Denise's insight that employment fulfilled more than material needs. Of course, Stacey needed stable, better-paying employment to keep a roof over her head, food on the table, and clothes on her back. But her desperation and sense of urgency to secure better employment were rooted in relational needs, specifically her commitments as a mother and sister. The stress and frustration associated with her employment search connected to the deep, internal work she was doing to transform her self. Failing to secure a good job kept her dependent on her sister and the recovery home where she lived and thus caught between the past *criminal-addict* identity she was working to leave behind and the rehabilitated woman she was trying to become.

Despite these frustrations, Stacey was one of the few women in this study who had secured full-time, permanent employment. Most participants were unemployed, and that status not only created financial dependence, but also prevented women from feeling as if they were able to move forward with their lives. Because of their felony convictions and subsequent unemployment, they remained stuck in limbo. Moon's earlier reflections about lack of employment and this sense of suspended progress took on additional meaning when she recalled how an employer had withdrawn a job offer after receiving the results of her background check. Moon explained:

> Some people don't want to even hire you for seven years . . . Seven years until you had been out on the streets, so in the meantime . . . how do I feed myself? How do I eat? I'm bonded by the state of Illinois, but by me being a thief, nobody wants to hire me. Target hired me. I went through the drug test. I passed that. I passed the interview and everything, and when I called to get my schedule for Target, they said to me, "Please tell us you gave us the wrong Social Security number." I said, "No, that's my right Social Security number," and they said, "Well, um, I'm sorry. We can't give you this job." You know, that crush a person, because it's like, "Damn, when in life [will] I ever get the right to pay my debt to society?" It's like they push you and instead of like help you get a job, whereas you can be a productive, conducive member in society, it's like, "Naw, because you did this, you just go keep payin' this debt all over and all over and all over again."

Moon felt stuck and helpless.[73] In this example, she was engaged with social services and had secured bonding by the state of Illinois, which would ensure payment to the employer should they lose any money because of Moon. Even with the state's backing, Moon could not convince the employer to recognize her as rehabilitated and give her a chance at employment. She faced perpetual judgment and punishment, despite completing her formal sentence; the "mark" of the criminal record felt insurmountable.[74]

It is this permanent "mark" that prevented many women from ever feeling truly settled or like they finally made it. While Nyla expressed relief at securing part-time employment at Dunkin' Donuts and described the job as "a door open," she also explained she could not slow down. Although she had checked the box on the job application disclosing her felony conviction, the manager had not asked about it during their interview. His decision not to ask her about it might indicate her conviction was irrelevant to her hiring. The lack of discussion, though, left some lingering uncertainty. Nyla knew the job could be taken away from her at any moment. She was especially cautious since she had not started the job and was not yet on the payroll. She elaborated:

> I still feel the need to get up and go. Like I have to be doin' somethin'. I can't get complacent. Because the thought is now what if, what if, what if. Because I guess that thought is there because I actually haven't started workin' yet, so I feel the need to not stop what I've been doin', get up every mornin', and travel the city of Chicago. And yesterday, somebody was like, "Just sit down. [*laughs*] Just sit down. You got a job now! [*laughing*] . . . Well, why don't you just be still? Make some meetings . . ." You know, she was pretty much sayin', "Relax. Get out the way." And I understand all that, Chez, and at the same time, I'm like, you know, I don't want to think the worst or anything, I guess you could say because I'm not there, and now I have the [employee] shirts and everything, right? And I filled out the paperwork, but I'm still not there yet, you see? I don't feel like, I'm still, I'm still not on the payroll. So until then I have to do somethin' to stay in this process.

Nyla tried to reassure herself that she could slow down, but she did not feel secure and remained stuck in this transitory space. She identified the same risk that troubled Moon: complacency. There was a frantic sense to Nyla's ongoing employment search, which reflected the never completed project of personal transformation. Nothing would ever be good enough to communicate permanent rehabilitation. Regardless of the amount of clean time amassed, the number of certificates of program completion earned, or the number of job applications submitted, Nyla could not be complacent. Even when she secured a job, she could not get comfortable. She must do the continuous work of self-improvement. She must "keep movin.'"

Nyla continued to connect with various reentry programs across the city that promised assistance with job training, resume writing, and interview skills. This was a frustrating ordeal that required a lot of appointments and waiting. Nyla was in the midst of a two-month intake and waiting process with one organization that offered a one-week job training program. Completing the program would not guarantee job placement. Rather, the organization would put Nyla's name on a list for employers.[75] Nyla laughed and commented, "What am I to do in the meantime?" She had completed an intake and orientation with another program, only to be unable to reach them when it was time for the training to begin. The program had moved, and the phone number no longer worked. Neither Nyla nor her case manager at yet another reentry program had been able to track down a working number.

Nyla captured the stress and satisfaction of "keeping it movin'" with a photograph that showed her seated at a table, surrounded by paperwork, in the recovery home where she resided.[76] Her hair was pulled back into a ponytail, and her small gold cross necklace popped against the long-sleeved black shirt she was wearing. Nyla looked at the camera, almost smiling. She held a pen in her right hand, which rested atop a sheet of paper. It was as if the photographer caught her in the middle of filling out an important form or writing a note. Additional sheets of paper were scattered on the table, as well as a yellow folder. Nyla's winter coat and scarf hung over the back of a chair at the head of the table, and her purse rested on the table in front of the chair. Nyla explained the photograph: "This one I was feelin', I felt very comfortable. I felt very comfortable in doin' what I was doin' because I like doin' this. I felt secure. I felt like I was workin' my mind, and I was puttin' all of everything together from all of this. Your project . . . and just the whole feelin' of it . . . and then I was also thinkin' on my sons . . . that this could all be used to help them, too. Bein' . . . that they're incarcerated. And so it's just not, I'm just not wastin' my time. That's what that picture was." Nyla started to cry. Referring to the photograph, I asked, "And that was just on your own that you're just workin'." Nyla replied, "Right . . . I'm actually sittin' down tryin' to regroup, you know, get all these things together 'cause I'm all over the place. You know, I felt like I had been all over the city of Chicago." She laughed. "Was this at the end of the day you were feelin' that way?" I asked. "Yeah," she said still laughing. "And I'm sittin' there and then I'm thinkin' on my sons, how to write them and, you know, so I just felt like, 'Nyla, it's all gonna come together.' That was that picture."

The photograph conveyed the fear and joy embedded in Nyla's continuous work to maintain the boundary between her past *criminal-addict* identity and her rehabilitated identity. Over just a couple of minutes, her description of the photograph shifted from comfort and security in her progress, to concern for her incarcerated sons, to feeling "all over the place," to confidence that everything is "gonna come together." For our PEI, she had asked people to take photographs of her at each organization she went to for assistance. She documented her work, and then, at the end of the day, she documented how it all felt, sitting exhausted at a table trying to regroup. There was a sense of pride in working so hard, running all over the city, refusing to be discouraged by the run-around she encountered at reentry organizations, and making things happen on her own. A friend, not a social service organization, had referred her to the Dunkin' Donuts job. There also was an ominous sense, however, that hard work might not be enough.[77] Nyla had been in this place, under the protection of God's umbrella, before, and she had slipped back to her *criminal-addict* identity. Once again, she was working hard to stay under God's umbrella. Her photographs documented her work to create her rehabilitated identity. Her healthy appearance and her employment were getting her closer to being the woman she wanted to be. Nyla felt joy in these accomplishments and concern about what the future held.

Employment is a complicated piece of the rehabilitated woman controlling image. On the one hand, it subjects women to surveillance and exploitation. The state and reentry organizations view employment "as a primary indicator of criminal rehabilitation," which compels formerly incarcerated people to accept whatever employment they can find.[78] Employers of "bad jobs" seize on this desperation, recruiting formerly incarcerated people to fill low-wage and temporary jobs that offer neither benefits nor upward mobility.[79] The precarious nature of this work creates distinct gendered risks for criminalized women who lack employee protections but face sexual harassment and assault on the job, widespread avail-ability and use of drugs in the workplace, and aggressive behavior by supervisors who scream, threaten to fire, and fire women without cause.[80] The majority of the women in this study had not secured employment since their release from jail or prison, and the jobs women did obtain rarely provided an income that made self-sufficiency possible.

This is the dilemma of employment for criminalized women. It is necessary to have a chance of making it on the outside, but it often is unattainable. When it is attained, it typically reaffirms the deeply engrained inequality that structures the postindustrial neoliberal economy.[81] Today's bifurcated economy depends on low-wage workers to fill jobs in an ever-expanding service sector that props up the unfettered accumulation of wealth in the hands of the professional classes.[82] As sociologist Loïc Wacquant argues, the neoliberal state disciplines low-income and poor people into these social roles through the interlinked projects of "workfare" (e.g., the restrictive work requirements imposed by the 1996 Personal Responsibil-ity and Welfare Reform Act) and "prisonfare" (e.g., the containment and control administered through policing, probation, parole, and prisons).[83] The simultane-ous necessity and severe limitations of employment that criminalized women con-front fit squarely into the neoliberal economy. While employment may enable a criminalized woman to pay her rent, access health care, swipe her debit card, and bail her child out of jail, it rarely provides security. Rather, it consigns women to a lifetime of just barely getting by, in other words, to living on the economic and social margins of society. And that outcome only is possible if women can hang on. If the ongoing precarity and stress become too much, or if a disruption like a job loss or eviction occurs, not even a position on the margins is guaranteed. Women risk slipping back to an unsafe living environment, the streets, drug use, and eventually jail or prison.

On the other hand, "employment is an implicit challenge to the cultural stereo-types" that poor women, women of color, and criminalized women encounter.[84] Women referenced employment to contest controlling images and craft identi-ties as rehabilitated women capable of taking care of themselves and their chil-dren. Striving for and securing employment provided women with deep personal meaning. Like Opsal found, the women who participated in this study viewed employment as "play[ing] a central role in creating and sustaining change as they set out to be different kinds of people."[85] Work was not only valuable for the nec-essary though insufficient financial means it provided; it was a key piece of the new identities women were creating. In contrast to past periods of unemploy-ment or illegal work, holding paid legal employment, even when it was a "bad job," provided evidence of women's changing selves. As such, women found personal meaning in their work and took pleasure in what employment allowed them to do.

This tension is precisely what makes the rehabilitated woman image a con-trolling image. Like the seemingly positive image of the respectable "Black lady," who has secured professional success through education and hard work, the rehabilitated woman controlling image, on the surface, connotes empowerment and achievement that result from perseverance. Yet, by existing in opposition to the "welfare queen" and "crack ho" controlling images, it presupposes and reifies those more obviously denigrating images.[86] Furthermore, the rehabilitated woman image propagates the lie that criminalized women will survive if they just work hard enough, while eschewing the question of why anyone should be content with mere survival in a society that denies their fundamental humanity and dignity. In this way, the rehabilitated woman image resonates with the analyses of feminist scholars who document how the carceral state's gendered goals of empowerment and independence do not actually help women but rather coopt feminist ideals in the service of the state's work to discipline and regulate the socially marginalized.[87] And yet, if we truly listen to criminalized women, we see how joy exists within this tension. Despite the overbearing requirements and restrictions criminalized women navigated daily, they did more than survive; they embraced moments of unbridled joy through claiming their humanity in a society where recognition of that humanity was not a given.

CONCLUSION

The gendered markers of rehabilitation that constitute the rehabilitated woman did not grant access to normative femininity, which remained closed off due to race, class, and the permanent nature of the *criminal-addict* label. They did, however, provide a way to navigate a postincarceration landscape beset with institutions and individuals that relegate criminalized women to a second-class status and a 12-Step logic that presents only two recognizable subject positions—clean or dirty.[88] These gendered markers also provided women with personally affirming evidence of their ongoing progress away from their past *criminal-addict* selves. In some respects, rehabilitation was an aspirational identity, particularly for women who were recently released, living in recovery homes, still using drugs, or under formal correctional supervision. When women had not yet achieved these gendered markers of rehabilitation, they foregrounded the work they were doing to move closer to accomplishing this identity, in the process distinguishing their current self from their past self. Women embraced the joy of crafting rehabilitated identities, while also contending with the fear and risk associated with a return to a past *criminal-addict* self, and used the clean/dirty dichotomy to navigate these competing identities.

The 12-Step logic provided women with a roadmap to follow after incarceration to ensure they remained on their path to recovery. While the path did not have a conclusion, the 12 Steps prescribed how women could engage faith and recovery discourses to demonstrate their commitment to their noncriminality and sobriety. These discourses facilitated women's boundary work, meaning the many ways they drew distinctions between their past *criminal-addict* identities and their present recovering identities. In this context, relapse was not a neutral, routine part of the recovery process; rather, it posed a threat of returning to these past identities. Relapse threatened women's identity work, as resuming drug or alcohol use signaled a return to criminality and the associated judgments that return could prompt regarding morality and spirituality. The *criminal-addict* identity was inherently racialized and gendered, as it was bound up with deep-rooted controlling images of deviant women who threaten gender norms, family stability, and social order.

Against the backdrop of the 12-Step logic, appearance and employment were two foundational gendered markers of women's ongoing identity work. Appearance was the most recognizable and oftentimes most quickly achieved gendered marker of rehabilitation. Even when women were newly released from prison and therefore at the very beginning of their postincarceration processes, a healthy, feminine appearance quickly signaled their commitment to recovery. Stable legal employment, independent housing, and reestablished relationships with children and loved ones were longer-term goals that would take time to achieve. In the meantime, women could work on their selves. A healthy complexion, appropriate weight gain, and kempt appearance were immediate attainable signals of sobriety and thus evidence that women were working the 12 Steps. These markers also helped women distance themselves from the controlling images of the "crack ho" and "welfare queen" that justified the gendered violence they had survived prior to and during incarceration. Appearance communicated independence from drug and alcohol use, which was the foundation upon which women's recovery and rehabilitation were built. Legal employment, even temporary, seasonal, or part-time work, communicated independence from institutions and others, as well as sound moral character and commitment to fitting into the existing social order.

5

"God Blessed the Child That Has Her Own"

Recovering Identity through Domesticity and Mothering

"This is a beautiful picture," Ann Williams said (figure 16). "It's gorgeous." We were looking at a photograph she had taken of the dining room table where we now were sitting at Starting Again, where she had been residing for almost a year since her release from prison. "It just shows . . . inspiration. It just shows beauty . . . the setup is just gorgeous . . . it just shows greatness." It wasn't immediately clear what made this routine image so beautiful, but the 44-year-old Black mother of six was adamant. "How do you feel when you look at this picture now?" I asked. "I feel good. It's beautiful," Ann responded. "'Cause, you know, when you look at things, you have to really look at 'em . . . This is really gorgeous, because I'm really seein'. I didn't used to see. I used to didn't see anything 'cause my eyes was blind. Now I can see! And it's just gorgeous, the little things are just beautiful." As this was our second interview, I knew how important Ann's faith was to her. She thoroughly credited God with holding her through the many years she had spent in and out of prison, unhoused, and struggling with drug use and with guiding her through her current work to turn her life around. The religious imagery of a lost person who gains sight and clarity only after being saved was not lost on me.[1]

Pressing further, I inquired, "Is there anything else this table, this picture tells or reveals?" Without hesitation, Ann explained:

> One day I'll be at my own table with my family, at a beautiful table like that. That's what it really reveals . . . the table, my home, me and my kids. And we'll sit at my table and have family time . . . That's the good thing about this table. You can come and talk. If things seem like it's a little shaky . . . like say me and my roommate be goin' through somethin' . . . this is the table to come and talk about it. Everything! That's with my family too, now that I know, now that I'm learnin'. This is the table that we

FIGURE 16. "One day I'll be at my own table with my family" (Photo credit: Ann Williams).

point out the issues and resolve 'em. . . Just one day I'ma have the same house. I'ma be at the same house with my [children] at my table.

The table became a powerful symbol Ann returned to throughout this interview and the next, particularly as she discussed her evolving relationship with her children, who ranged in age from 5 to 17. She had lived separately from them for most of their lives. Four separate stints in prison and multiple years of being "out in the streets," as Ann put it, while using heroin or cocaine had pulled her away from being physically and emotionally present in her children's lives. She explained, "I never really was in their lives . . . I was there when I was tired and I was off drugs, comin' off the withdrawals. You know what I'm sayin'? I did a lot of damage . . . once I started usin' drugs, always ran." The image Ann described of having all her children under the same roof, gathered around a table, eating and talking together symbolized a goal she was working toward—to be able to provide for her children materially and emotionally.

The table did not just represent a future goal, however. It also celebrated Ann's current identity work and the incremental progress she was making to rebuild her family. She valued the process as much as the goal, and to this point, the process was going quite well. Ann had not used drugs in over a year. She regularly attended 12-Step meetings and had a sponsor whom she trusted and admired. Although she did not yet have a job, she was looking into several job-training programs, as well as a GED program. Perhaps most importantly, she had maintained stable living arrangements through Starting Again since her release from prison. At no point over the past year did she worry about ending up back on the streets, in a shelter, or living again with her children's father—all moves Ann knew would jeopardize her progress. Alluding to the common 12-Step directive to avoid "people, places, and things" associated with one's past drug use, Ann explained why she moved into Starting Again directly from prison: "I had already made the decision that I'm gonna go to a recovery home and keep the process goin'. 'Cause I knew . . . I don't wanna go back to that same familiar places."

Ann's stability at Starting Again was a reflection of her progress. Between our first and second interviews, Starting Again's director, Miss Dorothy, had moved Ann to the agency's second site. The move was a privilege granted only to residents whom Miss Dorothy determined were serious about their recovery and could handle the relaxed rules and additional freedom the second site provided. The first site was similar to many of the recovery homes I visited and heard about in interviews. It was a communal setup, where women shared bedrooms and common living areas with one another and were required to follow program rules, such as attending groups and adhering to a curfew. A staff member was always on site, which meant support was always available, but so was constant surveillance. While Starting Again's second site still had rules and programming, it was a more independent setup. Ann explained:

> That's a level one, this is a level two . . . you pay the rent over here, you get a job . . . you have more business, you have more . . . leeway . . . Over there you have to do groups, groups, groups, groups. Over here, it's like you're responsible now, so you know what to do, you know to go to your meetings, you know to do the necessary right thing . . . It's like bein' a big girl. Grown up.

Ann now had her own bedroom and shared an entire apartment with just one other resident. Women living in this apartment typically had to pay rent monthly, but Miss Dorothy, knowing Ann did not have the financial means, allowed her to live there rent-free. Ann continued to turn over her monthly Supplemental Nutrition Assistance Program (SNAP, commonly known as food stamps) benefits to Starting Again, as she had done at the first site, but she would not have to pay rent until she secured an income. The move was an affirmation of Ann's progress and new identity. She explained, "It's a good move for me because it's another level . . . It's a next level and it's another, you know, phase and everything . . . showin' them my growth, my character."

The increased freedom at the second site also provided Ann with the chance to spend uninterrupted, private time reconnecting with her children. Miss Dorothy allowed two of her children at a time to stay with her overnight on the weekends. Ann was using those visits to have in-depth discussions with her children about their past relationships and how to move forward. Looking at a photograph of her oldest child, Ann reflected on the work they were doing to rebuild their relationship:

> Ann: That's my baby, oh my God! That's my daughter, my 17-year-old daughter. This is the one I told you we really didn't have a relationship because of my drug use and now she's, we're building, we tryin' to build that relationship. She's comin' around. I'm tryin' to open up to her, and . . . it's like, somebody meeting somebody for the first time . . . 'cause I never was a mom, I mean . . . I never knew how to be a mom, it's like me learnin' how to be a mom . . . learnin' to open up, listen to her . . .
>
> CR: What does it mean to be a mom today?
>
> Ann: To be open-minded, to be loving, to understand, to be responsible. You know, to be there every step . . . It's a lot. To be a mom . . . It's a lot, but I'm willin' and I'm learnin'. Every day with my kids, okay, I wasn't there in the past, but I'm here now . . . I can't go back to the past, but I can only do what I can do now in the present and the future . . . That's what I tell my daughter . . . She said, "Mama, I forgive you" . . . I was like making amends, so I said, "That wasn't the person I was when I did that, when I did those drugs, that was not me. That was a monster inside of me. That wasn't me. The real me, this is the real me." And I'm learnin' to know who I am and be comfortable with who I am . . . That was not me. That was some person that I don't know . . . She was like, "Mom, I forgive you . . . I know that wasn't you."

Ann drew clear boundaries between her past *criminal-addict* and current *rehabilitated* identities to demonstrate her progress as a mother. Whereas in the past she was homeless and absent from her children's lives, today she had secured safe, stable (though temporary) housing. She was finding ways to be fully present during their time together, in stark contrast to her memories of laying on the couch while going through withdrawals, physically present but not really there. She acknowledged she had a lot to learn about her children and how to be a mother, and she embraced that work, finding joy and meaning in the learning process.

Ann grounded her progress in her sobriety. Generally, she made clear that her accomplishments were only possible because she no longer was using drugs. Resuming use would send her back down the same path she had followed the previous three times she had been released from prison. Specifically, she used the 12 Steps to frame her relationship building with her children. Step 9 involves making direct amends to the people one has harmed. Ann described the conversation where her daughter forgave her as "making amends." She acknowledged the harm she caused and affirmed that because of her sobriety, she was and would remain a different person—a present mother on whom her children could rely. Ann indicated how making amends was an active, ongoing process integral to her rehabilitation. She suggested that as she became more certain in her own identity, she also would grow as a mother.

Ann's faith was as important as her sobriety for her identity work. As noted in chapter 3, Ann believed God had saved her through incarceration. She also believed God was making her ongoing rehabilitation possible. Reflecting on her developing relationships with her children, Ann explained, "I see the difference. I see some healin'. God came along, and God is healin' us . . . back then, they didn't wanna be close to me. They didn't even wanna look at me, they didn't even wanna say, 'That's my mama' . . . So now they're able to say, 'That's my mom.'" She referenced a recent school event her oldest daughter had asked her to attend: "That was openin' up a door, and God was answering my prayers. He was opening up a door." Ann alluded to her rehabilitation as a pact with God. Echoing the 12-Step logic, she had admitted powerlessness, turned her will over to God, and was ready for God to remove her defects of character.[2] As long as she put in the work, God would keep opening doors and helping her move through them.

Ann's photographs and reflections provided further insight into women's identity work and centered the next two gendered markers of recovery—domesticity and mothering—that constitute the rehabilitated woman controlling image. Securing housing and reestablishing relationships with children are challenging tasks most people face following release from prison. Yet, the meaning and experience of working to accomplish these tasks differ for criminalized men and women in nuanced ways, with gendered impacts on identity. As such, I use the term *domesticity* rather than *housing* to reference the broad care work encapsulated in criminalized women's reflections on housing.

As with appearance and employment, domesticity and mothering are complex components of identity that subject women to ongoing judgment and surveillance, while also providing opportunities for healing and growth.[3] Domesticity and mothering also reflect ways criminalized women are judged not only for breaking the law, but also for violating feminine norms. Drug use and incarceration undermine women's ability to fulfill gendered expectations related to domestic and care work. Regardless of how unrealistic those expectations are, deviations from those ideals subject criminalized women to damaging assessments of their character. These assessments intersect with race and class, reflecting the controlling images of the "crack ho" and "welfare queen." The moral judgment the *criminal-addict* label bestowed on women tapped into something much deeper than criminalization and drug use. It suggested a weak, immoral self that prevented women from fulfilling their social roles and thereby threatened the stability of families, communities, and society overall.[4]

In this chapter, I use the clean/dirty and fear/joy framework established in chapter 4 to examine how women engaged domesticity and mothering discourses as part of their personal transformation processes. There was a constant push and pull between the *criminal-addict* identity women were trying to shed and the *rehabilitated* identity they were working to accomplish. In reflecting on domesticity and mothering, women drew boundaries between their past and current identities, highlighting the positive changes they had made even if their goals remained out of reach. They engaged the 12-Step logic, the overarching discourse women encountered throughout the criminal legal system and postincarceration landscape, with its focus on sobriety, faith, and personal responsibility, to structure this boundary work. A sense of fear and vulnerability was associated with resuming drug use and the subsequent risk it would bring. There also was a sense of joy and excitement as women's goals related to housing and mothering grew within reach. Along with appearance and employment, domesticity and mothering were critical components of women's identity transitions that refuted racist stereotypes about criminalized women of color.

HOUSING: A FORMIDABLE TASK

Securing housing arguably is one of the most important and challenging tasks people face following release from prison. A wealth of research documents that housing, like employment, is crucial for people to end their involvement with the criminal legal system. Meeting conditions of release, finding employment, pursuing education, participating in drug treatment, reuniting with children, reconnecting with family, and abstaining from drug use are exceedingly difficult without a stable residence.[5] As feminist scholars Megan Welsh and Valli Rajah summarize, "Home doesn't just mean shelter; it means a stable and safe place that is symbolic of full reintegration into society."[6] Housing is central to postincarceration life because so much hinges on it.

Yet, similar to employment, a host of discriminatory laws, policies, and practices systematically exclude formerly incarcerated people from housing.[7] In the private market, landlords regularly use background checks to justify not renting to applicants who have a criminal conviction. In a particularly exploitive move, landlords may charge application and background check fees, fully knowing they have no intention of renting to an applicant.[8] Federal legislation allows, and in some cases even encourages, public housing authorities to deny housing to people with criminal backgrounds.[9] The bans are so extensive that in many cases formerly incarcerated people cannot even move in with a family member who lives in public housing.[10] These prohibitions impose financial and emotional strain, as the state limits how residents can offer support to newly released loved ones.[11] These policies exacerbate a host of historical and ongoing discriminatory housing laws and practices that have created and maintained entrenched racial and economic residential segregation throughout the United States.[12] As such, formerly incarcerated people typically return to the same disadvantaged communities where they lived before their incarceration and thus to the same challenging living conditions produced by community disinvestment and hypersurveillance that keep people caught up in the criminal legal system.[13]

These challenges are amplified for criminalized women, particularly criminalized women of color, who deal with intersecting oppressions related to gender, poverty, criminalization, and race.[14] Given a general lack of affordable housing, gender inequality in the labor market, the feminization of poverty, and women's disproportionate caretaking responsibilities, securing housing is a formidable task for women, even without a criminal record. The added stigma and discrimination caused by criminalization make a formidable task even more difficult. In her research with formerly incarcerated women, sociologist Beth E. Richie found participants felt overlooked by community organizations that focused on other groups needing assistance, concluding, "Women of color returning from jail or prison do not feel embraced by their communities, and they are not identified as having the right to demand services from it. The sense of being marginalized within the context of a disenfranchised community has a profound impact on the ability of women to successfully reintegrate into it."[15] Additionally, housing insecurity increases women's vulnerability to gendered violence, such as sexual harassment and assault while unhoused and by landlords and family members on whom women rely for assistance.[16] Similar to the ways employment discrimination funnels criminalized women into low-wage, precarious, and often unsafe work, housing discrimination keeps criminalized women contained in racially segregated communities shaped by generations of targeted economic disinvestment and subject to ongoing interpersonal, community, and structural violence.

Women's mothering responsibilities intersect with their housing needs.[17] The majority of incarcerated women are mothers and were the primary caretakers of minor children prior to their incarceration.[18] Whether they are biological mothers or not, women often fulfill important caretaking roles within their families and communities. As a result, women's incarceration creates severe disruption for families and long-lasting psychological impacts on children and women themselves. The separation from their children that women endure throughout their incarceration is a gendered pain of imprisonment.[19] Given this separation, reunifying with children is a central part of postincarceration experiences for most women.

Reunification efforts take a variety of forms, from reconnecting with adult children to regaining legal custody of minor children. Many women have formal Child Protective Services (CPS) cases, often for no other reason than their incarceration and not having anyone who can care for their children. As such, women must not only meet postrelease conditions and requirements of any programs with which they are engaged, such as drug treatment and recovery homes; they also must follow stringent case plans with CPS. The competing demands imposed by these various agencies and the degree of intersecting surveillance can be overwhelming.[20] Securing stable housing is a minimum requirement women must meet in order to regain custody of their children. Shelter and recovery homes typically do not fulfill this requirement, especially as most do not allow minor children to live with their parents at these sites. Indeed, Ann Williams's ability to have her children stay with her overnight at Starting Again was a unique privilege. In a very basic way, housing is intertwined with criminalized women's ability to mother their children and, particularly for women of color, to contest perceptions of maternal deviance.

Housing is further gendered in the ways it impacts identity.[21] Like employment, housing fulfills more than material needs. There is a psychological benefit to having safe, stable housing. Public health scholar Alana Rosenberg and colleagues found housing insecurity among formerly incarcerated people undermined ontological security, meaning the sense of feeling at home and at ease, with negative impacts on identity. Sociological research has documented a reciprocal relationship between housing and identity for formerly incarcerated people: "Just as housing access could support the construction of positive post-incarceration identities, the reverse was also true. Participants described how housing insecurity inhibited their ability to build credibility and distance themselves from stigmatized incarceration histories that were considered legitimate grounds for exclusion from resources."[22] Both men and women in Danya E. Keene, Amy B. Smoyer, and Kim M. Blankenship's study revealed how housing is "a symbolic good in the context of widely circulating American values of self-sufficiency and independence."[23] As such, housing is a critical type of reparative identity work for criminalized men and women.

Given controlling images and discourses surrounding criminalized women, however, self-sufficiency and independence mean particular things for women. Independence, specifically economic independence, typically is gendered masculine, as men's perceived worth continues to be equated with (in)ability to financially provide for oneself and one's family. But for criminalized women, particularly women of color, dependence is a sign of pathology and ongoing criminality.[24] Thus, housing is a distinctly feminine goal in the context of intertwined discourses about criminalization, gender, poverty, and race. It is a resource women can use not only to increase their physical safety and support reunification efforts with their children, but also to contest dependency discourses and establish a positive rehabilitated identity.

THE IMPORTANCE OF HAVING ONE'S OWN

Women's attention to domesticity was a key component of the rehabilitated woman controlling image and a prominent way to distinguish between past and current selves. Similar to appearance, domesticity largely reaffirmed traditional femininity scripts. Stable housing represented women's ability to take on the traditional feminine task of caring for domestic spaces. It also offered protection from the gendered violence women had experienced in their homes and communities, as well as at the hands of the state.[25] In a practical manner, having a space of one's own separated women from past physical spaces that had been sites of violence. Symbolically, it also marked women as *not* deserving of the violence that, according to mainstream addiction and dependency discourses, their past behaviors had made them vulnerable to experiencing.

Rose's photograph of the alley where she was sexually assaulted, the photograph that opens this book, illustrates what housing means for criminalized women's

FIGURE 17. "Trying to live like a person's supposed to live" (Photo credit: Rose).

safety and identity. In addition to the alley photograph, Rose took photographs of her bedroom at Growing Stronger (figure 17). This was Rose's second stay at the recovery home. At the end of her first stay, she had moved into her own apartment. She eventually resumed using drugs, lost her apartment and job, and was incarcerated again for drug possession. Rose explained the bedroom photographs:

> I could look at these now and say, "Well, I got all, I'm getting most of my stuff back." So I will know how to appreciate it, you know. 'Cause last time . . . I had all this stuff, I got rid of it. Due to me going back out there . . . just looking at . . . it just makes me feel good to know that I'm trying to live life. I mean, I'm trying to live like a person's supposed to live.

The bedroom provided Rose with a safe place, in contrast to the dangers she faced in the alley. The items that filled her bedroom showed her progress away from drug use, homelessness, and vulnerability to sexual assault and toward her new identity as a sober woman able to provide adequate shelter, clothing, shoes, and hygiene items for herself. By documenting her skill at creating a safe domestic space, Rose constructed a positive feminine identity, despite her inability to have her own apartment. Like Ann Williams, she took pleasure in the process and enjoyed displaying her accomplishments. By doing so, she resolved the dilemma of living in a society where affordable housing is not available and self-sufficiency is not yet within reach. Her memories of the trauma and hardships she endured were persistent reminders of the risks associated with failing to maintain her new identity. Juxtaposing Rose's alley and bedroom photographs provided a striking visual of the relationship between her past and current identities and what was at stake while navigating between them.

When women first move into Growing Stronger, they are assigned to a shared bedroom. As women advance through the program, they earn the privilege of moving into a single room, where they enjoy greater privacy. Denise talked about her single room at Growing Stronger as a sign of her progress and contrasted having her own room to her past experiences living with abusive partners in a way that resonated with Ann Williams's reflections on moving to Starting Again's second site.[26] Denise recalled, "When I . . . got my own room in Growing Stronger, this was the first time ever in life that Denise's had her own room, that I ain't had to worry about waking up and there's somebody next to me." Despite the recovery home's rules and having to answer to staff, Denise enjoyed a relative freedom at Growing Stronger compared with the extreme surveillance and control she had endured from her violent partner and while in jail and prison.[27] She looked forward to the further peace and independence she anticipated would come with having her own apartment, "even if it's just a kitchenette or a studio," that she could decorate any way she wanted. As Denise summed up, "It ain't nothin' like havin' your *own*. You know, God blessed the child that has her own." The practical safety and symbolic redemption housing provided would further distance Denise from her past identity and move her closer to the new woman she was working so hard to become.

The Lioness also discussed how her room at Growing Stronger symbolized the better woman she was becoming. She took a photograph of the door to her room (figure 18) to show, like Denise, she had earned the privilege of staying in her own, single-person room, where she found "a peace of mind." She contrasted the privacy she enjoyed in her room with the complete lack of privacy she experienced in prison: "See I was in prison for two years with women . . . I never had privacy, you know? So to get in this room it was like . . . oh my God, I could breathe." The suffocating description of prison mirrored Denise's recollection of being in a domestic violence relationship. Like Denise and Rose, the Lioness enjoyed the relative freedom, safety, and ability to breathe that the recovery home provided. Having her own private room enabled her "to plan my day or plan my week, what move I wanna make, what goals I have for myself, so now, it's just my safe haven."

The Lioness also proudly described how well she cared for her room. While wearing a stylish pink sweat suit, she explained the significance of a photograph of her bed (figure 19): "This is my bed . . . I love pink." She added, "My momma used to dress me in so much pink. You know, my momma was the type of person that she wanna have little girls be always beautiful and clean. I used to have, my hair was always pretty and my clothes was never dirty." She continued, "I love

FIGURE 18. The Lioness's door (Photo credit: the Lioness).

FIGURE 19. "I like my bed nicely made" (Photo credit: the Lioness).

my room. I love everything. But the bed, it shows that, organized. I'm always keepin' it nice and clean, I keep my linen clean . . . now I make my bed, I mean I'm
organized. I don't like to be no scattered, I like my bed made nicely." On the one
hand, the Lioness's description reflected her internalization of the disciplinary
regimes, structured living, and rigid routines many residential facilities attempt to
impart to criminalized people.[28] An organized room and routine communicated
rejection of an unruly, disordered self that was associated with the chaos of the
streets and the drugs lifestyle.

There also was a gendered meaning to the Lioness's burgeoning organization
skills. She used the photograph to show not just that she was working on her
rehabilitation, but that she also was working to cultivate normative femininity.
Her mother had taught her what it meant to be a proper woman ("beautiful and
clean"). The Lioness suggested her drug use and participation in the streets lifestyle had compromised that identity, but she now was reclaiming it. Her repeated
mention of being "clean" countered the judgment she faced as a Black woman
without a stable home who had used drugs and engaged in sex work. The color
pink, which for the Lioness "is a sign of woman . . . pretty in pink," represented
that she was getting back to the type of woman her mother wanted her to be. Her
housekeeping also reflected this transformation. She explained, "I have a ritual
that I do. I clean my room in the mornin', vacuum my floor, make my bed." The
cleanliness of her room reflected her rehabilitated gendered identity. She was a
far way from the woman who stole soap, toothpaste, and deodorant and was condemned by the corner store worker as being not a real woman.[29] Similar to the
way external changes in feminine appearance reflected internal changes in one's
self, the chaotic or orderly presentation of one's room provided a window to what
was going on internally.[30] The Lioness displayed and described her domestic skills
in ways that contested the *criminal-addict* label and, more specifically, the "crack
ho" controlling image. She still was poor, unemployed, and technically unhoused,
but the social marginalization she now faced differed from what she encountered
on the streets and in jail and prison. She was moving toward the rehabilitated
woman controlling image, and being clean—with the multiple meanings the word
connotes—was affirmation of that progress.

"BACK TO SQUARE ONE"

While a small minority of women had secured apartments either on their own or
through a housing program, the vast majority of women's housing circumstances
were much more precarious. Women's stays at recovery homes were limited, and
the living conditions at many of these homes made many women eager to move out
as soon as possible. Just as some women referenced positive experiences at recovery homes as indicators of their personal transformation, other women described
problems at recovery homes as signs of their suspended progress. Women who
did not have their own apartment or reside in a recovery home bounced between

temporary stays with friends and family members and periods of homelessness. Lynn and Xenia shared particularly turbulent housing trajectories throughout the period we were in contact for this project.

The living arrangements of Lynn, a 33-year-old Caucasian mother of two, frequently and at times unexpectedly changed during the nearly five months we were in contact. Between our first interview at Starting Again and our third interview at another recovery home, Lynn reported living in a hotel, being back in jail, being on the streets, staying inpatient at a psychiatric hospital, completing an inpatient drug treatment program, and briefly residing at multiple recovery homes. She made an explicit connection between being unhoused and her ongoing drug use, noting, "My main problem is somewhere to live, and, you know, I don't want to be in the streets. 'Cause that's a big trigger for relapsing, too, is being in the streets . . . I don't want to be sober in the streets."

Lynn faced a dilemma when it came to housing, though. She was anticipating receiving the second installment of a payout from a class action lawsuit against Cook County Jail for illegally shackling women during childbirth. Lynn was considering finding an apartment and using the installment to pay rent for several months in order to have secure housing, thereby eliminating one of her greatest stressors. She thought the apartment could provide a solid foundation for her girlfriend, Faye, and her. She anticipated the assurance that would come with having their own place would support both of them in their recovery and provide much-needed time to either find employment or for Lynn to finally be approved for Supplemental Security Income (SSI) due to a disability. Lynn had been kicked out of Starting Again two previous times for rule infractions, once for getting drunk and staying out overnight and, most recently, for being caught having a romantic relationship with Faye, who also was living at Starting Again. Lynn described how the resulting housing instability contributed to a familiar cycle where she would increase her drinking and drug use, miss check-ins with her probation officer, and be worn down from dealing with the general chaos of not having a place to stay. Perhaps, she reasoned, having a secure place of her own, where she did not have to worry about program rules or being kicked out, would help her break this cycle. Plus, Faye was advocating for this plan.

The challenge, though, was Lynn was not certain she wanted to leave the new recovery home where she and Faye were staying. Although Lynn had only been there for about a week, she explained she thought the program might be able to help her. She summed up how it was distinct from other recovery homes where she had stayed: "This is not like a slop house. This is not like, you know, just somewhere to live and not do what you're supposed to do." Plus, she described it as "relationship-friendly . . . This is like the only place you can have a relationship at . . . that's big, you know, because . . . there is a lot of gay couples that are trying to get clean together, and they don't want to be separated, and they shouldn't have to be." She and Faye had been kicked out of two recovery homes because of their relationship. At the current program, they did not have to hide their relationship, even though they had to stay on separate floors, and program rules prohibited any sexual activity in the house.

Additionally, Lynn was not confident she was ready for her own apartment. She explained:

> When I get my money, I wanted to stay [at this recovery home] for like a month . . . 'cause I am fresh in recovery once again . . . My mom put in my head that I've been, I'm gonna need to be institutionalized for the rest of my life, 'cause, you know, I've been in recovery homes for like the past 10 years, and I've never really lived on my own. So, you know, she's [Faye's] tryin' to get me out of that, "You don't need to be institutionalized, and you can just jump out on faith" . . . I'm just kind of scared [*laughs*] to . . . go out there. And it makes her so mad. [*laughs*] She's like, "You cannot keep depending on people for the rest of your life."

Lynn hoped the current recovery home would provide her with "some stability," which to her meant "being able to wake up and stay sober, be around sober people, just to be around recovery . . . I want to be clean . . . I want to, you know, like the meetings and stuff, you know. I'm getting up on time. Makin' my bed. You know, structure, I guess you could say." Attempting to clarify her point, she defined stability in opposition to her past lifestyle. "Because I was all over the place. You know, takin' my medicine here and there, you know, just doin', you know. Here you gotta take your medicine at a certain time. You gotta make sure you take it. You know, you have morning med, you have to get up for morning group at 6:30. You have to be on the floor at 6:30, you know, you *have* to go to groups, you this, you know. You're supposed to be goin' to IOP [intensive outpatient treatment], too . . . every day." Lynn described how she had tried numerous times to stop using drugs on her own or to be able to just drink casually, but one drink always led "to the harder stuff." She commented, "I think I'm an addict." She seemed to be searching for a different way forward.

Lynn's ambivalence about what housing would be most beneficial for her at this point in her life alluded to dominant dependency discourses, the 12-Step logic, and the rehabilitated woman controlling image. Faye suggested dependency was a weakness and encouraged Lynn to become independent as soon as possible, even if doing so felt risky. Lynn, however, focused on the meaning of dependence associated not just with drug use, but also with her *criminal-addict* self. In Lynn's explanation, she would not be able to abstain from alcohol and drugs and stop depending on institutions until she did the deep work required to bring about a true, lasting identity change. Resonating with the 12-Step logic, Lynn suggested true recovery required a transformation of self. In this respect, dependency on institutions was an acceptable temporary state while she committed to the lifelong project of recovery. Lynn implied she had to accept she was an addict. Provided she was willing to put in the work, the recovery home's programming might help her develop a structured life out of the current chaos that reflected her disordered, undisciplined self. Lynn revealed the reciprocal relationship between identity and housing and how, in some cases, a recovery home that felt accepting and stable might provide a greater sense of ontological security and support for positive identity development than an independent apartment.

Xenia's experiences throughout the course of our interviews affirmed Lynn's concerns about preemptively leaving the recovery home. The 41-year-old Puerto Rican mother of eight also had lived briefly at Starting Again. Unlike Lynn, Xenia left on her own terms. She identified multiple frustrations with the program, such as the requirements to attend Miss Dorothy's church with the other Starting Again residents every Sunday and to turn over her food stamps, which staff used to purchase food for the entire house. Xenia said she ultimately decided to move out because she wanted to be with her family, and her niece invited Xenia to move in with her. After a couple of weeks, though, Xenia's niece told her that if she could not contribute to rent, she could no longer live there. With no income, Xenia moved out and was staying "here and there," including living out of her car. Although Xenia did not miss Starting Again's rules and restrictions, she noted she was missing out on Miss Dorothy's resources and referrals and having a stable place to stay.

Beyond the physical hardships she endured due to her homelessness, Xenia also reflected on being pulled back toward her *criminal-addict* identity. Xenia explained she was trying to hold on to the insights she had learned in the 12-Step-based drug treatment program she attended in prison. She was trying to "let go and let God" and accept her "powerlessness," as she now worked to abstain from drug use and stay out of prison. Lack of housing and poverty were making it difficult, however. "I don't have a stable place to go. So I'm back to square one again," Xenia said. "Yeah, it's kind of difficult . . . for me to live and survive I have to try and, you know, find ways and means of survival. You know, I didn't want to go back to prostituting, what I'm used to doing. I didn't want to go back to that. Didn't want to go back to selling drugs . . . I just want to do it the positive way."

Two months later, at the time of our third interview, Xenia's situation had not improved. She was staying at an overnight shelter that required her to leave daily between 8 a.m. and 4 p.m. Having nowhere to go during the day was especially hard on her arthritis during Chicago's cold winter months. She needed to purchase a new battery for her car, which was parked in the shelter's lot. She had started spacing out her psychiatric medication, taking one pill a day instead of two as prescribed, since she was unsure when she would be able to afford a refill. With no assurance she would be able to secure a legitimate income or stable housing anytime soon, Xenia noted the draw of past behaviors: "I don't wanna get out here and sell no drugs. And I know people ask me all the time, you know, 'Just stand here and be our lookout, you know?' And I'm about to do it because I need that battery before, it's getting to the point where now they're telling me that they're gonna tow my car. Now I'm in a bind between a rock and a hard place. Now I have to make a choice of what I'm gonna do." Xenia linked having a place to stay with more than physical shelter, safety, and protection from Chicago's brutal cold. She linked her ongoing housing instability with a potential return to her *criminal-addict* identity.

While Lynn's and Xenia's experiences at Starting Again drastically differed from those of Ann Williams, all three verbalized an understanding of rehabilitation as a process of personal transformation and of housing's central role in that process. Lynn and Xenia were earlier in their recovery than Ann and did not express as much joy or hope in the process. Unlike Ann, they did not share a vision of their future selves. Rather, their comments seemed to center more on risk, insecurity, and even fear. Lynn did not want to repeat what she had done with the first install-ment of her lawsuit settlement—spending much of it on drugs and ending up back at the beginning of yet another recovery attempt once the money ran out and she landed in another institution. As a result, she doubted Faye's advice. She suggested independent housing maybe was not what she needed at the moment. Lynn won-dered if maybe she needed to first focus on internal change, which would allow her to confidently secure her own housing, which in turn would support the identity transformation process she had begun. Xenia did not want to return to sex work or selling drugs. She had turned her will over to God, and if she could just find a stable place to stay and hold on to enough money to pay for her car, medication, food, and personal items, she then could focus more intently on her rehabilitation. Without some stability, though, her progress was suspended. The positive reflec-tions and hopeful outlook Ann shared seemed to indicate what could be possible once women had the foundation that safe, stable housing provided.

"MY OWN PLACE, MY OWN KEY, THE LEASE IN MY OWN NAME"

Photographs representing women's future homes further revealed women's use of domesticity discourses to narrate their personal transformation processes, as well as the importance of women's imaginings of their future selves. Women's discus-sions about their future homes often intersected with their desires to reconnect with their children. In this way, women illuminated a strong connection between a structural need and a relational need.[31] Beyond fulfilling a basic material need, housing provided support to fortify relationships, and those relationships were central to women's identity shifts.

Chicken Wing, who took the photograph of the police officer, visually rep-resented this connection between structural and relational needs with another evocative photograph (figure 20). The image of a building represented her goal of home ownership. She referenced her four children, who ranged in age from 23 to 36, while reflecting on the photograph:

I can't wait to get my own place so I can have my kids over for dinner. So they have somewhere they can go. When they get tired of runnin' the street, they can come

FIGURE 20. "I can't wait to get my own place" (Photo credit: Chicken Wing).

home to their mom's house, you know, bring their friend over, "This my mom!" You know what I'm sayin'? So that's a beautiful thing. I can't wait for that, to cook for them.

Although she had maintained a relationship with her children during her 21 years of incarceration, being on the outside now gave her opportunities to mother in ways that had been out of reach for decades. Securing her own home would expand those opportunities, as the program rules at Growing Stronger and the conditions of her mandatory supervised release limited how and when she could be available to her children.[32] Like Ann Williams, Chicken Wing envisioned her home as a gathering place for her children, a refuge they could rely on and a space where she could care for them in ways that were meaningful to her. Establishing a safe, stable home for herself and her children was a central part of the rehabilitated identity she envisioned. Like her employment and appearance, home ownership would further establish her identity as a dependable mother, refuting her self-described past identity as a "crackhead" and contesting racist controlling images and dependency discourses.

Iris, a 49-year-old White mother of two teenagers, took a photograph similar to Chicken Wing's that also represented her long-term housing and family goals. Iris had been living at Growing Stronger for a few months at the time of our interviews. She had been living apart from her children for much longer. After her most recent arrest and stay in jail for a DUI charge, her husband had filed for divorce. He had won custody of their children, who now lived with him in another state. In order for the judge overseeing their divorce to approve a visit where Iris's children could stay with her, Iris had to secure permanent housing. During our second interview, she shared a photograph of what she described as a nice condo building down-town.[33] The building looked like the typical mixed-use structure that had been popping up in Chicago's west loop, a gentrifying area that was steadily extending west. Six floors of condominium units stood above a Starbucks that occupied the ground floor. Each unit had one to two large windows that stretched from nearly floor to ceiling and faced onto one of two busy downtown streets. Iris noted that in addition to the Starbucks, a dry cleaners across the street, a nearby sandwich shop, and multiple public transportation options made the location particularly desirable. Her driver's license had been suspended as a result of her most recent DUI, and Iris explained it would be a long process to reinstate it. Until that time, she would continue to rely on public transportation.

Iris explained how the photograph represented a number of her goals, and in doing so linked her sobriety with domesticity and mothering. She explained the building represented "the next steps in terms of my permanent address, if you will. It doesn't have to necessarily be a fancy condo downtown, but obviously since June of 2010, I've been pretty much institutionalized, meaning living in the treat-ment centers, recovery homes." The past nearly three years of her life had been characterized by instability and an inability to make sustainable forward progress. Like Lynn, Iris attributed this cycle to her addiction and used the 12-Step logic to make sense of it. Specifically, she referenced the dangers of institutionalization. A popular maxim within 12-Step circles is that addiction leads to one of three ends: jails, institutions, or death. Iris and Lynn suggested they had covered the jails and institutions options; ending their alcohol and drug use was a matter of life and death. Securing "a nice, not super huge, fancy place, but a place big enough, and safe and secure enough to accommodate" her children, similar to the condo building she depicted in her photograph, would affirm Iris's ability to avoid all three devastating ends and escape the cycle in which she was caught.

Iris continued to engage the 12-Step logic to explain her life trajectory as she reflected further on the photograph:

> Ultimately this is what I want. I want my own place, my own key, the lease or what-ever in my own name. And see the thing is that I've had all of that, so . . . I know what I'm, hopefully with this sobriety being the only focus, huge priority, because that's the thing that took everything away from me. Because I knew how to get a good job, how to even maintain a good job when I was still drinking, for 18 years I had a career going, how to make good money, how to maintain a home, because I was paying the bills. So, once I can get this other side of the street cleaned up and be able to maybe work with the sponsor and stay in the recovery circles and go to meetings and, be-cause at some point I was still functioning, but then the addiction finally progressed

because they say it's not only cunning, baffling, powerful, but it's progressive, deadly. So it had progressed to the point where I just couldn't function anymore, and then as a result of that, I lost everything.

Iris implied her internalization of the 12-Step logic's conceptualization of addiction. Using the common 12-Step phrase "cunning, baffling, powerful," she suggested she was powerless over her alcohol use and shared her understanding that unless she committed to working the 12-Step program in perpetuity, she would end up again in jail or an institution, or potentially even dead. Her past experiences of getting clean and resuming her normative behaviors and roles, only to relapse and lose it all, reminded her she could not control her addiction on her own. Like Ann Williams and Lynn, Iris expressed she needed more than just housing. She needed to make and continue to nurture a deep internal change. As such, Iris suggested a reciprocal relationship between stable housing and her rehabilitated identity, with each supporting the continuation of the other.

There is a gendered component to this relationship between housing and identity. When Iris commented her addiction had taken everything away from her, she referred, in part, to her identity as a woman. She had been a successful working mother who skillfully "maintain[ed] a home." She indicated if she was unable to maintain her sobriety, then she also would be unable to fulfill these responsibilities. Furthermore, Iris's ability or inability to "maintain a home" would directly impact her ability to mother her children. She was working hard to win back visitation rights, and the judge would determine her fitness as a mother based, in part, on her ability to maintain a home. Iris indicated a similar self-assessment, as she linked her recovery with her ability to again "have a nice place" and provide a safe, loving environment for her children.

Despite varied housing circumstances at the time of our interviews, women consistently used housing to demarcate different phases of their lives. A few had enjoyed relatively stable home lives that had been disrupted by their drug use. Many more described chaotic home lives, marked by poverty, insecurity, and sexual violence throughout their childhoods and adulthoods that precipitated any drug use. Across the board, criminalization exacerbated women's housing challenges, contributing to ongoing instability that jeopardized other areas of women's lives, specifically recovery, safety, employment, and mothering. Yet, women did not only talk about housing as a barrier. Many referenced housing, verbally and visually, in positive ways to show the progress they had made, were making, and would continue to make in their personal transformation processes. Additionally, women talked about housing as more than a physical place to stay. They noted its connections to care work and safety, for themselves and others, such that domesticity was a more accurate, comprehensive term to describe what housing meant. Women referenced domesticity in joyful ways that allowed them to claim dignity and a positive sense of self as independent women and as mothers. Their reflections also suggested fear, as women considered the risks they faced and what they stood to lose if they resumed drug use and slipped back to their past identities. A similar dynamic structured their reflections on mothering.

RENEGOTIATED MOTHERING

Research on criminalized women's mothering documents the many challenges women face to maintaining and reestablishing relationships with their children during and after incarceration and what mothering means for women's sense of self. Oppressive cultural ideologies about mothering, discriminatory policies and practices, and material needs make mothering particularly contentious terrain within the postincarceration landscape. While the intensive mothering ideal that demands women's selfless devotion to child-rearing is an impossible standard that constrains all women, it has particularly devastating consequences for women of color and poor women.[34] The ideal presumes a significant degree of social privilege—Whiteness, heterosexuality, marriage, middle- to upper-class status—and is central to creating oppositional definitions of femininity in which normative Whiteness is defined against deviant racial others.[35] While structural oppression and material conditions have precluded access to the intensive mothering ideal for socially marginalized women, the ideal has never been ideologically available to this group, particularly women of color. Sociologist Patricia Hill Collins's work on controlling images again is relevant, as so many of these images explicitly evoke assumptions of women of color, and Black women in particular, as inherently deviant and incapable mothers.[36] In sum, motherhood is a social position that bestows reverence to some and is an ideology that, by denying motherhood claims to many, supports oppressive social structures that reinforce hegemonic ideals of Whiteness, wealth, and heterosexuality.

Mothering is a site of gendered surveillance that disproportionately subjects poor women and women of color to criminalization. Sociologist Dorothy Roberts's extensive work on the child welfare system, for instance, documents pervasive racial discrimination and the disproportionate breakup of Black families through placing children in foster care as opposed to providing services while keeping the family intact. This disparity reveals the disproportionate scrutiny Black mothers face by social institutions, which increases the likelihood of child welfare involvement, as well as the increased surveillance Black mothers then are subjected to through case plans that may include supervised visits, drug testing, and mandatory participation in a variety of classes and services.[37] Criminal charges related to child abuse and neglect further underscore the state's punitive orientation to Black mothers. Seeking a prison sentence rather than providing support is a choice. Comparing the prison system and child welfare system, Roberts concludes, "Stereotypes about Black criminality and irresponsibility legitimate the massive disruption that both systems inflict on Black families and communities."[38]

These practices and controlling images perpetuate the systematic denial of mothering by women of color that extends back to slavery and colonization.[39] This denial persists postincarceration in material and subjective ways.[40] As previously explained, formerly incarcerated women face numerous challenges to securing safe, stable housing and permanent employment that pays a wage sufficient to support their children and themselves. These material resources often are prerequisites for Child Protective Services (CPS) to allow women to regain custody of their children. Even when CPS is not involved, many women express the need to have these resources in place before they are ready to physically reunite with their children. Additionally, parole conditions may prevent women from living with their children, such as in situations where women are required to live at a recovery home or residential drug treatment program postrelease. Similar to parole, CPS typically imposes a list of tasks and programs women must complete before reunification is considered. The ongoing separation from their children creates significant stress for women who are limited in their ability to ensure their children's safety and well-being while they are in someone else's care. The measures women take to keep their children safe may violate parole conditions or recovery home rules, ultimately leading to women's reincarceration.[41]

Subjectively, criminalization adds another layer of stigma, further cementing the perception of criminalized women as maternally deviant.[42] In addition to racist and class-based stereotypes that already frame them as bad mothers, criminalized women also face judgment for abandoning their children and shirking maternal responsibilities. As Brittnie L. Aiello and Jill A. McCorkel note in their ethnographic study of a program through which children visited their mothers in jail, strict rules shaped how mothers interacted with their children, undermining mothers' authority and ability to parent. The visits also subjected women to further judgment of their mothering: "When children expressed 'negative' emotions like sadness or anger, staff blamed it on mothers' inability to follow the program's rules and used this as a basis to evaluate women's selves."[43]

Mothering constitutes an important dimension of incarcerated and formerly incarcerated women's reparative identity work.[44] Research investigating this identity work uncovers a number of resilient strategies women employ to renegotiate their mothering identities, including embracing religion and spirituality;[45] reframing their past mothering practices as evidence of their identities as good mothers;[46] employing a forward-orientation focused on what they will achieve as mothers rather than dwelling on the past;[47] and taking intensive measures to protect their children from state intervention, abuse by caretakers, and community violence.[48] Collectively, this research foregrounds criminalized women's agency, despite structural and ideological impediments to mothering. It also shows criminalized women are aware of the stigmatized mothering discourses that shape others' perceptions of them, as well as women's perceptions of themselves. Finally, it suggests successfully renegotiating mothering identities is not a given. Despite women's best efforts, barriers to mothering may derail physical reunification and emotional connection with children, as well as development of a positive mothering identity.[49]

Thirty-one of the 36 women who participated in this project were mothers, and all discussed how their drug use and incarceration had impacted their relationships with their children in long-lasting ways. Women did not avoid the disparaging discourses that labeled them as "bad" mothers. They confronted these discourses, openly acknowledging the ways they had not been there for their children in the past due to drug use and incarceration. For the most part, however, women refused to be trapped by their pasts. They foregrounded the ways they were present in their children's lives today, often despite significant constraints caused by poverty, lack of independent housing, and legal restrictions. The familiar pattern of drawing distinctions between their past *criminal-addict* and *rehabilitated* identities structured women's reflections on mothering. As they contested controlling images of mothering, women engaged another dominant discourse, the 12-Step logic, to structure their narratives.

BUILDING A STRONG FOUNDATION: "IF I'M NOT RIGHT, I CAN'T BE RIGHT FOR THEM"

At the time of our interviews, none of the women were living with their children. Many children were adults and living on their own. Most of the younger children were living with family members, sometimes as a result of involvement with the Department of Children and Family Services (DCFS) but more commonly because family members had stepped in to assume a caretaking role when women's drug use interfered with their mothering or when the women were arrested. While women frequently discussed their desire to have their children live with them again, many took a measured approach to their reunification plans. They spoke candidly about the importance of not rushing physical reunification and taking the necessary time to build a strong foundation. Similar to Ann Williams's, Lynn's, and Rose's cautionary reflections about leaving recovery homes prematurely, women explained that moving too fast could lead to relapse, which would just harm their children. Thus, taking a long-term orientation was a critical part of some women's work to renegotiate their mothering identities.

While reflecting on a photograph her five-year-old daughter had taken during a weekend visit at Starting Again, Ann Williams discussed how the visit helped her honestly assess whether she was ready to have her children all living under the same roof with her. That vision remained her goal, but Ann realized it would be some time before she was able to make it a reality. She recalled how energetic her daughter had been throughout the weekend and described it all as a bit overwhelming:

> Sometime they say, "You be careful what you ask for, you just might get it too fast"
> . . . That's why I know things don't happen by mistake, it happen in orderly fashion,

in a reason. You know what I'm sayin'? 'Cause I'll be so quick to say, "I want 'em [her children] back, I want 'em back," but it's a lot of workin' on me that I gotta do. 'Cause I gotta be honest with me. I love my kids, and God knows I do, but He's settin' me up . . . to be prepared for 'em. So, I'm not confused . . . When she [her daughter] came, I gotta tell you, I was a little like, "Oh boy, I don't think I want to do this right now." [*laughs*] I really was, I was like, "Oh my goodness!"

She added that God was showing her "'so, this is what you gon' be ready for. So, you think you ready right now?' No. You know, it's goin' all in a straight path." In addition to providing Ann and her children with quality time to connect, the weekend visits provided a reality check. Taking care of her children full-time would be hard work that would demand her full attention and require much more than providing material necessities.

Ann realized that despite her strong desire to be the primary caretaker for her children, she was not mentally and emotionally ready for that responsibility. She returned to this point later in our interview, commenting, "Now that I'm tryin' to change . . . I gotta be honest with myself. Yeah, this is what I'm lookin' towards the future, my kids gettin' back in my life, but I gotta work on me. If I'm not right, I can't be right for them." Getting right required continuing to work on her recovery, through her commitment to the 12-Step program, and trusting in the linear path God had laid out for her. Becoming the mother she wanted to be was a process. She explained that her children also needed time. In response to my question about what problems she had faced since her release, Ann said, "The guilt, the shame, the things that I did to them [her children]. All that came back. But I'm takin' it in a positive aspect. 'Cause I'm trustin' the process in time, the healin' process. 'Cause I know they still, some things that they goin' through is things that I put them through. I reflected back on all that, but I was sick." As painful as these realizations were, Ann welcomed them. Rather than discourage her, they made her mothering goals seem actually attainable. She was leaving behind her *criminal-addict* identity and trusted that her sobriety and faith ultimately would repair her mothering identity.

Iris similarly focused on the importance of taking time for herself before reuniting with her children. The urgency she felt to secure an apartment so her children finally could visit collided with her pragmatic understanding that rushing the process could jeopardize her own recovery, thereby fracturing their relationship further. Iris explained:

> I just need to really, changing more on a, from the inside and building a strong foundation and just going forward not just surface-wise. And not just trying to grab bits and pieces and maybe a job, an apartment, or buy a few things here or there, open a bank account, I just need to have something little more substance and a foundation like a solid program and some steps, and the sponsors.

Having a job, stable housing, and financial stability all were requirements to gain visitation with her children, but Iris stressed these achievements alone were insufficient to mother appropriately. Without doing the deep work of personal transformation, Iris suggested she could lose each of these things just as she had before. The only way to provide true stability for her children was to foster a deep change of her self that went beyond the surface.

Like Ann Williams, Iris put her trust in the 12-Step program, her sponsor, and God to help her facilitate this interior change. Iris also reasoned the extra time could benefit her children. She recalled a recent meeting with her attorney where Iris provided proof of her 12-Step meeting attendance and a negative drug test from Growing Stronger for her attorney to submit to her ex-husband's attorney. Her attorney asked Iris, "'So, what's the worst case scenario? The kids see that the mom is clean and sober. If they don't come in the summer, they come for Christmas. Perfect time because they don't see winter in [the state where they now lived with their father]!' . . . She brought a good point! The kids could never be happier than hearing that I'm doing okay."

Stacey Williams (no relation to Ann), a 41-year-old African American mother of six children, expressed a similar mix of urgency and pragmatism regarding reuniting with her children. As discussed previously, her sister had cared for Stacey's youngest two daughters since they were born. Due to poor health, her sister could not continue to be the girls' sole caretaker indefinitely. This development intensified housing and financial pressures for Stacey and posed potential risks to her recovery. Stacey explained:

> First I have to get myself together to let them [her children] know that, well, she's sayin' one thing and then down the line she's gonna do another thing. So I'm gonna have to make sure that I'm OK. You know. 'Cause you never know what tomorrow brings. I might wake up and say I want to use drugs. I don't know. That's the type of person I am. I don't know where I go from the next moment.

Having been out of prison for only about three months at the time of our interviews, Stacey knew she had a long way to go before she would feel secure in her recovery. She had been incarcerated four separate times throughout her adult life, meaning family members and her children had witnessed her come home before and eventually return to prison. Stacey wanted to take the appropriate amount of time to feel secure not only for herself but also to prove to her family and children that this time would be different. She suggested that type of security only would follow an identity change. She attributed her ongoing drug use and criminalization to her nature ("the type of person I am"). Beyond behavioral changes, Stacey implied she would have to achieve a change in self. That type of deep work would take time. Repeatedly, women stressed a "clean" identity was foundational to their rehabilitated gender identities as mothers.

BEING THERE

While working toward their long-term mothering goals, many women discussed their efforts to be there for their children as much as possible in the present. Despite structural constraints, such as poverty, DCFS cases, parole conditions, and recovery home rules, women found joy in the moments of genuine connection they shared with their children. These moments were a gendered type of identity work, as women contrasted their current presence with their past absence as mothers. Women used the clean/dirty dichotomy to demarcate these oppositional mothering identities.

New Life, the Black 30-year-old mother of two whom Pastor Geraldine had convinced not to leave Growing Stronger, provided a vivid illustration of the difference between absence and presence in her children's lives. Her reflections were particularly insightful since New Life had lived with her children prior to her incarceration and had been their sole caretaker throughout their lives. In contrast to many of the women who participated in this study, New Life did not discuss repeated stretches of being physically separated from her children. New Life's self-described 'addiction' to marijuana, rather than drugs like heroin and cocaine, further distinguished her from other research participants, as did her housing and financial stability prior to her incarceration. Despite these distinctions, New Life shared a similar process of personal transformation and referenced changes in her mothering to illustrate the deep identity shift she was cultivating. Two specific examples of New Life's current presence and past absence illustrated her renegotiated mothering identity.

New Life recalled participating in a surprisingly meaningful family event at Growing Stronger.[50] She had planned to skip the event and enjoy her weekend pass away from the house, but Pastor Geraldine specifically encouraged her to attend with her daughters. New Life complied and experienced what she described as one of her best days at Growing Stronger:

> I got here, and it was like, wow. It was some women singing, they was all recovering addicts, and they just sounded like angels. Like, and all the women here had their family and people here . . . and I don't know why she [Pastor Geraldine] pinpointed me, but she was like, "There's a very special young lady who came, and I'm so grateful she came" . . . And she said, "God has a calling on your life . . . You're here for a reason." And at first I didn't know she was talking to me, but I got tears coming down, because I know God saved me. And He does have a calling for my life, you know. And all my kids, you know, they, "Mom, you okay?" I'm like "Yeah, yeah." She's [Pastor Geraldine's] like, "New Life, come on up here so I can let them know who I'm talkin' about." And I said, "Me?" And I got up there and everything . . . and she was like, "Sing that song I always hear you sing" . . . And it's "Grateful." You know, in the song say [singing], "Grateful, grateful." 'Cause I am so grateful, you know, I never used that word so much in my life until I was released. And I sung that song, and my kids sung it with me, and everybody just started singing 'cause it's a very popular

song, and you know it was just hugs and kisses, and it was just, I don't know, I don't know. I could honestly say I think that was one of my breakthroughs. I think I really loosened up and started getting more out of the meetings and the groups that we have. I really started opening up more because all I [had] wanted to do [was] just run out here. I didn't never want to stay. When I got my [weekend] pass, it was my pass. I didn't want to have to come back for anything. So I really think that day was one of my breakthroughs.

The event marked a critical turning point in New Life's postincarceration process when she shifted from just doing the minimum that was required to fully engaging with Growing Stronger and its lifestyle. The intermingled faith and recovery meanings embedded in this memory were particularly noteworthy. New Life came to believe Pastor Geraldine was correct that God had a calling on her life and had saved her and that she must respond by engaging deeply with the 12-Step logic, specifically investing more in "the meetings and groups" and "opening up more."

This deeper engagement supported New Life's identity change, not just from *dirty* to *clean*, but also as a mother. New Life's participation in Growing Stronger's family event demonstrated her growth as a mother, underscoring a shift from absence to presence. This display of family togetherness contrasted with her past absence from her children's lives. Although drug dealing had allowed New Life to provide more than adequately for her children financially, the lifestyle required her to spend considerable time away from them. She recalled that while participating in parenting classes in prison, she began to realize she had "made them [her children] happy with a lot of material things," but she had not spent enough time "communicating" with them and developing a "bond." New Life regretted this trade-off and vowed to correct it going forward.

To illustrate her point, she recounted a birthday party she threw for one of her daughters a few years ago. After her daughter opened her birthday cards, many of which contained money from relatives, New Life had to leave to meet a customer. She explained:

> My daughter looked at me, she like, "Mom! What you fittin' to do?" I said, "I'm fittin' to go and pick up somethin'. I'll be back, OK?" She said, "Mom, I'll give you all my money I got, Ma. You know what I really want for my birthday? I want a whole day with my mama." Oh my God. Do you know how many days I cried thinkin' about that day? Do you know I still walked out that door? Because I thought my baby was just talkin', you know how kids say little stuff? But in reality my daughter wanted me there for her birthday!

New Life implied she was becoming a better mother today because she was spending "quality time" with her children, such as at Growing Stronger's family event. Her orientation to motherhood shifted from being a sound financial provider to being present and attentive. This shift was just one reason New Life declared:

I was gone, though, for a long time. I was. I mean a long time. I thought I was gonna sell drugs forever. You know, I hate it took for me to do them three years, but I can truly say I walked in there kind of lost and confused, but I walked out with a lot of goals, determination to do good. I walked out there a better woman, out of Decatur Correctional Center. I walked out of there a better woman. You know, with my head on right. You know, and I still got some growing to do, but it's nothing like knowing that I'm in the right place to grow.

Being gone referred to the totality of her time away—her time in prison and selling drugs. But that absence marked the past. Today, New Life was present—for her daughters and for herself.

Lynn provided an instructive contrast to New Life's reflections on the relationship between mothering and rehabilitated identities. As discussed above, Lynn was cycling through drug use, homelessness, recovery homes, and institutions during the course of our interviews. This instability was reflected in the way she discussed her relationships with her two young children, who lived with two different family members. During our first interview, I asked Lynn how she was a mom to her kids today. After a pause, she replied, "I'm really not." I pointed out that she still saw and spoke with her children, that she was in their lives. Lynn countered, "But I don't [pause] not, you know, I'm not, I'm their mom, but I don't take care of them." I asked her what she would like her relationship to be like with her children in the future. After another pause, Lynn said, "You know, I want to be the one to take care of them, send them off to school, and help them with their homework, and, you know, do things for 'em, teach them life." In response to my questions, Lynn explained, while quietly crying, this goal did not feel realistic, because she had so much going on in her life and felt stuck. She was kicked out of Starting Again shortly after this interview, catalyzing the cycle detailed above.

During our third interview, Lynn reflected on a phone call with her daughter while Lynn had been hospitalized at a psychiatric hospital: "She was mad at me because . . . she's goin' through a lot, my daughter, just a lot . . . she's gettin' to that age where she's like, 'Damn. When am I gonna get it?'" I asked Lynn what that question meant. She clarified, "When am I gonna get clean? When am I gonna, just, you know, be a mom that I need to be? . . . She just wants to spend more time with me. You know, she just wants to be with me." Lynn explained that she wanted to be present in her children's lives, but her ongoing drug use and run-ins with the criminal legal system continued to pull her away. She made clear how her *criminal-addict* identity undercut her ability to renegotiate her mother identity. Lynn did not make a connection, at least not explicitly during our interviews, between the trauma she experienced approximately four years prior of giving birth to her son while shackled to a hospital bed and then being separated from him almost immediately and returned to Cook County Jail. It is plausible, however, that violent experience deeply influenced her description of herself as not really being a mom to her children today, as well as the cycle in which she continued to be caught. The earlier state-imposed absence continued in a new form.

NAVIGATING THE CRIMINAL LEGAL SYSTEM

Multiple women shared their concerns regarding their teenage and adult children's own troubles with the criminal legal system.[51] By modeling their own survival of the system and sharing lessons they had learned about navigating the postincarceration landscape, women provided encouragement and practical guidance to their children. This support constituted a distinct type of mothering that deepened women's connections with their children and strengthened their renegotiated mothering identities.

Sharon was a 44-year-old African American mother of one child, a 28-year-old son. She had been incarcerated six times and explained prison's dehumanizing impact in clear detail. At the time of our interviews, she had been living at Growing Stronger since her last release, approximately seven months prior. Sharon described how her progress since her release and the relationships she developed with Growing Stronger staff members were now benefiting her son. During our second interview, Sharon had just found out her son, who was being released from prison later that week, could not parole to her sister's house as planned. About two months later, during our third interview, she explained her son initially had paroled to a large homeless shelter, but he now was staying at the men's recovery home that was run by the same parent organization as Growing Stronger. Pastor Geraldine had helped her son secure a spot.

Sharon now was helping her son adjust to living in a recovery setting. He was feeling overwhelmed by the recovery home's requirements, such as attending NA meetings, parenting classes, anger management groups, vocational programs, and school. She recalled:

> He got distracted and upset about it because he said, "Mom, this is too much at one time." So I said, "Just calm down and just talk to somebody . . . I'm sure they can work around your schedule" . . . 'cause he wanted to leave. He wanted to pack his stuff and leave. I said, "No, that ain't the way out." I said, "God sent you . . . through stuff for a reason, for you to open your eyes and to realize . . . That's just a stomping ground, just to prepare you to get out into the real world." So I said, "Don't get frustrated, because I get frustrated sometimes. But by me being here at Growing Stronger almost seven months, I know the format. I know what I have to do to stay clean and sober and not to go back out there and use drugs. And you have to do the same thing."

Sharon offered her son a needed perspective he had not yet developed. Based on her lived experience, she was able to normalize her son's frustrations and assure him the recovery home had a reason for its many requirements and that, by following its program, he would be better prepared for "the real world." Although he did not yet understand the "format," Sharon reassured him she did and encouraged him to follow her lead. Because she no longer was incarcerated, Sharon could be there for her son. Furthermore, because she had stayed at a recovery home and remained "clean and sober," she could give him specific guidance on how to navigate his own postincarceration process. Sharon explained:

So I talk to him on a daily basis and tell him, "It's gonna be okay. We gonna have stumbling blocks we have to go through to get it right." So I told him, "It's okay. But you don't have to jump up and run every time you get in a situation." So because, like . . . I do it, too, but I know I can't run. Because if you just get up and take off and wanna go back out there, you ain't gonna do nothing but find trouble.

Sharon merged her son's experience with her own, noting "*we* have to . . . get it right." She mothered through modeling a successful postincarceration and recovery process and passing on lessons she had learned.

Sharon reflected on how her close relationship with her son today was a stark contrast to the relationship they had for most of his life. She explained, "I was young when I had him, so I really didn't know how to raise a child." DCFS removed her son when he was about four years old, and Sharon's mother took custody. Sharon added, "I really didn't have a bond with my son due to me using drugs and stuff like that, etcetera. And due to that . . . he stayed in the neighborhood with drug selling and a lot of that. So he grew up to that, and so he started selling drugs, and due to that, he was getting locked up and stuff . . . We really didn't really have a mother-and-son bond. We mainly had like a sister-and-brother relationship." The self-blame implied throughout Sharon's reflection suggested her absence as a mother caused the problems her son was grappling with today.

Sharon effectively contrasted that past absence with her current presence, explaining how through regular communication, their sister-brother relationship transformed to a true mother-son bond. That communication began with letters they wrote to one another when they both were incarcerated. Now that they both were out of prison, Sharon said her son "calls me on a daily basis and tells me how he feels now and what to expect of him and stuff like that." They were continuing to get to know one another and committing to the active, daily work of relationship building. Due to her own recovery work, Sharon was able to pass on wisdom to her son and guide him, embracing her newfound identity as a mother. Sharon explained how her renegotiated mother identity was a central part of her overall rehabilitated identity: "And today, I'm a new person. Even though I'm still working on some things in my life, but I know it's gonna get better as I go. Long as I stay in this program and do the right things, and I've been doing that, God been truly blessing me. And he blessed me with my son back in my life, and he close to me . . . We can talk. So it's truly a blessing to me."

Nyla, a 42-year-old Black mother of six children, shared a particularly vivid example of helping her 20-year-old son navigate the criminal legal system. She described how about a week after her release from prison, she attended her son's sentencing date for a burglary conviction. Prior to sentencing, the judge gave Nyla an opportunity to speak on her son's behalf. She recalled her impromptu statement:

"I would like to apologize on behalf of my son and us bein' here today as a result of the crime committed against the young lady." Um, and I don't know quite verbatim, but it was geared in that direction. And how the time that my son had spent in the

Department of Corrections, I believe in my heart without a shadow of a doubt that he, too, is very remorseful and is sorry for what he's done. And if given the opportunity, I believe also in my heart that he will do the right thing, as a result of havin' to have sat down and having had the time, the time that he sat to take a look at the error of his ways and the pain that it has caused someone else. And it was very emotional that day.

Nyla described how the judge listened attentively to her, turning all the way around in his seat to face her and even putting his pen down. The judge sentenced her son to three months in boot camp, and her son's public defender told her that her statement influenced this relatively favorable outcome. Before the sheriff's officer led her son out of the courtroom, he instructed Nyla, "'Hug him. Hug him. Hug your son . . . He's gettin' ready to go. Hug him now!'" In these ways, Nyla gained recognition from influential others as a caring mother who had stepped up to support her son, signaling her achievement of a credible identity.

When I asked Nyla how she felt about her statement, she said, "I'm glad that . . . I was able to be there and that I was in the mentality that I was, because, truthfully, I don't think that anyone knew that I had just come back from the penitentiary. And that I also had a background. Wow. Somethin' to think about, huh?" Nyla's physical presence in the courtroom that day allowed her to advocate for her son and publicly demonstrate her love for him. It also reflected her transformed "mentality" and shifting identity from a *criminal-addict* to a rehabilitated woman, which was interconnected with her renegotiated mothering identity. Importantly, throughout our three interviews, Nyla suggested she would continue this mothering beyond the courtroom experience. As discussed previously, Nyla used photographs to document the many reentry organizations she visited as part of figuring out how to navigate postincarceration life. She explicitly connected that work to both of her incarcerated sons. When reflecting on those photographs, Nyla indicated that leaving prison, trying to find a job and an apartment, and staying out of trouble with the law would allow her to provide her sons with a model of how to turn their lives around once they also were released from prison.

CONCLUSION

While women consistently expressed remorse, guilt, and shame for past absences from their children's lives, they consistently articulated a forward-looking orientation to mothering.[52] As Ann Williams plainly stated at the beginning of this chapter, "I wasn't there in the past, but I'm here now . . . I can't go back to the past, but I can only do what I can do now in the present and the future." Women focused on ways they were present in their children's lives today through spending time together, showing up to important events, and drawing upon their experiences to help children navigate their own involvement with the criminal legal system. They also stressed how they were building relationships with their children in order to remain involved in their lives and continue to deepen their mother-child bond. These efforts were rooted in women's commitment to their own recovery. Although women were anxious to reunite with their children, particularly when there were external pressures from family or an open DCFS case, they took a measured approach and explained that rushing things would only cause more problems down the road. A renegotiated mothering identity was anchored in sobriety, in other words, in a *clean* identity.

Women also applied a forward-orientation in their reflections on housing. While supportive recovery homes provided temporary refuge from gendered violence, women consistently stressed their desire to find their own place. A place of their own would further protect them from the vulnerability and violence they had survived, in their homes, on the streets, and in jail and prison. In some cases, having a home also would support women's efforts to strengthen relationships with their children. Practically, a home would provide the physical space for women to mother their children in immediate, close ways rather than through the more restricted avenues of letters, telephone calls, and monitored prison visits. Symbolically, providing children with a safe, structured living environment would contest the controlling image of the absent, drug-addicted Black mother whose instability undermines family values, thereby perpetuating social disorder.[53]

This forward-orientation connected all components of the rehabilitated woman identity. Threat and judgment persisted, but women remained vigilant in their commitment to find a way. Rather than dwell on the past, they sought a better future. As with employment and appearance, women engaged the 12-Step logic to distinguish how their identities related to domesticity and mothering were different today, often identifying specific approaches and behaviors as evidence of change. Through these examples, women implicitly and at times explicitly contested controlling images, like the "crack ho" and "welfare queen," and dependency discourses that always already frame criminalized women as deviant women and "bad" mothers. Additionally, in line with the 12-Step logic, women frequently wove references to God into their reflections on housing and mothering, suggesting how their faith provided reassurance about their value.

Despite limitations, women shared moments of joy and connection they were experiencing in new housing arrangements and with their children, which not only reminded them they were on the right path but also provided hope for the future. The limitations were real, however. External restrictions, such as precarious housing situations, DCFS cases, and parole conditions, limited some women's ability to find stability or be present in their children's lives. Additionally, some women doubted whether they would be able to maintain their sobriety and thus secure permanent housing or make the relationships they envisioned with their children a reality. Women's housing and mothering joys often existed in tension with their housing and mothering fears.

6

"I've Gotten So Much Better than I Used to Be"

Recovering Identity through Relationships

Reading the transcripts of my three interviews with Chicken Wing, I was struck by the amount of laughter that peppered our conversations. After serving 21 years in prison, the 55-year-old Black mother of four adult children clearly was loving life. Indeed, the photographs she took for our PEI documented the joy she described feeling in what to many people would be unremarkable everyday activities, like getting a cup of coffee at Dunkin' Donuts, riding the bus to work, and eating breakfast at the Billy Goat Tavern and Grill for four dollars and some change. She commented that the cheap breakfast was a notable improvement over the "slop" she had grown accustomed to in prison. Chicken Wing appeared in several of the photographs and was beaming in each one, including a photograph of her boyfriend and her at a church event on Christmas night just a week and a half prior. They were nestled together, their arms wrapped around one another. The three poinsettias in front of which they were seated and the fluffy Santa hat perched atop Chicken Wing's head left no doubt this was a festive Christmas celebration. But the real feeling in the photograph came through in their wide smiles and what I perceived as an excited yet content look in their eyes. Chicken Wing's smile was so big that her nose was scrunched up, creating a few wrinkles between her eyes. I asked Chicken Wing what the picture revealed. She immediately replied, "Happiness. 'Cause I'm happy with him." They had been dating almost the entire time Chicken Wing had been home from prison, since meeting at a 12-Step meeting. Chicken Wing explained, "We were in a AA meeting. And he gave me that look. And that was it."

Chicken Wing explained how their relationship had grown over the past seven months. In response to my question asking what she valued about this relationship, she replied:

Just how we do things together all the time, you know. Really I never had a relationship like this. Even when I was in the street, I never had a relationship where I felt that we love each other at the same time. It's always I love you more or he love me more. We never was, you know, right there at the same time with it, like me and him, we love each other right at the same time. We like bein' with each other. We like talkin' to each other. You know what I'm sayin'? We like eatin' together. We like doin' things together. Like they had dancin' under the stars this summer downtown. We went there for the steppin' set. We had a good time. He videotaped it. We had a good time down there. We do a lot of things together. We go to the show. We just do a lot of things together that I never had that type of relationship with another man before.

Chicken Wing marveled at how different this relationship was. The sense of togetherness, mutual care, and fun she was enjoying had been absent from past relationships that had been characterized by her partners' infidelity and physical violence.

Chicken Wing held herself responsible for those past issues. She made a direct link between her sense of self and her previous partners' abusive behavior, noting how her insecurities and character flaws compelled her to act in ways that strained relationships with her partners. She explained:

Chicken Wing: I had real low self-esteem . . . I was glad somebody wanted me that was nice looking, you know. I never thought I was nice looking . . . I didn't like myself back then. You know, so I was always more into them than they was into me.

CR: So what, I mean, what type of problems or issues did that cause?

Chicken Wing: That caused a lot of problems, because I was like needy. You know what I'm sayin'? Don't nobody want no needy woman. You know? I argued a lot. If they wanted to go somewhere, I argued. I'm jealous-hearted. You know, like I'm sayin', because I never thought I was pretty. I never thought I looked good enough. You know. But now I do . . . But today I feel good about me. I like me. You know, back then I didn't. So I can see why the men really didn't like me. 'Cause I didn't like myself!

Chicken Wing explained how her changed behavior in her current romantic relationship reflected a deeper change in her identity: "God said He would make your latter years better than your first years, and I believe that now, because my latter years are better than my first years. And I was in the world! I'm a better person now since I did 20 years." When I asked her how she was a better person today, she responded:

I just can feel it. I just know I am. How I treat people, how I talk to people . . . I *give* now. I was selfish back then. You know, I was a taker. I'm not like that now. I don't mind volunteerin' for somethin' now. Back then I would've never did that! I don't mind sharin' what I got now. Back then I wasn't like that. I was just out for myself. I'm not like that today . . . It's better . . . to be a giver, it's better.

In Chicken Wing's mind, since she no longer was a "needy," "jealous-hearted" woman who lacked self-esteem, she finally was able to enjoy a relationship with a man who treated her well and loved her for who she was. She explained this relationship only was possible after she became a new woman and learned to love herself. Stressing this point, she commented, "I'm not that *person* no more. I'm not the Chicken Wing that went to prison . . . He got the *best* Chicken Wing. He didn't want that Chicken Wing before I went to prison, so he got the better Chicken Wing. He got the best deal."

The photographs of Chicken Wing and her boyfriend and her reflections on their relationship were additional sites of identity work. As much as she was demonstrating how deeply she valued this unique relationship and the joy it had introduced to her life, Chicken Wing also was verbally and visually presenting a new identity. To do so, she used a similar narrative technique she and other women in this study used to discuss other parts of their identities: appearance, employment, domesticity, and mothering. She drew a clear boundary between her past *criminal-addict* self and her present *rehabilitated* self, and she used the familiar touchstones of the 12-Step logic, specifically independence, sobriety, and faith, to establish that boundary. Chicken Wing was no longer dependent on a man to have a positive view of her self, because, as she asserted emphatically, she liked herself today. She recognized her many positive qualities, which existed independently of what any man thought of her.

Chicken Wing further made clear that this positive, independent self was anchored in her sobriety and faith—commitments she and her boyfriend shared. They had met at an AA meeting and were both "in recovery from drugs," as Chicken Wing put it. They also had begun a formal process to attain recognized leadership roles within their church, which demonstrated their commitment to serving God through helping those in need. As Chicken Wing had commented, God was fulfilling His promise of making her "latter years better than your first years." For Chicken Wing, her new relationship, life, and self were signs of God's work and affirmation she was on the right path.

Chicken Wing's photographs and reflections centered an additional gendered marker of recovery—romantic relationships—that constituted the rehabilitated woman controlling image.[1] For the women who participated in this research, romantic relationships were the least salient part of their personal transformation processes. Unlike employment and domesticity, romantic relationships were optional. Whereas all of the women who were mothers discussed their relationships with their children, many women did not discuss current romantic relationships as part of our interviews. Still, the way women who mentioned relationships talked about them was telling. For these women, relationships were an important site of identity work. Romantic relationships were not an essential part of the rehabilitated woman image, but they could only be achieved through personal transformation.

Romantic relationships that were free of drug use, coercion, infidelity, and abuse brought women in line with conventional notions of femininity. Despite significant changes in work and family relationships over the past several decades, women continue to shoulder the primary responsibility for care work in the United States, in practice and ideology. Similar to intensive mothering ideals, women's social value often is connected to romantic relationships, specifically marriage.[2] Failed relationships, particularly heterosexual relationships, often are read as reflections of women's inability or refusal to prioritize their partner and devote themselves to the work required to maintain the relationship. In contrast to the cultural trope of the happy, unencumbered bachelor, a single woman faces presumptions about her unsuitability for marriage, a sign of gender deviance since it violates deep-rooted social norms. These social expectations constitute the ideological scaffolding that supports systemic gender inequality.

Race and class shape these gendered social expectations about relationships. As discussed previously, normative femininity is a privileged social category defined in opposition to those whom it excludes. Similar to the ways slavery, colonization, and immigration policies have systematically denied women of color's mothering, these dehumanizing systems also have systematically disrupted loving interpersonal relationships. Criminalization is one vehicle through which these "enduring legacies" persist, systematically fracturing communities and relationships.[3] Violent practices of family separation rely on the ideological justification controlling images provide. If women of color and poor women are not real women, then they lose any claim to the protection and reverence the social roles of mother and wife extend to socially privileged women. A host of race-specific controlling images paint women of color as inherently sexually deviant and promiscuous. As such, these images justify sexual violence against women of color by constructing them as unrapeable. These images also label women of color as incapable of and uninterested in maintaining a mutually respectful loving relationship with a romantic partner. While women of color are framed as incapable of such relationships, they also are blamed for not having them. Moral panics over the so-called breakdown in family value are laid at the feet of women of color.

The added layers of stigma associated with drug use and criminalization further cast criminalized women not just as social deviants, but also gender deviants. Sociologists and criminologists who study criminalized people's postincarceration processes have identified romantic relationships as noteworthy factors that support desistance.[4] Social bond theory posits that prosocial attachments help people feel more connected to others and create disincentives for continuing participation in criminalized behavior, since people have something to lose. Along with education and employment, relationships consistently are noted in this research as a significant social attachment. Research that incorporates an explicit gender focus suggests relationships are particularly important for women.[5]

For the women who participated in this study, relationships worked on an individual and ideological level. Individually, women frequently contrasted current relationships or imagined future relationships with past abusive relationships, much like Chicken Wing did. Ideologically, relationships characterized by mutual respect, trust, love, and sobriety countered controlling images of the "Jezebel" and "crack ho" that present Black women as inherently sexually promiscuous and immoral. The "crack ho" image, in particular, suggests a link between Black women's drug use and immoral sexuality, invoking images of an unclean, unhoused woman who trades sexual favors for drugs. Depending on the context, the image is employed for cheap comic relief or to stoke fear and condemnation of depraved Black femininity. Either way, the image justifies the violence and derision leveled against these always already deviant women, whether by an intimate partner, community member, or state actor.[6] In short, women's depictions of their romantic relationships were a way to demonstrate their personal transformation regarding drug use and criminalization and contest controlling images.

Because relationships were such an important site of identity work, I conceptualize them as part of the rehabilitated woman controlling image. As with previously discussed gendered markers of rehabilitation, my intent here is not to critique women's relationships. The absence of physical, sexual, and emotional relationship violence is an unqualified positive aspect of women's lives. This absence should have been a given, and the fact that women had to work so hard to cultivate lives free, to various degrees, from this violence was telling. The feelings of fulfillment and being appreciated that women described were undeniable positive developments in their lives, as was the confidence women exuded when reflecting on a decision to end a relationship or to remain single. In analyzing women's depictions of their relationships, my goal is to show how romantic relationships fit into a larger cultural script about what criminalized women's recovery and rehabilitation should look like. It matters that women did not talk with me about having multiple sexual partners or, for the most part, romantic relationships with women. The similarities in the ways women talked about their relationships suggest they were engaging a cultural script about how relationships should be.

For the remainder of this chapter, I continue to use the previously established clean/dirty and fear/joy framework to examine women's relationships as identity work that furthered overall processes of personal transformation. Romantic relationships were yet another gendered and raced way women created rehabilitated identities that brought them joy and affirmed their dignity. In the second half of the chapter I discuss women's reflections on their friendships with other criminalized women. These reflections revealed how, throughout their incarceration, women relied on other women to survive the daily stresses of prison life and do their time. Similarly, postrelease, women found a sense of community as they connected with other formerly incarcerated women and helped one another manage the challenges and setbacks they encountered. Women grew stronger in their own personal transformations as they did the work of recovery and reentry with supportive peers. I present romantic relationships and friendships together since both provided affirmation of women's value and dignity. Both mirrored back to women positive images of their selves as good people who were deserving of love and care, despite their past mistakes. That recognition of one's inherent worth was nurtured through deep personal connections and mutually affirming relationships.

TAKING THE TIME TO GET IT RIGHT

A common point women made when talking about positive romantic relationships today was the importance of not rushing into things. They shared a recognition that it would take time to build a stable relationship with a partner they could trust and be sure they both were invested in the relationship for the right reasons. Similar to the way women viewed their personal transformation as a work in progress, they indicated the need to be attentive to their relationships and address potential problems as they arose. Taking time to get to know a partner and ensure their priorities aligned was an important part of this relationship work.

Ann Williams, the 44-year-old Black mother of six who had taken the photograph of the dining room table at Starting Again, reflected on the slow process of building from a friendship to a relationship with a man she had met about a year ago at a 12-Step meeting. She hoped they would become "significant others" and explained, "I'm believin' in it, but it takes time. 'Cause you got to get to know each other. I always, in my relationships, I had never get to know the person. I just got into the relationship. So now, that's somethin' new for me." For the past year, they had been getting to know one another by "spendin' time, talkin', we call, we talk to each other every day on the phone. If he ain't called me, I'm callin' him. Every mornin' we talkin' and say good things to each other on the phone. We go out and we spend time. He helps me, I help him. A friend."

Like Chicken Wing, Ann made an explicit contrast between her past and current approaches to relationships and how that change was making things better today. She used similar language to describe establishing a strong foundation for this relationship as she had when discussing rebuilding her relationships with her children. Taking the time to physically be present, honestly talk, and actively listen to another person were new ways Ann was trying to establish genuine connections with people about whom she cared. She suggested that in the past, she had not invested in the relationships in her life. But that was the old Ann, who was distracted by drugs and periodically removed from her loved ones' lives by incarceration.

Like Chicken Wing, Ann attributed this new relationship to her sobriety and to God. She reflected on how her friend also wanted to take things slow. He told her he was not ready to be in a relationship, in part because he was living with his parents and could not financially provide for Ann. She welcomed this explanation, noting, "I was like, 'Wow,' I was sayin' to myself, 'God, this must be the man sent from you.' 'Cause all other guys I had they didn't think all the good stuff like that. So I'm like, okay I don't wanna mess this up." She reaffirmed her hopefulness for their relationship: "All I gotta do is just keep doin' what I'm doin' and it's gonna fall into place . . . I think we think the same way. We on the same level. We both know what we want." Ann trusted things were happening for a reason, and she attributed the noteworthy turning points, like her most recent incarceration, and positive developments, like her growing relationship with her children, in her life to God's work. As long as Ann remained committed to working her recovery, she believed this friendship would grow into the relationship she desired. As pillars of the 12-Step logic, sobriety, faith, and personal responsibility were discursive resources Ann could use to make sense of her past, have hope for her future, and find joy in the required work to get there.

As hopeful and joyful as Ann seemed, she still noted the threat of falling back to her past life and past self, suggesting that concern remained a constant presence in her life. She did not just contrast the nature of her current friendship with past relationships in general; she made a specific distinction between this friendship and her past relationship with her children's father. She reflected on her vigilant work to prevent that past relationship from upending the progress she had made. When I asked Ann what problems she had faced since her release, she replied, "My kids' father. He's actively usin' . . . me and him used together [in the past] . . . he was everything to me. Like, everything. I thought I couldn't live without him, like everything. We did everything together." Her entire life prior to her last incarceration had centered around him, and while Ann did not blame him for her own problems with drugs, she recognized that his use had encouraged her own. Being "on the same level" as her current romantic interest, who also was working the 12-Step program, encouraged Ann's commitment to working her own recovery. For example, Ann explained how she was following the 12-Step directive to avoid "people, places, and things" associated with her past use: "It's different now, I don't hang out no more . . . as my thinkin' done changed. I don't go up there . . . kick it with them thinkin' I can still. No. I can't do that." Ann added that when she saw people with whom she used to get high, she just would "keep it movin'. 'Cause this ain't what I want no more. And I ain't lookin' down on you 'cause I ain't sayin' I arrived . . . I ain't exempt neither. I can easily be right back there again."

Even though the father of Ann's children was the person perhaps most strongly associated with her past drug use, she could not avoid him. All six of her children lived with him. In order to have a relationship with her children, she had to engage with him.[7] As such, Ann took care to limit the types of interactions she had with him and set firm boundaries on their relationship today. During a recent visit with her children at their father's home, Ann brought a case manager with her so she would not be alone. "That's like me goin' to a drug area and I'm clean," she commented. "I'm not gonna set myself up no more. I don't care, I'm just not. When you know better you just do better. So, if I go over there . . . I have to take some people with me. I got some people that I can just take with me inside. Used my tools. I'm learnin'. Use your tools. Don't go in the fire by your[self] . . . My life is on the line."

Ann suggested the precarious nature of her recovery and rehabilitation. It would have been easy to reunite with her children's father and have her family living under one roof immediately. But she identified that option as "moving backwards," and that direction would lead back to "hurt" and "trauma." She added, "Why would I go back? And that was like even when I was with him, I didn't really, it was pain, I didn't wanna be with him for real. It was always strife, argument, everything, so. I'm not confused about that." She identified her certainty about that decision as an indication she was on the right path. In the past, "I would've just stepped out there and went back to the usual. So I know there's growth."

Ann's thoughtful considerations revealed the connection between her romantic relationships and her identity.[8] The nature of these relationships reflected how strong she felt in her newfound sense of self. Her ability to define the terms of these relationships in ways that felt safe and aligned with her personal goals reflected her growing independence and confidence. The nature of these relationships also reflected how strong she felt in her recovery. Her past *criminal-addict* identity was wrapped up in her past relationship with her children's father. Her *rehabilitated woman* identity made possible and was reaffirmed by her current friendship that, with enough time and care, had the potential to develop into a mutually supportive romantic relationship. By rejecting and redefining her relationship with her children's father and by asserting her hopes for her current romantic interest, she presented herself as a woman who had learned from her past and was committed to her ongoing personal transformation. Her relationship work was one and the same as her identity work. Through all of her identity talk, Ann credited God with the progress she was making and noted the importance of trusting God's plan. Again asserting she had moved on from her children's father, Ann explained, "See God, He do things in a divine order . . . And I don't even have that second thought. Nah, I'm not even fittin' think that. Why would I go backwards?"

Ms. Fields, the 47-year-old Black Afro-American woman who had explained recovery as working through the 12 Steps from start to finish repeatedly, also discussed how renegotiating her relationship with her ex-husband was a critical piece of her overall personal transformation process. As with Ann Williams, the 12-Step logic provided Ms. Fields with guidance on how to do so. Across our three interviews, Ms. Fields repeatedly referenced the 12 Steps as a framework she was using to make sense of and guide her life. Within the first 15 minutes of our first interview, Ms. Fields plainly explained, "My whole reliance right now, you know, first on God and the program of Alcoholics Anonymous has helped me really see the truth in my whole addiction, which caused me to go to jail, lose my family relationship, lose my marriage, lose me goin' back to school, lose my housing." Ms. Fields departed from Ann, however, in that she was trying to reunite with her ex-husband and hoped they eventually would remarry. She believed her independence, sobriety, and faith would make that goal possible.

According to Ms. Fields, she had "manipulated" her ex-husband and used him for his money in the past when she was using drugs. Now, with just under four years of clean time, she explained she was capable of being a better partner to him because "I know how to love today . . . And I'm not that person who I was. You know. And I would not now do anything to hurt anybody deliberately, you know, I just won't do it now . . . I've been transformed." Ms. Fields said her ex-husband was interested in remarrying only after she could show him she had changed, particularly through her participation in AA and NA. He attended Al-Anon meetings, she explained, and "he heard that after a person works 12 Steps, that they have, you know, really allowed God to go in and, you know, let them see who they really are . . . so that's what he's waitin' on." Working through the full 12 Steps would reassure her ex-husband that she "won't resort back to the old way."

When I asked Ms. Fields how she felt about his stipulation, she said it gave her "hope" for their future and agreed she needed to work more on improving herself before becoming his wife again. She elaborated, "I do really want to be married, but I want to be able to be marriage material." Ms. Fields clarified how she would know when she was marriage material:

> One would be for me to have my own finances because I used to depend on his money so much and take all of his money. Yeah, I need to have my own money. I need to be able to bring somethin' to the table. You know, school will allow me to do a lot of that . . . School teaches me so much discipline. And see once I do 12 Steps, it'll allow me to do a balance. This is your space, this is your husband's space, you know. Now if he lets you do all that stuff you do, 'cause you know you work, you go to school, you sponsor women, you praise dance, you holy ghost dance, you be with your sponsor, you go to all these meetings and all that, then you can't invade on his . . . So, those [12] Steps'll teach me how to be a wife, how to be a friend, how to be a neighbor, how to do everything . . . I've gotten so much better than I used to be. That's why I can see that I'm getting to be, I can be that material. You know. It's still gonna take some work.

Ms. Fields explained that only after she had attained foundational components of the rehabilitated woman controlling image—appearance, employment, and domesticity—would she be able to have a genuine relationship with her husband characterized by balance and mutuality.[9] As she described, her past self was undisciplined and disordered, qualities that had undermined her marriage. The 12-Step logic imposed a rigid structure and was helping her cultivate a disciplined, ordered self. As she saw it, those developments would make her a better wife. The success of her new marriage would reflect the changed person she was working so hard to become.[10]

ASSERTING AGENCY

Discussing positive romantic relationships in relation to personal transformation was not the only way women incorporated relationships into their identity talk. For some women, ending a relationship or not starting a relationship reflected their new self. Denise, the 45-year-old Black mother of five who had come to see Judge Hopkins as "Heaven sent," shared perhaps the clearest example of this dynamic. In our final interview, Denise seemed conflicted when recalling breaking up with her boyfriend earlier that day. She explained he had hepatitis C, which he had contracted years prior through intravenous drug use. He had pressured Denise to have unprotected sex with him. She reluctantly complied and was worried not only about possibly contracting the disease but also about why he pressured her to do something that could harm her. She explained:

> Sometimes I be wanted to tell him, "I don't wanna be with you no more, because if you love me like you say you do, you wouldn't have unprotected sex with me." Now I don't put the whole blame on him because I'm partially to blame, too . . . But I'm just saying, had I had any type of life-threatening disease and I know somebody say they care about me, and I know what I'm going through, these liver transplants, taking all this med[ication], if I loved you I don't wanna see you go through that . . . So I had to try to tell myself, "Denise, he don't love you, because if he did, he wouldn't, not under any circumstances would he put you in harm's way."

His response when Denise ended their relationship reassured her she had made the right decision. Denise recalled:

> The things that he was saying to me, it just really just told me he don't care. He was like, "You know what? You know, you still the same dope fiend ass lady you was before you came into the program. You ain't shit. You ain't got shit. You never was shit. You ain't never gonna be shit." And I'm just sitting up here like, "Damn. You know, if he really cared about me, he wouldn't say nothing like that to me."

Although Denise expressed she wanted to get married someday, she determined this man was not whom she wanted as a lifelong partner. Their relationship echoed past relationships in which partners had abused and taken advantage of her. In previous interviews, Denise shared detailed accounts of the physical, sexual, and emotional abuse she had survived. She recalled how trapped she had felt in these relationships and how she would leave small, folded-up handwritten notes to God, asking Him to show her a way out, hidden in the pockets of her clothes in her dresser drawers. Denise's current boyfriend's abusive behavior took her back to that time and to her *criminal-addict* identity. She commented, "I ain't been talked down like that since I was sober." She made a decision that prioritized her well-being and protected her *rehabilitated* identity. Ending this relationship reflected the new woman she had become.

In thinking through how she knew she made the correct decision, Denise recalled the many risks she faced in the past when she was using drugs, engaging in sex work, and partnered with abusive men. She described how lucky and grateful she felt that she had not contracted HIV or another serious disease throughout her drug use, and she attributed her relative good health to God. When deciding whether to end the relationship, she had thought to herself:

> "But you sitting here, you throwing your life on the line after God done blessed you so many times. You know, you think you invincible. You know, that you exempt from the whole world. Everybody else can get this and get that, but God done blessed you so much. Girl, you covered in the blood of Jesus." You know, and I really struggle with that because I don't wanna keep putting myself in harm's way.

Denise's reasoning recalled Nyla's imagery, discussed previously, of being under "God's umbrella" and "in the light" while in her sobriety versus being outside "of His protection" and "in the darkness" while in her addiction. Even though Denise was not using drugs, the relationship with her boyfriend exposed her to the same risks she encountered when she had been. She noted, "I didn't catch this shit when I was in my addiction, and now I'm sober. I'm still doing some crazy, dumb shit when I should be able to think clearly now." It also is noteworthy her boyfriend's hepatitis C status was the result of his past drug use, and stigmatized diseases such as hepatitis C and HIV often are associated with dirtiness. Although selflessly caring for relationships and nurturing partners align with conventional notions of femininity, this relationship could not be a marker of a "clean" *rehabilitated woman* identity. Rather, it pulled Denise back toward a "dirty" *criminal-addict* identity she still was working to leave behind. In this case, the absence of a romantic relationship reflected positive developments in Denise's identity work.

Carmel, a 44-year-old Black woman who had been living at Growing Stronger for about nine months at the time of our interviews, also reflected on how *not* being in a romantic relationship was a sign of her new self. Throughout our three interviews, Carmel discussed how powerless she had felt to end her heroin and crack use. She commented, "I just thought I was gonna just die getting high. I wanted to stop, but, you know, it was like the feeling wouldn't let me, or I just, I couldn't stop usin' it. No matter how I tried, I could not stop." For approximately seven years during that time, Carmel had been in a relationship with Joseph. During our PEI, she reflected on a photograph she had taken of a building where they had lived together. Throughout their entire relationship, Carmel had used drugs. Joseph also had used for most of that time, with some periods of recovery.

According to Carmel, her ongoing drug use had made it difficult for Joseph to maintain his own recovery. Looking at the photograph of the building, she recalled:

> He always thought that I would clean myself up, you know. I didn't wanna think about cleanin' myself up. I was in my own world and hey, you in yours, you payin' the rent, or whatever, so I'm gonna do what I wanna do up in here. And I would come in there and go in the kitchen and close the door to the bathroom and sit there and just, get high. You know, when the stuff ran out I would go in the room and I would bug Joseph for more money, you know, and he was like, you know, "I'm not giving you no more money," or whatever, and I start cussin' him out. You know, getting mad because he wouldn't give me more money to buy more drugs with. So I went outside the building, around to the front of this building, like right there, this is the front entrance of it. And, you know, I got to know the guys out there that was sellin' drugs. So, they let me work. They let me sell the drugs. I would take the drugs back around the corner to the house and take 'em upstairs and I be hiding them in the house where Joseph you know, he was even on parole, and that wasn't good for me to have drugs in the house and he on parole. You know, and he would never say nothin'.

As Carmel told it, she had caused many of the problems in their relationship. While describing what their relationship had been like, she commented, "I didn't wanna be a good woman to him, because I didn't know how to stop using drugs. You know, even when he was on drugs, he still was a good person and a good man to me." She elaborated, explaining how Joseph had taken care of her financially, was patient with her, and encouraged her to better herself, such as by going to school to finish her high school diploma. She summarized, "He always wanted the best for me. I can't even say he disrespected me, cursed me, abused me. He just didn't do none of that to me, you know. He was always somebody I could depend on."

According to Carmel, her ongoing drug use coupled with a death in the family eventually pushed Joseph to relapse. Together, their drug use escalated, and they both began selling drugs. They stopped paying their rent and lost their apartment. Each moved in with different family members. It was just a matter of time before they each were arrested on separate drug charges, Joseph first and then Carmel. Carmel participated in the women's drug treatment program at Cook County Jail and then was released on probation. Joseph was sentenced to prison and had been released a little over a week prior to Carmel's and my second interview. They had seen each other twice already, for the first time in two years. They had met privately for dinner and talked for a few hours. Having just been released, Joseph needed essentials, like his state ID and help with transportation. In a role reversal, Carmel was able to provide for him. She gave him a few bus cards, cigarettes, and some movies. "All the help he done for me . . . I shared what I have with him," Carmel said. Two days after their dinner, Joseph accompanied Carmel and some of her family members to church and then joined them for a meal at her aunt's home. Carmel shared two photographs of her and Joseph from that day. In both photographs, their arms are wrapped around one another, in a sideways embrace, and broad smiles are plastered on their faces. Carmel commented, "I can see the happiness in the picture, for both of us."

A lot had changed in the two years since they had been together, so it was not a matter of simply picking up where they had left off. Carmel explained they were at the beginning of a new process of getting to know one another. She elaborated, "He don't know me. But I know him sober, and I know him clean. But he don't know me . . . He don't even know the person I am. And he said it. He said, 'You totally, you know, like a stranger.' And I know I am . . . You know it like put him in a state of shock or somethin'." Carmel was so different from the woman Joseph had known throughout their seven-year relationship that he was uncertain how to interact with her. She commented, "I had to tell him it's okay to hug me. He wouldn't even hug me . . . 'cause he didn't, he don't know how I would've reacted."

While Carmel still cared for Joseph and was happy to see him again, she did not want to resume their romantic relationship. Commenting on her different feelings for Joseph today, she explained, "But I can't see us bein' together. I don't see it, and I see us bein' friends." She stressed she was focused on her own plans, a focus that even was reflected in their getting together on a Sunday and attending Carmel's church. I asked Carmel why they met at church rather than at a restaurant as they had a couple of days earlier. She replied:

> 'Cause I wasn't gonna let him distract my goals and my plans that I had been doin' for me. He either could've waited 'til I got out of church and I would have met him somewhere or he could've came and joined church because that's what I do every Sunday. And that's my schedule . . . I'm not turnin' around my schedule for him or nobody.

She had not contacted Joseph throughout the following week, because she was busy with her schoolwork. Carmel was focused on maintaining "the new me," and the foundational components of her new identity were her relationship with God, sobriety, school, and independence. She was not going to let a relationship, even a supportive one with a "good man," disrupt the structure she had put in place to nurture her recovery.

These findings offer important nuanced insights about the connection between romantic relationships and identity for criminalized women. Romantic relationships did provide an important "hook for change" that could facilitate identity transformation.[11] But at times that transformation was reflected through *not* being in a relationship. Furthermore, being in a relationship was far less important than the meaning women attached to those relationships. The ways women negotiated, understood, and talked about romantic relationships provided opportunities to affirm the rehabilitated woman identity. These relationships were a significant site of gendered identity work to the extent women made them so. Thinking and talking about these relationships provided women with an opportunity to reflect on their personal transformation processes and take stock of the progress they had made. Whether talking about past partners or potential romantic relationships with new partners, women consistently framed the nature of their relationships as a reflection of their selves. Women associated chaotic, contentious, and outright abusive relationships with their *criminal-addict* identities. They were self-critical of what they had contributed to these relationships and, at times, identified problems in the relationships as reflections of their own personal flaws, such as Chicken Wing's self-described jealousy or Ms. Fields's self-described manipulation. For women who now were enjoying mutually fulfilling romantic relationships, they described those relationships as possible because of the deep identity work they had done.

Additionally, much like personal transformation, romantic relationships were a dynamic process characterized by movement forward and backward.[12] The women in this study revealed that such movement was interconnected. As a marker of the rehabilitated woman, romantic relationships moved between the familiar poles of fear and joy, "dirty" and "clean," and dependence and independence on the spectrum of criminalized women's identity work. Women discussed reuniting with partners who had been part of their past drug use as a risk that could lead them right back to the *criminal-addict* identity. Relationships with new partners that mirrored dynamics in past relationships posed a similar risk. For some women, any romantic relationship was too risky, as it could divert focus from their attention on their continued self-improvement. In this framing, women's overall personal improvement—as evidenced by markers like sobriety, commitment to the 12 Steps, and employment—allowed them to experience the joy of romantic relationships free of exploitation, coercion, and abuse. Whether women decided to commit to, end, or abstain from a relationship, the decision was theirs alone, reached after careful consideration about what they might gain or lose. Those decisions reflected growing autonomy and confidence in one's self.

There likely was not one single discourse that shaped women's evolving views on relationships.[13] Along with parenting classes and 12-Step meetings, however, domestic violence and healthy relationship classes were a regular part of programming available to criminalized women in jail, prison, and community settings. Recovery homes, including Growing Stronger and Starting Again, frequently hosted relationship groups on-site. Some women also were required to attend domestic violence counseling as part of probation or parole conditions or Child Protective Services (CPS) cases. Ranisha, the 34-year-old Black woman who gave birth to her youngest child while detained at Cook County Jail, initially did not understand why her CPS caseworker required her to participate in domestic violence counseling, because she did not think she had experienced domestic violence. After participating, though, she learned "a lot of it did apply to me, you know, mentally and emotionally, so I mean I learned and I benefited from it." When I asked for an example of how she benefited, Ranisha replied, "As far as like being controlled emotionally, or mentally . . . I know how to set boundaries with that. You know, I know just what I'm not gonna accept period. You know, no ifs, ands, or buts about that. I know that."

Based on the reflections of Ranisha and other participants, these classes seemed to provide education about warning signs of abusive behavior and encourage women to have a strong enough will to reject such behavior. Additionally, these classes seemed to stress to women they did not deserve to be abused, real love did not hurt, and they were not alone. Manipulative, exploitive, and violent relationships were signs of a disordered life where women were not in control. Such relationships also made women vulnerable to further surveillance and judgment, from the criminal legal system and CPS, and even reincarceration.[14] Asserting self-worth in relationships was one way for women to gain control over their lives. This connection between a healthy self and a healthy relationship might help explain why participants did not necessarily identify partnering with a man as a sign of accomplishing femininity. Developing a relationship that was free of coercion, violence, and drug use—or remaining single—was the paramount concern. This conceptualization of a healthy relationship could be deployed by women who identified as lesbian or bisexual, despite service providers potentially holding discriminatory views.

CONNECTION AND COMMUNITY:
"NOT BEING THE ONLY ONE"

Women frequently reflected on friendships they developed with other criminalized women, throughout their incarceration and after release, as important relationships that provided critical support and reaffirmed their humanity. These moments of connection were particularly important given that incarceration was a deeply isolating experience. Women were separated from their family members, friends, and communities, as the Illinois Department of Corrections (IDOC) shipped them to distant locations in central and southern Illinois to serve their prison sentences. Keeping to themselves was a common survival strategy women practiced to avoid problems with correctional officers and other incarcerated women. Despite frequent references to conflicts that erupted among women in jail and prison, women also focused on the care they received from and offered to other women. A sense of community emerged as women shared resources and strategies on how to get by, and that community, both literal and abstract, extended beyond the prison walls.

Ann Williams and Sharon, the 44-year-old African American mother who had helped her son secure a spot at a men's recovery home after his release from prison, were just two women who noted the critical support they received from other women throughout their multiple prison sentences. Ann stressed how alone she had felt while incarcerated, because she had no family members on the outside to put money on her commissary account. The other women helped her, though, by letting her know that she could submit a request with one of the correctional officers for a care package and by sharing their items. Birthdays could be particularly painful, with no cards or gifts arriving from loved ones on the outside, but Ann fondly recalled the last birthday she spent in prison:

> They went out of their way and showered me and made a card. See, they say the little things can touch your heart, and . . . I was thinkin', you know, what they gon' do? They made that day really special for me! And I still to this day got that card . . . they sung happy birthday, they made food for me . . . we had like a little grab bag, and then they had little stuff on my bed. I went and took my shower, and I came back, all my little treats and stuff was on my bed, my card. It was really nice. I really enjoyed that . . . they really made me feel loved and excited and happy . . . that was a great experience for me.

The community of love and support Ann experienced carried her through particularly difficult days and helped her make it through her sentences.

Although she described herself as someone who kept to herself, Sharon also reflected on the relationships she developed while in prison. She discussed growing close with one woman, who ultimately died after correctional officers ignored her pleas to see a doctor for her asthma. Sharon recalled being "heartbroken" by the woman's death: "I was so hurt because when I first came on the unit with this young lady, she didn't know me, and she walked right up to me and just start, she had a care package, she didn't even know me, she gave me food, deodorant, and stuff . . . and ever since, we became close." Like Ann, Sharon stressed how important these moments of connection were in prison and how something as seemingly simple as giving someone deodorant was a humanizing act in a deeply dehumanizing place.

As women left prison, they also developed friendships with other women with whom they lived at recovery homes. In fact, women commonly learned about recovery homes from other incarcerated women who recommended which places could offer the most help. During one of our interviews, for instance, New Life referenced the staff member who was working at Growing Stronger's front desk. She commented, "My friend Monique . . . she was in there [prison] with me, and when she left, she said 'I'm goin' to Growing Stronger, New Life, and it's a beautiful place.'" Once Monique was released and moved into Growing Stronger, she wrote to New Life in prison and told her all about it. New Life continued, "She was like, 'Girl, Christmastime, they gave me so much stuff, and we're so clean here you won't even think it's a recovery home.' And it's like it never left my mind, Growing Stronger." As discussed previously, New Life now considered Growing Stronger and its staff a pivotal source of support that was helping her maintain her sobriety, deepen her faith, and strengthen her relationship with her children. She had Monique to thank for connecting with that community.[15]

While women noted conflicts and tensions that arose in these communal living spaces, they highlighted how women helped one another. A theme that emerged across women's photographs was the sense of connection they felt to other criminalized women, frequently represented in pictures of housemates and recovery home activities. Sharon, for instance, took photographs of a close friend at Growing Stronger:

> She's a sister that I always wanted . . . She's down to earth . . . she talks to me, because like my real sisters never talk to me and . . . on a daily basis she asks me what's wrong with me. She . . . calls me on a regular basis, asks me how I'm doin'. Even when I take my weekend pass, she calls and checks on me. And my real family don't do that, but she does it . . . and it makes me feel good and it makes me feel loved . . . She talks to me about anything, and I can talk to her about anything and it stays there. It don't go anywhere.

Red, the 41-year-old Puerto Rican woman whose photographs of Starting Again presented in chapter 3 symbolized God and the 12 Steps, similarly took a photograph of a couple of residents at Starting Again to show the impact they had on her life. She described how much she appreciated one resident who voluntarily cooked for everyone in the house and explained that the women depicted in the photographs were "here like me" and symbolized "a second chance in life, you know, that I'm not alone, 'cause I'm really not alone with them . . . They don't let me be alone." Prison fundamentally changes the nature of family relationships, structuring when and how incarcerated people can be in their loved ones' lives, if at all. The consequences of those changes persist long after release. Friendship networks helped fill in the holes prison had "punched" into women's care networks.[16]

Denise also used photographs to show the togetherness she felt with fellow Growing Stronger residents. During our PEI, she commented on a photograph a friend had taken of Denise standing next to a Michael Jackson impersonator. In the photograph, Denise and the man stand side-by-side, posing playfully for the camera as they wait for the red line L train. The man wears a version of Michael Jackson's iconic red and black leather jacket, adorned with multiple zippers, Jackson's trademark black fedora, and a sparkly, silver glove on his right hand. Denise stands to his right, mimicking his body language. Both lean slightly, with their right hips jutted out and their left legs slightly bent. Their right arms are raised, the man seemingly waving at the camera with his single gloved hand, and Denise making a peace sign with her purple-gloved hand. Denise looks stylish in a cropped black leather jacket, cozy gray turtleneck sweater, light gray jeans, and black snow boots. She flashes a bemused smile, while a full smile extends across the impersonator's face. Next to the impersonator is an advertisement for Coors Light that reads, "GET ON THE RIGHT TRACK," a noteworthy irony since Denise and her friends were on their way to a 12-Step meeting. Looking at the photograph, Denise commented, "I just seen an opportunity . . . to get some entertainment, you know, 'cause they say that you can have fun in recovery, so I caught myself creating some."

Similarly, Moon, a 40-year-old African American woman, shared photographs from a bowling trip Pastor Geraldine had organized for Growing Stronger residents. "I haven't been bowlin' since I was a kid," Moon said. She laughed while flipping through photographs that showed several of the Growing Stronger residents, including Moon, in action as they bowled, posing for the camera, and cheering on each other. In one image, a woman has fallen down on the alley, after a presumably failed bowling attempt. In another, Moon watches her ball roll toward the gutter. In several images, Moon plays to the camera, looking over her shoulder and striking a quick pose before hurling the bowling ball down the lane. In one, she has stopped mid-approach and strikes what looks like a dance move from a musical, both arms outstretched, holding a bowling ball in one, and dipping forward as if she's about to touch the floor with her free hand. The images leave no doubt it was a fun trip, as all of the women are smiling and laughing in each photograph. In one photograph, Moon and New Life stand back-to-back, posing for the camera. New Life holds her bowling ball in front of her chest, as if she's getting ready to take her turn. Moon leans back onto New Life, her bowling ball resting on her left thigh. When I asked Moon what the picture showed, she replied, "That picture shows us happy at the bowlin' alley . . . it's just like a sister thing . . . it was like a come together and like a fun thing. It's like she's [Pastor Geraldine's] teachin' us to have fun in our new life."

In the context of what the women had been through and the many challenges they continued to face, these moments of silliness and joy took on added meaning. The photographs evoked a sense of freedom associated with being able to get lost in the moment, having fun with a street performer or revisiting a childhood activity. Such activities were not possible while women were incarcerated, and they likely were improbable while women were in the midst of their drug use, typically struggling with poverty, homelessness, and routine violence. Photographs that may have seemed unremarkable at first glance actually conveyed significant meaning about women's lives and identities. These joyful moments reflected women's rehabilitated identities. Denise and Moon, for instance, explicitly connected these moments to their sobriety. Furthermore, women's rehabilitated identities were nurtured through relationships. Being part of a community provided a sense of acceptance that largely had been absent from women's lives and assured women they were deserving of love, support, and a second chance.

Women also used photographs to document more formal group experiences. Carmel shared a photograph of her classmates and her at an adult high school where she took classes and eventually earned her high school diploma. Reflecting on the photograph, Carmel said, laughing, "They mean a lot to me because we struggle, all of us struggle . . . We're trying to stay clean. All of us in this picture are recovering from alcohol and drugs and prison, coming out of prison and stuff. That little group right there." She explained how school was a collective experience that promoted connection: "There's no one in there arguing and fighting and stuff like that. Everybody is a help to one another, and we worked so hard . . . We give each other hope and strength . . . 'Come to school tomorrow, you're gonna get it. We're gonna get this graduation and stuff. We're gonna graduate together.'" The students were not just committed to their individual success; they were committed to their collective success. Carmel clearly valued the community she found at school and the opportunity to both give and receive encouragement and support. The students' shared life experiences—positive and negative—created a bond that strengthened their commitment to their personal transformation processes.

Some women noted the importance of connecting specifically with other women who had similar life experiences. Denise shared a photograph from a Growing Stronger event where alumnae spoke about their accomplishments since leaving the recovery home. She said the photograph revealed "recovery. Everybody in here is sober and got a new start. That's why I asked to take it. I said, 'These are all my . . . sisters.'" Nyla similarly noted the importance of being connected to women who personally could understand what she had been through and the challenges she continued to face. Referring to Women Helping Women, the month-long peer health education group where we had met, Nyla said:

> I felt a part of a group of women, I was around a group of women . . . I don't want to get to the point where I don't want to talk about stuff . . . I don't want to get to the point where I shut down. I don't want to get to the point where I start believin' the lies again . . . and I truly don't want to get to the point where I feel that I'm inferior, I'm less than . . . I don't measure up, and I'm not worthy.

Nyla implied the tenuous nature of her rehabilitated identity and how being alone could undermine the positive sense of self she was working to maintain.

Through her photographs, Moon documented her participation with other Growing Stronger residents in a One Billion Rising event.[17] She described how much she enjoyed the afternoon:

> We danced and celebrated ourselves . . . we don't have to be quiet and sit back and take it . . . it was just like a good thing to do with a bunch of women . . . we're not the only ones, even though we've been to prison and rehab, and . . . drug abuse and stuff. It was women there that wasn't been through that, but they been through the traumatic part like rape and . . . beat up and . . . just abused period. And they was all there celebrating the fact that you don't gotta take that anymore . . . It was wonderful. I've never . . . seen anything like that. So it was wonderful to see so many women comin' together just to celebrate being a woman, you know . . . We got rights and stuff like that, so it was like a feminist sort of thing . . . It was all women . . . together on one accord, to celebrate freedom . . . especially freedom of not being the only one. That's what was the most important thing to me . . . Not being the only one who's gone through some of these hard experiences.

Like Denise and Nyla, Moon stressed the collective nature of her recovery, not only from drug use but also from violence, as the critical factor that was helping her move forward. She knew she was not alone, and this knowledge provided her with a sense of power and strength. Formal events like this one and informal events like bowling provided Moon with critical reminders of her self-worth and her connection to a larger community, both literal in the sense of her Growing Stronger sisters and abstract in the sense of the countless women around the world who were survivors like Moon.

Importantly, the sense of community women began to develop spanned the prison walls. Once released, women did not forget about the women they had left behind. Women frequently expressed concern about specific friends, as well as the thousands of women, in general, who remained behind bars fighting to survive the daily cruelties of prison. Ella, the 46-year-old African American woman who successfully had her record sealed and now worked at Growing Stronger, commented on the women she met in prison who were serving life sentences: "For some people to know that they're never leavin' there, I don't know how I would deal with that. I think for me knowin' that I had a out date made it better for me, because I knew each day that I'm in there, I'm gettin' closer to my out date. But if I knew that this was it for the rest of my life, that's a lot to swallow." Similarly, Ida, a 49-year-old African American mother of three adult children, empathized with women who remained in prison. She noted, "I've got to meet a lot of young ladies at Dwight, a lot of young ladies in Lincoln . . . and a lot of them have shared their stories with me . . . and they say, 'You know what? You can go back home to your family, we can't.' Some of us girls that's locked up in prison, will never come from behind those bars."

Through communicating with one another in prison, women learned there was more to people's stories than the charge for which they had been convicted. Ann Williams described slowly getting to know the other women with whom she was incarcerated and "understanding [them] . . . getting that connection, feeling them . . . There's some women in there ain't never gon' leave . . . And just looking around and seeing . . . we all made bad choices and mistakes. You know, but we still good people." Rather than distance herself from the "lifers," Ann related to them, using "we" to refer to their common experiences of criminalization and imprisonment. Regardless of their "mistakes," they all are "good people."

Ella, Ida, and Ann Williams revealed how the effects of incarceration linger long after release. In addition to the well-documented collateral consequences of incarceration, these women suggested how the experience of incarceration shaped their beliefs and values. Now that they knew about the thousands of women incarcerated throughout the country, many of whom shared similar life experiences, they could not forget them. They were transformed by these women's stories. Even though they no longer were physically bound by the prison, its presence loomed. Ella suggested as much with a photograph (figure 21) she took of the window out of which she looked during her daily shifts at Growing Stronger. Now an employee who took joy in supporting Growing Stronger residents, Ella had lived at Growing Stronger upon release from her last incarceration approximately seven years prior. The window served as a daily reminder of how far she had come. Ella wrote a poem to accompany the photograph:

FIGURE 21. Ella's window (Photo credit: Ella).

Looking out that window so many days, so close but yet so far away.
Well, not today.
Because I'm finally looking and seeing from the other way.
Appreciate and celebrating just being free.
The window that I used to look from and see was when I was in the penitentiary.
Now that I'm free, it's really made a big difference for me.
I thought that I appreciated the gift of life, right? Nope. Wrong.
I appreciated being able to smell the flowers, the grass, and looking at the trees.
Being able to open up a window or a door or going to the store.
In the penitentiary, it's called commissary.
And it's only done once a week.
That's if you have money and you fill out a commissary sheet.
Today I can truly say that I'm grateful for whatever comes my way.
If it's a bad or a good day, it's ok, because I'm out here living and not locked up
      in a way.

While Ella's reflection on the window centered on freedom, I was struck by the way the window also provided an ever-present reminder of her incarceration. The window's connection to Ella's daily work to keep women out of prison added yet another layer of meaning for me. With women continuously cycling through Growing Stronger, some moving on to their own apartments but others returning to past lifestyles and eventually prison, the window symbolized how "reentry" is a liminal space with porous boundaries. Prison was not a past experience. It was a constant presence.

CRITICAL CONSCIOUSNESS

Women's memories of others with whom they had been incarcerated and their friendship networks with other criminalized women and survivors of gendered violence fostered a growing awareness of how their individual stories connected to a larger social story about women's incarceration. Through its efforts to punish, reform, and monitor criminalized women, the state paradoxically brought them together in jail, prison, and recovery homes, creating opportunities for a collective consciousness to grow, despite the individualizing focus of the 12-Step logic. As women began to view their situations as part of a collective experience and not just an individual problem, they began to critique how the criminal legal system operated. If they could be transformed, why could not other women who still were locked up? If they benefited from drug treatment and supportive services, why did prison have to be so harsh? Women's embrace of the 12-Step logic and their commitment to personal transformation did not foreclose critiques of the criminal legal system as unfair, racist, and needing reform. In fact, the opposite occurred. Because this personal work happened in community, it fostered such critiques.

Corrine, the 63-year-old African American woman with a master of social work degree, described the tension she felt between accepting personal responsibility for her past behaviors and being critical of how little support she received to deal with what she had described as years of trauma that was the underlying cause of her ongoing drug use and criminalization. She remembered "having good desires and intentions after serving time to go home and do the right thing . . . and not finding that the community support was . . . there for me. Or the family support." Now, as a social worker who worked for a women's treatment program within Cook County Jail, Corrine walked a fine line daily between encouraging women's individual change and recognizing the odds were stacked against them. Her goal with her work was:

> To educate and empower and to give women hope that . . . their lives can change with some determination and strong willpower and footwork. However, even in promoting that, it's sad because women often do not have the adequate resources once they leave the jail. And that's a big impact on them succeeding in their reentry process back into the communities, and when I mention the resources I'm thinking more of housing, safe living environments . . . many of them will be forced to return right back to their communities, but also without the skills that they need in order to be successful in their reentry process.

As a result, Corrine saw the same women return to her program and described jail and prison as a "revolving door." Rather than blame the women, Corrine recognized "the state today plays a big part, because they have removed funding . . . for rehabilitation for these women, and . . . the money is just not there for services." Based on her own criminalization experiences and now working with criminalized women, Corrine developed a structural critique of the criminal legal system.

FIGURE 22. "Having fun being kids" (Photo credit: Moon).

She suggested a personal commitment to change was not enough; systemic change also was needed.

Women's critiques also centered on how racism and economic inequality structured the criminal legal system, specifically whom the system targeted and how the system treated them. Moon, for instance, discussed the unequal life chances children faced based on whether they were born into rich or poor communities. She noted that children who lived in well-resourced communities benefited from private educational programs, while children in underresourced communities were left to struggle on their own, as she had as a child. Reflecting on a photograph she took while attending a basketball game at a local university, Moon described how hopeful she felt for the young people she saw in the stands (figure 22): "I was like, man, now that's what's up, showin' these little kids that it's more to life than just the block, you know?" She was happy someone was encouraging these young people to see ways their lives could be different from what they routinely observed in marginalized communities.[18]

Moon was so moved that she had approached the adult chaperone for the youth group and told her:

"Take the kids and let them see like the Black colleges, Morehouse and stuff like that. Let them see Arkansas, Pine Bluff, Mississippi State, let them see that there are Black kids doing other stuff, too, besides the 'hood" . . . It gave me a good feeling to see all these kids in a good place. No funeral. No Ceasefire [a local community-based antiviolence program]. This was a game. They were there having fun being kids, and I like that.

By mentioning historically Black colleges and universities and noting the importance of Black youth having positive Black role models, Moon indicated how Chicago's racially and economically segregated communities created structural disadvantages for young people. She also recognized that structurally disadvantaged communities largely supply the Black and Brown bodies that fill Chicago's jail and Illinois's prisons.[19] Moon described prison as "a modern day slavery" and noted that when she started getting in trouble with the law, she always encountered White people in positions of authority (i.e., state's attorneys and judges), who reinforced her grandmother's warnings throughout her childhood that White people did not want her to succeed. Moon explained, "It made it seem like [what her grandmother said] was true, because they didn't send me to . . . rehab, they didn't send me nowhere to like get . . . help. They sent me to jail . . . And jail wasn't the answer."

Olivia, the 49-year-old Afro American woman who talked about judges' consideration of past convictions when determining sentences as a type of "double jeopardy," similarly critiqued the criminal legal system's racism. She referenced the image of Lady Justice, whose blindfold represents fairness and balanced scales represent equality, and called it inaccurate. Olivia said in an accurate representation "her blindfold is crooked. It's not actually straight . . . and then the scales [are] not balanced. They're uneven. That's not fair. That's what justice is." A crooked blindfold, Olivia elaborated, would symbolize how the criminal legal system treats defendants differently based on their "nationalities," "class," and where they live: "In the city, they have a real high conviction rate. And if they have somebody from the suburbs, they've got a better chance of giving them probation or rehab or something, as to where us in the city, they want to send us straight to the penitentiary." According to Olivia, the courts "figure the people in the suburbs, the middle class and upper class, they come to the city to get their drugs or whatever. OK, but they're grown like me. Them the choices they made. You can't be mad at the city for it, 'cause they're doin' what they want to do." Olivia expressed an intersectional analysis in which "prejudices" based on race, class, and place intertwined to result in more punitive sanctions for low-income and poor people of color who live in the city.

Tinybig, the 51-year-old Afro Native American Indian woman who had shared photographs of *The Life Recovery Bible* and a 12-Step meeting directory, represented this disparity with a photograph she took of news trucks parked outside of the Chicago Police Department Headquarters (figure 23). She had gone here to request a copy of her criminal background, which was required to begin the expungement process. It happened to be the same day local news outlets were reporting on Chicago reaching the tragic milestone of its 500th homicide for

FIGURE 23. Chicago's 500th homicide of the year (Photo credit: Tinybig).

the year. Tinybig took the photograph because "it's interesting how some features or events show up on the news and some don't . . . Like a lot of times in the Black community . . . or even [the] Hispanic community, it may not come across the news where somebody died of an overdose, of a bad heroin purchase. But in the suburbs, it may." Tinybig explained this uneven news coverage reflected the way society devalued the lives of people of color. If she had died while on the streets, she said, "it may not be broadcast, but because it might be a political figure's daughter, a judge's daughter, an attorney's daughter, it's all over the news." Similar to Olivia's analysis, Tinybig recognized certain lives mattered more than others and how this social reality played out in the criminal legal system.

RESILIENCE AND RESISTANCE

Women's personal experiences and relationships with other criminalized women fostered a number of insights about the system. First, many women understood how racism, bias, and inequity were embedded in and perpetuated by the criminal legal system. Second, they recognized how commonly criminalized women were survivors of gendered violence. Third, they developed an analysis of how the untreated trauma resulting from that violence often contributed to the behaviors and circumstances that kept women entangled in a wide carceral web of surveillance, judgment, and punishment. These insights undergirded women's efforts to challenge the system in subtle individual ways and explicit collective ways.

At the individual level, women sought recognition of their personal transformations and attainment of the rehabilitated woman identity from authority figures, such as judges, parole and probation officers, recovery home staff members, and treatment providers.[20] Doing well in recovery homes, drug treatment programs, and reentry programs; holding a job, however low-paying and unstable it was; securing an apartment, even if it was a single-room occupancy (SRO) unit where children could not live; and *not* getting in trouble again with the law were ways women resisted the criminalization of disadvantaged communities. Women's resilience *was* resistance, because it subverted one of the carceral system's main functions—to maintain existing social hierarchies. As scholar-activist Angela Davis argues, the state responds to social problems by criminalizing and imprisoning poor people and people of color. This response attempts to "disappear [social problems] from public view," while leaving systems of inequality intact. "But prisons do not disappear problems, they disappear human beings . . . vast numbers of people from poor, immigrant, and racially marginalized communities."[21] Neoliberal policies that deregulated the economic market, facilitated deindustrialization, and allowed corporations to exploit a global labor pool contributed to growing wealth inequality and social stratification. The resultant economic and social insecurity felt by the middle class contributed to support for harsh law-and-order approaches to maintain social control.[22] As Davis summarizes, "The massive prison-building project that began in the 1980s created the means of concentrating and managing what the capitalist system had implicitly declared to be a human surplus."[23]

Given this historical, social, and political context, women's abilities to complete parole and probation, pass drug tests, maintain their stays at recovery homes, move into their own apartments, attend school, and find employment mattered. Women's resilience made them visible, as they refused to allow the criminal legal system to disappear them. Furthermore, as documented throughout previous chapters, women's personal transformations helped them feel better about themselves and establish meaningful relationships with children, family members, romantic partners, and friends. Women grew to love and accept themselves and felt they were in a better position in life. Their attainment of the rehabilitated woman identity did not come without complication, but the access it extended to reclaiming humanity and dignity in a fiercely unforgiving world should not be downplayed. By not just surviving the state systems that bear down on their lives, but actually finding ways to make these systems benefit them, women reinterpreted and resisted these systems in everyday ways that were significant.

Women's resilience and individual success also made it possible to participate in more overt collective forms of resistance aimed to bring about broader changes in the criminal legal system that would improve all women's experiences. Three women discussed being part of class action lawsuits, one for illegal shackling during childbirth and two for illegal strip searches (one at Cook County Jail and one at Lincoln Correctional Center). Correctional officers had conducted strip searches with groups of women, rather than individually, while male correctional officers were present. In addition to wanting restitution for the state violence she endured throughout her 21-year prison sentence, Chicken Wing hoped the lawsuit would bring about broader change:

> I hope they stop that, you know. Men ain't supposed to be looking at us, and they was talking about women and looking at our bodies, and we have to squat and all this, stand up there for like 15 minutes, you know, and all that. You can't put on a pad or tampon, you know, it's just disrespectful . . . they should stop that . . . they should sue their butts off. And the warden should get fired behind that.

The lawsuits were one way women collectively attempted to hold the state accountable, reduce the violence of incarceration, and institute reforms that would benefit criminalized women broadly. Such efforts were bigger than individual redress and healing. They demanded recognition of gendered violence that often remains invisible and institutional change.

For the five women who were employed at programs that provided services to incarcerated or formerly incarcerated women, their employment allowed them to turn their personal experiences with the criminal legal system into valuable information that benefited others. Women who worked in these jobs stressed how much they enjoyed giving back and being able to help other women who were in situations similar to those they had overcome. Corrine, for instance, reflected on her work at Cook County Jail:

> I listen to myself sometimes when I'm talkin' to the ladies and tellin' them how important it is in raising your children, building that trust, and the love and the nurturing, and so I share with them there's nothing like a child being with their own parent. Because I'm seeing a repeat of everything that I've done on a daily basis when I talk to those ladies. "Well, my mom got my kids and, you know." And I see these ladies that go right back out there, come right back in and many of them never even touch base with their children and stuff, and so the work that I do today is still a healing process for me. And even more so when I feel that I have had an impact on somebody's else's life . . . even if it's just startin' to think about takin' a different route in their life. It's very rewarding for me.

Ella also commented on the joy she felt from observing Growing Stronger residents' personal transformation processes:

> I love welcomin' the ladies when they come and then continuin' on to show them that you are loved. You know. People need to know that. People need people . . . Some of 'em will tell ya, "I don't need nobody!" You know, but it start changin' somewhere down the line, and it really gets to me like when they don't even realize they have changed, but then one day they'll see it and be like, "Oooh! I remember!" Or like when another lady come in, and they used to be in a bad way, and they greet them,

too, you know. "Ooh. You'll love Growing Stronger . . . Welcome to Growing Stronger!" And I'll be like, "Mm. This the same one that was kickin' and screamin'. Now, 'Welcome to Growing Stronger! You're gonna love it. What room you in? You need a big sister? I'll be your.'" And I'll be like, "Oh, wow." You know. So, yeah, Growing Stronger helps.

Through their work, both Corrine and Ella refused to allow the carceral system to disappear other women. They drew upon their own success to create humanizing experiences for women as they moved through the system. They offered knowledge and support in an effort to help women avoid recriminalization. Even though their efforts were not always successful, Ella and Corrine continued to do the daily work of resistance.

Five women spoke of their advocacy and organizing efforts to bring about larger change in the criminal legal system and social service field. Chunky, the 56-year-old Black woman who critiqued the negligent health care in prison, discussed her volunteer work with an organization that provided direct legal services to incarcerated women and advocated for criminal legal reform policies at the state level.[24] As part of its policy work, the organization organized formerly incarcerated women to work on legislative campaigns. This organizing work included strategies, such as lobbying trips to Springfield to meet with state legislators, public demonstrations, petition drives, and meetings with officials within the criminal legal system. Chunky talked about a recent trip she made with the organization to the Illinois women's prison where she had served time and her participation in a meeting with IDOC officials to advocate for better living conditions at the prison. Chunky specifically talked with the officials about the need for better health care services and to lower the fee women had to pay to see the doctor. In some cases, the fee prohibited women from seeking needed health care which they had a right to receive. Chunky asked, "So what? So now we into crime and punishment instead of corrections? What? You're punishing me already, I'm away from my family, I'm away from my kids, I'm away from everything." She also informed the officials of the need to "change your guards, 'cause I think you know you got some guards here that is not right." She recalled the racist insults correctional officers used and their gossiping about incarcerated women during her imprisonment. "It felt really good," Chunky said, to speak her mind and give input to the wardens and deputy director. "They took our suggestions, and they wrote them down. They were duly noted, and we felt like . . . it wasn't wasted. They were actually communicating with us. That was a good feeling . . . I felt hopeful."

Iris, the 49-year-old White woman who was trying to secure visitations with her two teenage children, also talked about her advocacy work with this organization, specifically a lobbying trip to Springfield to encourage support for a bill that would allow people to petition the court to seal certain nonviolent felony convictions four years after completion of their sentence. Although the bill would not benefit Iris directly, since her felony conviction was for one of the excluded offenses, she valued the opportunity to contribute to a "good cause to improve people's life conditions, to give them chances, to be of service, and just get outside of myself and do something for a good cause." She also benefited from the lobbying experience because "it empowers me, and it motivates me. Because I have a voice! You know, and the voice needs to be heard."

Julia, the 51-year-old African American woman who took a photograph of her certificates on her windowsill, also gained lobbying and organizing experience with another organization that led a successful campaign to end felony convictions for prostitution in Illinois. When I was at Growing Stronger for an interview one day, Julia proudly showed the organization's newsletter to me. It featured a picture of her, as well as a short bio explaining her contributions to the campaign. Julia and I remained in contact after I completed data collection, and she periodically sent text messages to me, updating me on how she was doing. She had been working at the Chicago Transit Authority (CTA) in an apprentice program for people with felony convictions and cleaned buses and garages. The temporary position paid minimum wage. Julia always spoke positively about the job and expressed her gratitude for the program. In one of her text messages, though, she said she planned to start a campaign to increase apprentices' pay. Tinybig also remained in contact after data collection and worked in the same CTA program. While stressing she liked the position, she also expressed frustration with the heightened surveillance apprentices experienced in comparison to the permanent employees, as well as the insecurity of the temporary position.

Reflections such as these indicated women saw themselves as part of a collective group of criminalized women who had experienced unjust treatment while incarcerated and remained subject to discrimination long after their release. While women were concerned with their individual well-being, they also expressed a commitment to helping other criminalized women. Even when a campaign or policy change would not benefit them directly, as in Chunky's and Iris's cases, the reform was important because it would offer protection to other women who shared a similar social experience. As women encountered barriers, they experienced the limits of personal transformation and the double bind of the rehabilitated woman identity. As such, many participants recognized the need for broad social change.

CONCLUSION

This chapter shows how romantic relationships and friendships nurtured attention to the necessity of social change. While women still used the 12-Step logic, with its clean/dirty dichotomy and moral implications, to make sense of relationships, these relationships did more than provide evidence of women's rehabilitated identities. Women received affirmation of their worth and dignity from partners and friends. That affirmation provided a solid base from which women demanded more from and better treatment by individuals, social services, and the criminal legal system.

7

The Personal Is Political

Moving toward Social Transformation

Toward the end of my third and final interview with Rose, the woman who took the alley photograph that opens this book, I asked her a closing question that I posed to almost every woman who participated in this project: how would you describe yourself today? Rose seemed a bit surprised by the question. After a brief pause, she chuckled, then said, "I describe myself as a different person today than I used to be. You know? Like I said, being open to suggestions. I describe myself as a helpful person. I like to help others if I can, in any kind of way . . . I would describe myself as more of a beautiful woman." "Could you say more about that? What makes you beautiful?" I asked. Rose responded, after another thoughtful pause, "I have a different outlook of myself, you know. I enjoy life. I enjoy this side of the fence [more] than I did last time." She paused again, seeming to search for just the right words to explain what precisely was different about her today and how this release from prison was different from her two previous releases. Rose continued, "I enjoy the things that I'm doing today. You know, I'm not out trying to manipulate or steal. So I enjoy myself today, very much so."

With her concise yet thoughtful response, Rose again summarized the core analysis of this book. She previously had done so visually, with her alley photograph, and now she had done so verbally, with her self-description. Rose explained that her identity today was rooted in difference and was defined in opposition to her past identity. Over the course of our three interviews, I had learned that maintaining her rehabilitation from drug use was a central focus in Rose's life, which would enable her also to end her entanglement with the criminal legal system. Rose was confident she had served her last prison sentence. She was certain this time would be different because *she* was different.

Each of the women whose stories open a chapter in this book shared descriptions of themselves that resonated with the positive, confident tone of Rose's self-description. In response to my closing question during our final interview, Tinybig described herself as being in a better place. Denise described herself as a caring person who loves to help people. She elaborated, "I done been through a lot, and I know it's hard to rise above a lot of things that people go through. So I have a lot of empathy for people." Ella also laughed before exclaiming, "I don't even know! Um, wow. I'm excited about life." After a pause, she added, "I'm a very happy person, and . . . I feel good about myself." Without hesitation, Ann Williams described herself as "confident. Confident, content, and enthusiastic. Courageous . . . On some days I just feel so energized and so, especially when I'm doin' the right things and, you know, accomplish things, I feel good, and then talkin' about God, you know, I just, I get boost with energy and good things." In her characteristic fashion, Chicken Wing was direct: "Today I describe myself as a good person. Yeah, somebody that know how to listen these days to somebody else. Yeah, somebody that's not too judgmental . . . Somebody that's trying to do the right thing in life. Somebody that's loving, you know, to a certain extent. Yeah. Not an angel, but I ain't what I used to be."

I was deeply moved by the women's self-descriptions. Especially in light of the accounts they had shared with me of sexual and physical violence, years of struggling with drug use and the associated vulnerabilities and challenges, and the dehumanizing treatment they experienced at the hands of police and correctional officers, there was something profound and resilient about their views of themselves as good people who cared for others, contributed to society, and truly enjoyed life today. Their descriptions signaled to me that they indeed were healing from the trauma that characterized much of their earlier lives and finally had reached a place where they felt genuine joy. They were not just getting by; they seemed happy and content.

Despite the joy and hopefulness women expressed, and that I felt as I listened to each of them reflect on their personal transformation processes and plans for the future, I felt a nagging concern. I knew the odds were stacked against them, for reasons detailed throughout previous chapters. I kept thinking, it should not be this hard for these women to make it on the outside. I knew these women would face lifelong legal discrimination due to their criminal convictions. Indeed, many had shared stories of being denied employment or housing because of their criminalization. This discrimination was not going to magically disappear, and it likely would constrain most if not all of these women to financially precarious lives on the margins of society. But these external factors were just part of the story. As I listened to each woman focus squarely on identity throughout our interviews, I became increasingly concerned about not just the external barriers they would continue to face, but also the internal work they would continue to undertake. Their identity work was not just related to their drug use or experiences of interpersonal violence. Their identity work also was necessary because of the systematic process of dehumanization they experienced throughout the criminal legal system.[1]

Even though these women welcomed the opportunity to transform their selves and expressed feeling deep joy in the new rehabilitated women they had become, I remained skeptical of the singular transformation narrative the criminal legal system offered. The 12-Step logic, with its focus on individual responsibility and change, might provide criminalized women with a small carve-out in a hostile society, but it did little, if anything, to disrupt the systems of power that contributed to women's criminalization in the first place. As women discussed the deep, intensive, and at times painful identity work they dedicated themselves to daily, I wondered, what were we asking criminalized women to work so hard for? The rehabilitated woman identity offered a chance to survive on the margins of society, where women likely would continue to face gender-based violence, navigate Chicago's racially and economically segregated neighborhoods, and find ways to take care of themselves despite systematic disinvestment in the neighborhoods where they lived. Throughout it all, the daily choice of whether to return to drugs as a way to cope or just numb out when things felt a bit too much would persist. In the face of these relentless challenges, women would be armed with a strong sense of self, the 12 Steps, their faith, and their connection to a community of criminalized women—women who, like them, had made it out and women whom they had left behind inside prison but had not forgotten.

THE MESSENGER MATTERS

My intent is not to critique women's general embrace of the 12 Steps or religion. Both were sources of strength and comfort that provided women with reassurance their lives could be different and with practical strategies to make those changes. My critique is of the carceral state's use of the 12 Steps and religion. For decades, the United States has advanced an agenda of criminalizing drug use.[2] This agenda relies on willfully ignoring the social causes of drug use, particularly systemic racism, community disinvestment, and a culture that condones gender-based violence. Every woman who participated in this research traced their ongoing drug use to the seemingly inescapable web caused by the intersection of trauma, poverty, and criminalization. Rather than address these social causes, the criminal legal system blamed women for the circumstances that led to their criminalization. Once women were pulled into the system, they almost exclusively encountered individualizing discourses steeped in moral judgment. These discourses tapped into cultural tropes about the inherent deviance of women of color, justifying the violent treatment women encountered throughout the criminal legal system and holding women personally responsible for extricating themselves from the carceral web.

The 12 Steps and religious programming were ubiquitous in jail, prison, and throughout the postincarceration landscape. In this carceral context, I argue this programming was neither voluntary nor neutral. Women might technically have had the choice to attend a 12-Step meeting or Bible study class in prison. The choice hardly was free, however, given the lack of other available services and pressure to prove they were reformed in order to secure release, as well as coveted spots at popular recovery homes. As discussed in chapter 3, the widespread imposition of the 12-Step model throughout the criminal legal system reflects a particular view of addiction and criminality as personal problems caused by individual defects of character and will.

The 12 Steps augment a range of personal responsibility discourses available to women under correctional control. Carceral scholars have extensively documented and critiqued these discourses across a variety of settings, including habilitation programs in prison,[3] alternative-to-incarceration programs,[4] residential drug treatment programs,[5] religious programming in prison,[6] and prison libraries.[7] These ethnographic studies provide important, detailed analyses of the ideological underpinnings of these programs, how they operate, and how people respond. *Recovering Identity* seeks to contribute to this critically important scholarship by suggesting how these discourses converge in the *12-Step logic*, creating a broad impact across the diverse settings with which criminalized women engage. The 12-Step logic shows the fusing of concerning punitive discourses that largely have been addressed individually in the literature. My research suggests these discourses are not confined to a single program or site.

The 12-Step logic's merging of recovery and punishment subjects women to the lifelong *criminal-addict* label and thus the lifelong project of creating and maintaining a *rehabilitated* identity. It asserts the addict is perpetually in recovery, never recovered. The carceral state's linking of addiction and criminality and its near exclusive reliance on the 12 Steps creates a social reality where criminalized women perpetually work on their rehabilitation but are never rehabilitated. Between the collateral consequences of a criminal conviction and the moral judgment it imposes, women remain vulnerable to ongoing criminalization.

The 12-Step logic also refers to the distinct fusing of faith- and abstinence-based discourses that emerged in carceral settings and instilled a lifelong commitment to rehabilitating the self. Comparing the experiences of someone who chooses to attend a 12-Step meeting, absent any coercion from the state or threat of punishment for not attending, with the experiences of a criminalized woman who cannot avoid 12-Step messaging and whose freedom and relationships with her children may depend on her ability to demonstrate a commitment to the 12 Steps is like comparing apples to oranges. The 12 Steps, with their moral and spiritual roots, take on a distinct quality in the carceral context and among the plethora of personal responsibility discourses extensively documented in the literature.

Discourse becomes a weapon when used by violent systems whose social function is to dehumanize, punish, and control. Discourse provides ideological cover for this institutional and systemic violence and suggests that criminalized women only deserve recognition of their humanity if they fit into the narrow image of the rehabilitated woman. But even then, that recognition is of partial humanity, not full. The *rehabilitated woman* identity exists in opposition to women's *criminal-addict* identity, an identity that is past but also still present given the threat it can potentially be reactivated at any time. As detailed throughout this book, the presumption of criminality never fully goes away. Additionally, the intense moral judgment, discrimination, and surveillance that follow women after release from prison effectively relegate them to a place on the margins of society. Ongoing challenges related to employment and housing made it difficult for the women in this study to be financially secure. While relationships with children were a source of pride, joy, and connection, they also could be a source of considerable stress. Whether women were dealing with Child Protective Services, helping their children with their own criminal legal system involvement, or trying to make up for lost time, mothering was a site where the perpetual impact of the *criminal-addict* identity made itself clear.

IDENTITY WORK AS JOY AND RESISTANCE

Despite the limiting nature of the 12-Step logic, women found ways to experience joy in their personal transformation processes. Even though the *criminal-addict* identity seemed always to be present, as women repeatedly contrasted their current identities with this identity, women expressed confidence that this identity indeed was in the past. As evidence, women commonly pointed to their appearance, employment, domesticity, mothering, and relationships as markers of the progress they had made in rehabilitating their selves. I refer to these markers as gendered, since they reflect distinct challenges formerly incarcerated women face. I argue that taken together, these gendered markers constitute a new controlling image in the era of mass incarceration: the *rehabilitated woman controlling image*.

Controlling images, by definition, are racist, sexist, and constraining. The rehabilitated woman controlling image is all of these things. By centering the voices of criminalized women, however, I show how women also experienced joy, confidence, and even empowerment through engaging and repurposing this controlling image. On the one hand, the gendered markers of rehabilitation that are recognized by actors throughout the criminal legal system and the postincarceration landscape prescribe particular ways of being. On the other hand, women explained finding deep meaning in changes related to appearance, employment, domesticity, mothering, and relationships. While women at times expressed concern and even fear about possibly returning to a past *criminal-addict* identity, they focused overwhelmingly on what they were doing to ensure that return did not occur. I sensed an undeniable joy in the progress they were making, and the gendered markers of rehabilitation provided specific evidence of this progress to which they could point in narratives and photographs.

IT SHOULD NOT BE THIS HARD

One of my significant concerns with the 12-Step logic, and the rehabilitated woman controlling image it offers as a solution to women's problems, is the dismissal of social factors. As with other responsibilization strategies, they effectively individualize social problems. It seems not only unfair, but also harmful, for the criminal legal system to demand personal transformation from women without attention to the need for social transformation. The lifelong moral judgment the 12-Step logic imposes on criminalized women is another significant point of concern. To respond to women who have survived gender-based violence, poverty, and a host of vulnerabilities connected to drug use with punitive discourses and practices only exacerbates the violence they already have endured. These responses further entrench the ongoing cycle of criminalization, creating additional barriers that marginalize criminalized women and their children. What if Lynn continued to relapse, for instance, not because of a weak, disordered self or lack of will, but rather because of the trauma caused by giving birth while shackled to a hospital bed and being separated from her newborn son? What if Rose struggled to make it after her previous release from prison not because of insufficient determination, but rather because of deep feelings of abandonment and loneliness in part tied to her multiple experiences of sexual assault and incarceration?

In contrast to the many individualizing discourses, steeped in moral judgment and punishment, that bracket out the social, we need a new discourse that allows for individual healing and accountability with analysis and organizing for social change. In short, we need discourses that connect personal and social transformation. Such discourses would support women in their identity work by affirming who they are and who they want to be without defining those identities in opposition to a presumed *criminal-addict* identity. Drug use, drug selling, sex work, shoplifting, child neglect, child abuse, and assault would be recognized as things women had done, not who women are. Drug recovery discourses would not judge women as "addicts," but rather acknowledge women's survival and address the root causes of problematic drug use. The discourse offered by the 12-Step model likely could do so, provided the 12 Steps were divorced from the imposition or threat of criminalization. But additional discourses and models of recovery must also be available. Women's reflections made clear it is not only the physical structure of the prison that is harmful; its very organizing logic of mortification must be uprooted. As Caleb Smith concludes in his extensive study of the origin and afterlives of the penitentiary, we must "discover a language that refuses both the prison's dehumanizing violence and its captivating vision of human redemption."[8] Revising this language only will produce slightly different types and degrees of dehumanizing violence. We need radically different discourses.

The women who participated in this research pointed out what was most helpful to them in their recovery and rehabilitation processes. In addition to material support, the ability to develop and receive affirmation for their identity work, specifically related to appearance, employment, domesticity, mothering, and relationships, was critical. Their insights suggested the value of providing targeted support for these very identity components. Rather than dehumanize women and tell them they are "nobodies," how can we introduce humanizing discourses that acknowledge the mistakes they have made while creating opportunities for them to develop in the ways they identified as important? Furthermore, becoming a part of a larger community of women who also had experienced criminalization was critically important. It provided opportunities to foster connections that helped women reclaim their humanity and dignity and critique personal responsibility rhetoric. Rather than isolate women from their families and one another through incarceration, what if our responses facilitated such life-sustaining connections?

These questions demand a new way of imagining. Working within the bounds of the current carceral system, such as through developing more gender-responsive and trauma-informed programs, ultimately will only fortify that system.[9] We have to divest from our social obsession with punitive logics that presuppose the value of mortification. As Megan Sweeney concludes, "Our current failure to approach communal safety and well-being from the perspective of social equality and social justice . . . represents an impoverishment of our social imagination."[10] As long as we remain socially invested in the prison as a response to social problems, we will reap harmful social consequences. We will reinforce patterns and systems of inequality and oppression. If we cannot imagine different ways of organizing society and our relationships to one another, we will fail to enact actual systemic change.

Prison abolitionists have been doing the hard, slow work of developing a new social imagination. As scholar-activist Ruth Wilson Gilmore steadfastly reminds us, abolition is not only about the absence of prisons. Abolition also is about presence, meaning the intentional, long-term work of creating and nurturing relationships and institutions that support the ability of people and communities to thrive. Abolition demands we divest from institutions, like policing and prisons, that cause death and invest in institutions, like education and health care, that affirm life.[11] Education and health care also can dehumanize, punish, and surveil, however. The divest/invest strategy does not only refer to funding. It refers to how we imagine these institutions. It requires replacing the current "sacrificial logic that pervades our culture and governs U.S. penal policy" with a logic that honors the inherent humanity and dignity of even the most marginalized.[12]

The women who participated in this research were candid about the mistakes they had made and the harm they had caused. None were looking for a free pass. All deserve the chance to heal, find joy, and fully participate in society, free from the lifelong discrimination and stigma criminalization currently imposes. As a society, we have a choice to hinder or to support those efforts. For far too long, we have made the wrong choice, responding to women's survival with dehumanizing violence. The women whose stories fill this book make a compelling case for making a different choice.

Methodological Tensions

Conducting research with socially marginalized women who have experienced gender-based violence is a challenging endeavor that requires extreme care and ethical considerations on the part of the researcher. Throughout this project, I struggled with issues of power, voice, and representation. I have written elsewhere about some of these challenges and how I attempted to resolve them, in part through the use of photo-elicitation interviewing (PEI).[1] In this brief methods appendix, I expand on some of those ideas and provide further details about how I conceived of this project, recruited participants, and related to participants, and how these issues impacted my analysis and overall findings.

INITIAL RESEARCH GOALS

I began this project as most eager PhD students do, with what I thought was a firm grasp of the literature and a clear theoretical framework. I suspected that criminalized women experienced similar kinds of interactions with the state across settings, whether the state took the form of a supposed helping organization (like Public Aid or a domestic violence shelter) or the form of a punitive organization (like a jail or prison). Heavily influenced by Lynne A. Haney's *Offending Women: Power, Punishment, and the Regulation of Desire* and Jill A. McCorkel's *Breaking Women: Gender, Race, and the New Politics of Imprisonment*, I conceptualized the carceral state as a decentralized network of public and private institutions and organizations that regulate socially marginalized women's lives through surveillance and service provision.[2] As such, I wanted to study the role of the state, in its myriad manifestations, in criminalized women's lives.

As a feminist scholar, I also wanted to decenter power in the research process by creating space for women to share what was most important to them, instead of simply respond to my inquiries based on my presumptions of what topics were most meaningful. Building upon the work of feminist sociologist Dorothy E. Smith, I strove to approach participants as research partners, rather than "objects of study," and develop an understanding of "the actualities of their everyday worlds."[3] Additionally, I was keenly aware of how my social position—particularly my identities as a White, cisgender, heterosexual, highly educated, middle-class woman—would create distance with participants. I worried about how to build rapport and ensure I truly heard what participants shared.[4]

To accomplish these goals, I turned to PEI with participant-generated images. This method entails having research participants take photographs related to the research topic. The photographs become the basis of an interview, during which participants select which photographs they want to discuss, in which order, and reflect on what they want to communicate with the images. As noted in chapter 1, PEI provides several benefits, especially when dealing with traumatic subject matter and working with socially marginalized groups.[5] PEI can help ensure participants have an opportunity to discuss what is most important to them through their selection and discussion of photographs. PEI also can provide a more accessible way to reflect on painful experiences than can a conventional interview format. Lisa Frohmann's use of PEI with domestic violence survivors was particularly influential. She found PEI to be empowering and healing for some participants who reported "gaining a better understanding of their lives."[6]

At the outset of this project, I hoped PEI would provide these benefits and help clarify my conceptualization of *the state* for participants. I intended for participants to take photographs documenting where they saw and felt the influence of the state in their lives, such as meetings with parole officers or a job or housing application that led to a denial due to their background. I cringe as I type these words, because it is so apparent now how, at the beginning of this project, I was not truly ready to cede control and center participants' voices. Quite frankly, I had a research agenda I was imposing on participants, despite all my talk of feminist research methods and decentering power in the research relationship. Luckily, as I discuss below, the women who participated in this project did not let me get away with imposing my agenda. I will forever be grateful for their patience with me and their perseverance to tell the stories they wanted to tell. PEI was critical, because it provided participants with a way to redirect my attention.

RECRUITMENT

To recruit participants, I worked with three nonprofit organizations that provide services to formerly incarcerated women. Two were recovery homes for women leaving prison: Growing Stronger and Starting Again. One was a nonresidential program: Women Helping Women. While both recovery homes were explicitly faith-based, sober living residences, they differed in notable ways. Growing Stronger was significantly better resourced, as it was part of a parent organization that ran multiple reentry programs, including educational and vocational programs and a recovery home for men. Starting Again was a much smaller operation, founded by an individual woman. Women Helping Women was a peer support and health education program for women who had been involved in the criminal legal system within the past year. The program offered workshops and trainings on topics such as HIV and STDs, sexual health, and healthy relationships.

Since my initial research focus was the role of the state in criminalized women's lives, I thought Growing Stronger, Starting Again, and Women Helping Women provided a diverse set of organizations through which to begin recruitment. Because I was not focused on religion, for instance, I did not limit recruitment to faith-based organizations. Since I was not focused on drug use and recovery, I did not limit recruitment to drug treatment programs or recovery homes. Between these three sites and referrals from interviewees, I hoped to hear a wide range of experiences.

To begin recruitment, I attended meetings at each site. I introduced myself as a PhD student who was conducting a research project on women's experiences with incarceration and reentry and was interested in learning about experiences that led to involvement with the criminal justice system, as well as experiences leaving that system. I noted I was focusing on the ways women receive help from different places and people before, during, and after incarceration, as well as the ways women are limited, restricted, and even harmed by various places and people before, during, and after incarceration. I explained participating would involve completing two to three one-on-one interviews with me and that all participants would have the option to include photography in their interviews. For the photography component, I would provide participants with a digital camera and memory card at the end of our first interview. They then would take photographs that communicated their experiences of incarceration and reentry for us to discuss during a second interview. If needed, we would meet for a third interview to discuss any important topics not yet covered. I noted participants would receive a $20 gift card to a store of their choosing as compensation for each interview and keep their digital camera and memory card. The only criteria to participate were for participants to identify as women and to have had some involvement with the criminal legal system.

Almost every woman in attendance at all three initial recruitment meetings signed up to participate. I also handed out a recruitment flier and encouraged women to share it with anyone who might be interested. I started receiving phone calls from women who heard about the research project from other women or had seen the flier. All women who called me were living either at Growing Stronger or Starting Again. As I began conducting some interviews on-site at Growing Stronger and Starting Again, I came to be recognized as "the lady with the cameras." Frequently, new residents at the homes would approach me to express their interest in participating.

INTERVIEWS

Between December 2012 and July 2013, I conducted 99 interviews with 36 participants. I met 21 participants through Growing Stronger, 8 participants through Starting Again, and 7 participants through Women Helping Women.[7] All 36 participants expressed an interest in completing a PEI, but only 32 participants ultimately did.[8] Table 2 presents a summary of selected characteristics about research participants. I conducted interviews at a location of the participant's choosing, which often was the recovery home where they resided. Other locations included Women Helping Women's office, public libraries, McDonald's, participants' homes, and a public park.

Although I anticipated completing three interviews with each participant, I did not conceive of this project as a longitudinal study. The number of interviews was a practical choice to facilitate PEI and ensure adequate time to discuss the range of topics included in the study. Interviews with an individual participant typically took place over a span of two to four months. The first interview typically focused on women's experiences with criminalization, specifically arrest, prosecution, incarceration, and release, and experiences

TABLE 2. Selected Characteristics of Research Participants

Name[1]	Age	Race[2]	Education	Employment	# of children	Approximate time since release at final interview[3]	# of interviews
Amber	47	Black[+]	not shared	none	4	not shared	2
Ann	47	Caucasian	less than high school	none	5	1 year, 1 month[^]	3
Ann Williams	44	Black	some high school	none	6	1 year	3
Brenda	55	Black	GED	part-time	6	3 years	3
Carmel	44	Black	high school diploma	none	0	1 year, 1 month[^]	3
Cathy Hill	52	White	some college	none	2	7 months[^]	3
Chicken Wing	55	Black	GED	part-time	4	8 months	3
Chunky	56	Black	some college	none	0	3 years	3
Corrine[*]	63	African American	master's degree	full-time	3	12 years	3
Darlene[*]	35	Black[+]	high school diploma	none	1	17 months	2
Denise	45	Black	some high school	part-time	5	2 years, 3 months[^]	3
Ella[*]	46	African American	high school diploma	part-time	5	7 years	3
Faye	46	Black American	high school diploma	none	4	7 months	3[X]
Ms. Fields	47	Black Afro American	some college	part-time	0	4 years[^]	3
Ida	49	African American	some high school	none	3	11 months	4
Iris[*]	49	White	bachelor's degree	full-time	2	4 years, 4 months[^]	2
Jean Grey	20	African American	some college	none	1	1 year, 3 months[^]	3
Julia	51	African American	some high school	none	3	8 months	3
The Lioness	49	African American	high school diploma	none	3	1 year	3
Lynn	33	Caucasian	high school diploma	none	2	1 year, 2 months	3[X]

(*Contd.*)

TABLE 2. (*Continued*)

Name[1]	Age	Race[2]	Education	Employment	# of children	Approximate time since release at final interview[3]	# of interviews
Mae	not shared	Black[+]	some college	full-time	4	17 years, 6 months	2
Maryann	not shared	Black[+]	less than high school	none	3	2 months	1[x]
Moon	40	African American	some high school	none	3	3 months	3
New Life	30	Black	some college	none	2	4 months	3
Nyla[*]	42	Black[+]	not shared	part-time	6	6 months	3
Olivia[*]	49	Afro American	GED	none	1	6 years	3
Ranisha[*]	34	Black[+]	not shared	not shared	3	4 months	2
Red	41	Puerto Rican	some high school	none	3	5 months	3
Rose	48	Black American	less than high school	none	0	1 year, 2 months	3
Sarah[*]	46	Latin, Native American	less than high school	none	4	2 months	3
Sharon	44	African American	less than high school	part-time	1	7 months	3
Stacey Williams	41	African American	high school diploma	full-time	6	3 months	3
Susan[*]	59	Black[+]	bachelor's degree	none	0	9 months[^]	1[x]
Tinybig	51	Afro Native American Indian	some college	full-time	3	4 months	4
Veronica[*]	48	Black[+]	not shared	not shared	not shared	not shared	1
Xenia	41	Puerto Rican	some high school	none	8	4 months	3

[1]All names are pseudonyms. Most participants chose their own pseudonym.

[2]Race is listed as participants described it.

[3]Most participants were released from an Illinois state prison.

[*]The author provided the pseudonym.

[+]The participant did not identify their race, and the author identified race based on information gleaned throughout interviews.

[^]The participant was most recently released from a county jail.

[x]The participant did not complete a photo-elicitation interview.

postrelease. I used a semistructured, in-depth approach and prioritized building rapport and pursuing noteworthy "markers" women referenced.[9]

At the end of the first interview, I asked participants if they were willing to meet with me again and if they were interested in including photographs in the next interview. I shared a photo instruction sheet I had prepared for the project and reviewed it with each participant. The sheet identified "the state" as a focus of my research and provided a working definition of the state as agencies, institutions, and people that do things like set laws and policies, enforce laws, put policies in place, monitor people's behavior, and provide social services. It also included a list of examples of "the state" (such as police, parole officers, Public Aid, and Child Protective Services) in an attempt to make the idea of "the state" more clear. I recognized a tension in my research design, in that by being too directive I could undercut the ability for PEI to decenter power and allow for participants to drive the next interview. In an effort to correct that tension, I included a list of additional questions and prompts on the photo instruction sheet, including the instruction to take photos of what was important to them and what they wanted to show me.

Second interviews typically took place about a month after the first interview to provide participants time to take photographs. Prior to the scheduled second interview, I met with participants to transfer their photographs from their memory cards to my laptop. I then printed two sets of photographs, which I brought to the second interview. One set was for the participant, and one set was for me. At the beginning of the second interview, I provided participants with their photographs and asked them to look through them and select about 10 to 15 photographs they wanted to discuss. For the entirety of the PEI, participants selected a photograph and reflected on what it meant to them. I asked follow-up questions before we moved on to the next photograph. Sometimes participants talked about photographs one by one. Other times, participants grouped photographs and discussed what each set showed. At the end of the PEI, I typically asked participants what all the photographs taken together communicated. Participants signed a photo release form, which provided me with ownership of the photographs, and we discussed which photographs I could include in presentations and publications. Most participants agreed to participate in a third interview, during which I asked follow-up questions that remained from the first two interviews and introduced remaining topics we had not yet covered.

ANALYSIS

Each interview lasted about one and a half to two hours and was audio recorded. Four undergraduate research assistants and I transcribed the interviews. I completed open coding of the transcripts, identifying "any and all ideas, themes, or issues . . . no matter how varied and disparate."[10] Initial codes centered on religion, recovery from drug use, interpersonal violence, state violence (such as police officers' and correctional officers' abuse, the overall jail and prison environment, and coercive court processes), relationships with children, employment, housing, moral judgment, and markers of rehabilitation. Personal transformation was the strongest initial theme that emerged, particularly the ways women contrasted their past and current identities. As I conducted more focused coding, I identified additional markers of rehabilitation, specifically appearance and romantic relationships, and noted the importance of friendships and community. Through memoing, I identified and clarified linkages among these categories and began to assess how the markers of rehabilitation were raced and gendered, as well as how they connected to faith and recovery discourses.

PEI deeply informed my analysis. As noted above, there was an inherent tension in my research design between my investment in the theoretical research questions I brought to this project and my desire to center participants' voices. PEI helped resolve that tension by pushing me to truly hear what women were telling me. At the outset of this project, I was not interested in recovery from drug use or mothering. Given the wealth of scholarship on these topics, I incorrectly presumed there was not much to add. The women who participated in this project would not let me ignore these issues, however. Through photographs and reflections, they pointed my attention to the centrality of drug use and recovery and how women's narratives of personal transformation, including becoming the mothers they wanted to be, revolved around the distinction between using and being in recovery. If I truly was committed to my feminist research aims, I needed to let go of my focus on the state, at least during my initial analysis. Without the photographs and the rich reflections women shared about them, I might not have truly heard them. I might have displaced their focus with my own.

My analysis also was informed by the time I spent at recruitment sites and informally talking with women and staff. While this project was not an ethnography and I did not conduct participant observation, I was not able to turn off my critical eye or pretend not to be impacted by the many hours I spent with criminalized women outside of our formal interviews. Since I completed many of the interviews at Growing Stronger and Starting Again, I spent a considerable amount of time at both homes. While waiting for participants to arrive and after interviews, I often hung out and chatted with whoever was present. I also accepted all invitations participants or staff extended to events, including a charity walk, a Mother's Day celebration, a family day event, and an adult high school graduation ceremony. As I recount in chapter 4, when Ella invited me to accompany her to her hearing to have her record sealed, I jumped at the opportunity. It was not planned that I would speak on her behalf; that development happened spontaneously in court. Rather, Ella wanted to share the experience with me as part of helping me understand the full picture of her life and the full story of criminalization. That desire to help me understand seemed to undergird every invitation I received. As I spent more time with the women, in interviews and informally, I think they saw my commitment to this project. Given how few spaces exist for them to truly be heard, I think they welcomed the opportunity to share their stories, with the hope that it would create some understanding in the world and maybe even some change.

The number of interviews I conducted with women also helped us build rapport, as did the PEI component. I suspect I looked and acted like many of the volunteers and service providers with whom participants routinely interacted. Women participated in numerous support groups, 12-Step meetings, and individual sessions where they frequently had to tell their stories. I think the use of PEI helped disrupt this routine, as women were pushed to think in different ways about how to represent their lives. As such, I do think we achieved a deeper level of exchange in our interviews than we would have without the photographs.

VOICE AND POSITIONALITY

As I wrote and revised my analysis, I struggled greatly about my role in this project and how much my voice should be included.[11] Frequently, I have wondered what right I have to write about these women's lives. Who am I to critique discourses that in many cases have served women well? What does it mean that women trusted me with their stories, and (how) should I present them?

Again, PEI helped me work through these questions. As I carried out this project, I recognized one of PEI's main benefits is how it can support the coconstruction of knowledge by creating space for both participants' and researchers' voices. As I gained a deeper understanding of the violence and discrimination criminalized women experienced, I also gained a deeper appreciation of women's ability to claim joy and dignity in their lives, while creating a positive sense of self. I realized my initial focus on the state had been disempowering and incomplete. Women challenged my biases and preconceived notions about the state's totalizing power and influence. They focused my attention on their agency. As I note in the concluding chapter, I increasingly felt it should not be as hard as it is for women to chart a path out of prison, especially when they expressed the determination and will to do so. I became dissatisfied with the limiting nature of discourses women encountered in jail, prison, recovery homes, and reentry programs about their identities and lives. The more I got to know these women, the more I wanted for them. Ultimately, I realized there were many dimensions to their stories, and it was my responsibility, as a researcher, to include as many dimensions as possible to tell the most comprehensive story. Rather than silence my critique, I grew to recognize its value. I came to see how all of us who participated in this project, the women and me, had a critical piece to contribute to the knowledge we together constructed about what it means for criminalized women to fight for freedom and dignity in a society that largely does not care about them.

I am not sure I satisfactorily resolved the inherent tension in my research design. Perhaps it was not possible to resolve. My imperfect resolution, however, was to embrace the coconstruction of knowledge, despite its messiness. As such, throughout parts of this book, I have included my own voice, while striving to center participants' voices. While some readers may critique this choice as egotistical, I view it as being honest and transparent. I also view it as a feminist practice. I am not pretending I was not moved by the stories women shared with me. I am writing from a place of deep care as much as from a place of rigorous theory. I felt a responsibility to connect women's personal transformation narratives to the larger ideological discourses that hold individuals responsible for systemic inequality and blame individuals when they stumble. To not do so would present an incomplete picture of criminalized women's experiences and exacerbate the individualizing, dehumanizing impact of those discourses. I only hope I have not drowned out the women's voices in the process of developing that critique.

LIMITATIONS

There are multiple noteworthy limitations to my research methods. Even though interviews generated an extensive amount of data, there is a limit to only meeting with participants a few times over a relatively short time span. Some women's lives changed significantly in just the one or two months that passed between our interviews, including developments like resuming drug use, losing housing, and being rearrested. Over the span of months or years, women's lives certainly changed in even more significant ways. Since I did not stay in contact with most participants, I cannot be certain their positive identity transformations were not interrupted by negative developments, such as reincarceration or an abusive relationship. Conversely, I do not know if some women went on to overcome the sense of never being recovered or rehabilitated that felt so strong to me throughout our interviews. As such, these interviews provided a snapshot of women's lives and identity work.

Retention and recruitment introduced additional limitations. I lost contact with seven women over the course of this project. Some might have lost interest, but it also is possible that negative developments and hardships prevented their ongoing participation. In those cases, not including those parts of women's stories and their impact on women's identity work is a significant omission. Similarly, all participants were connected, at least temporarily, to a social service program. Thus, I did not include women who were most disconnected from services and therefore likely most disadvantaged. Formerly incarcerated women who were not engaged with services might not have spoken as positively about identity transformation as did the women who participated in this project. Furthermore, disconnected women might not have been as well versed in the 12-Step logic. Although I recruited from a mix of residential and nonresidential programs and a mix of faith-based and non-faith-based programs, most of the women who participated in this project came from Growing Stronger or Starting Again, two faith-based recovery homes. Had I recruited from a wider range of programs or more word-of-mouth referrals, the prevalence of faith-based and recovery discourses might not have been as strong.

The biggest limitation of my study was not actualizing one of the most important benefits PEI provides—working with participants in groups. Scholars have developed several exciting advocacy projects that grew out of using PEI in group settings, where participants worked together to decide what topics they wanted to address, shared photographs with one another, and developed a collective analysis that often turned into a public education project or exhibit.[12] The public nature of such work supported personal empowerment and social change, as people who were directly impacted by a social issue raised awareness about the harms that issue caused. It also fostered community.

Because some of the women who participated in this study were on parole, I was not able to receive Institutional Review Board (IRB) approval to meet with participants in groups. The "prisoner advocate" on the IRB noted that a condition of parole is that people on parole are not able to co-mingle. Thus, participating in groups for this project potentially could make participants vulnerable to a violation of parole charge. As I have written elsewhere, this prohibition reinforced the state's individualizing impact on socially marginalized people.[13] Keeping people separated, by design, thwarts critique and community. Not surprisingly, critique and community are exactly what is needed to end the personal and social harm criminalization causes.

LANGUAGE

One of the central arguments throughout this book is language matters. As such, I am intentional with the language I use to describe women, their lives, and the systems that impact them. I use the term *criminal legal system* rather than *criminal justice system*, since the criminal legal system in the United States has not been designed to achieve justice; rather, it administers legal codes and punishment. Similarly, I have come to view the terms *reentry* and *reintegration* as inaccurate, since most incarcerated people were not fully integrated into society prior to incarceration, due to historic and present day patterns of discrimination that exclude people from full social membership. Additionally, the stigma and discrimination that follow people long after release from prison relegate them to a marginal place in society. Thus, I use terms like *postincarceration*.

I strive to use people-first language and avoid labels that reduce people to an individual characteristic, action, or event. Labels like *criminal, addict, victim,* and *prisoner* are dehumanizing.[14] I use the phrase *criminalized woman* to center women's humanity and acknowledge criminalization is a process that happens to women. Similarly, *substance abuse* is a medical term that connotes varied theories, presumptions, and moral judgments. I prefer the more neutral term *drug use.*

NOTES

1. WOMEN, INCARCERATION, AND SOCIAL MARGINALITY

1. All names of participants and organizations are pseudonyms. Most participants selected their own pseudonyms.

2. I use the terms participants provided to identify race and ethnicity.

3. Owen (1998); Leverentz (2014).

4. Roberts (1997, 2002); Collins (2000); Haley (2016); Ritchie (2017). Throughout this book, I capitalize *White* and *Whiteness*, as well as *Black*, *Latinx*, and *Native American*. In earlier drafts, I did not capitalize *White*, primarily because I worried that doing so reinforced the reification of Whiteness and aligned with White supremacist practices. Following the work of sociologist Eve L. Ewing (2020), I have come to understand the value in capitalizing *White*. Doing so makes Whiteness visible as a racial category and encourages us to critique what the social construction of Whiteness means. It still feels uncomfortable to write and read phrases like "White femininity" and "White supremacy" throughout this text. I think that discomfort is the point, however. The capitalization of *White* in front of *femininity* disrupts the deep-rooted ideology that femininity is normalized as white. As I argue throughout this book, that disruption is necessary to create a more safe and just society for all, particularly for women and gender nonconforming people of color. For further discussion of the value of capitalizing *White*, see Appiah (2020), Nguyen and Pendleton (2020), and Painter (2020).

5. Roberts (1997, 2002); Collins (2000); Haley (2016); Ritchie (2017).

6. Garland (2001).

7. Smith (2009); Sweeney (2010); Erzen (2015).

8. Leverentz (2014); Sered and Norton-Hawk (2014).

9. National Research Council (2014).

10. Sawyer and Wagner (2022).

11. Ibid.

12. Ibid.

13. Davis (1998, 2003); Wacquant (2009); Alexander (2010); McCorkel (2013).

14. Alexander (2010).

15. Wacquant (2009).

16. Haney (2004); Wacquant (2009).

17. Beckett and Western (2001, 46).

18. The Sentencing Project (2022).

19. Schlesinger and Lawston (2011).

20. Amnesty International (1999); Davis and Shaylor (2001); Davis (2003); Flavin (2009); Law (2009); Richie (2012).

21. National Research Council (2014).

22. Bush-Baskette (1998). See also Richie (1996, 2001, 2012); Davis and Shaylor (2001); Chesney-Lind (2003); Covington and Bloom (2003); Gaskins (2004); Sokoloff (2007).

23. Wacquant (2009); Bumiller (2013).

24. Davis (1998); Beckett and Western (2001); Garland (2001); Haney (2004, 2010); McCorkel (2004); Wacquant (2009, 2012); Bumiller (2013).

25. Wacquant (2009).

26. Haney (2010); Bumiller (2013); McCorkel (2013).

27. Gowan and Whetstone (2012); Kaye (2012); Miller (2014).

28. O'Malley (1992); Hannah-Moffat (2000); Garland (2001).

29. Hannah-Moffat (2000); McCorkel (2004, 2013); McKim (2008); Goodkind (2009); Haney (2010); Bumiller (2013); Hackett (2013).

30. Collins (2000); Davis (2003); Haley (2016); Ritchie (2017).

31. Petersilia (2003); Pager (2007); Sokoloff (2007); Alexander (2010); Middlemass (2017).

32. Ibid.

33. Richie (2001); Leverentz (2014).

34. National Research Council (2014).

35. Dodge and Pogrebin (2001); Richie (2001).

36. Maruna (2001, 87).

37. Leverentz (2014); Opsal (2011).

38. Leverentz (2014); Sered and Norton-Hawk (2014).

39. Please refer to the appendix for further details.

40. Harper (1998, 2002); Collier (2001); Frohmann (2005); Gauntlett and Holzwarth (2006); Lapenta (2011); Rumpf (2017).

41. Twenty-six participants completed three interviews, five participants completed two interviews, three participants completed one interview, and two participants completed four interviews.

42. When identifying a participant's race or ethnicity, I use the term she provided.

43. Please refer to table 2 in the appendix for a summary of selected characteristics of the research participants.

44. Emerson, Fretz, and Shaw (1995).

45. Snow and Anderson (1987); Opsal (2011).

46. In her research of incarcerated women's reading practices in prison, Megan Sweeney (2010, 17) describes a similar goal, noting, "As I understand it, my task as a cultural

critic is to build a bridge between the daily work that imprisoned women perform through their reading practices and the work of transforming structures and institutions that keep so many women in prison."

2. "THEY JUST LOOK AT US LIKE WE AIN'T NOBODY AND WE DON'T HAVE RIGHTS": THE VIOLENCE OF INCARCERATION

1. Occupying 96 acres, Cook County Jail is the largest single-site jail in the United States (Gaspar n.d.).

2. In the years since I completed data collection, efforts to end money bond have made significant strides in Illinois, culminating in the Illinois legislature passing the Illinois Legislative Black Caucus's criminal justice reform bill, HB 3653 SFA2, in January 2021. The bill includes the Pretrial Fairness Act, which effectively will eliminate the use of money bond in Illinois. See Coalition to End Money Bond (n.d.).

3. Smith (2009, 28); Rodríguez (2006).

4. Goffman (1961); McCorkel (2013); Lempert (2016).

5. Sykes (1958). See also Crewe (2011); Fleury-Steiner and Longazel (2014).

6. Goffman (1961); Davis (2003); Rodríguez (2006); Richie (2012); McCorkel (2013).

7. Collins (2000). See also Roberts (1997, 2002); Ritchie (2017).

8. Goffman (1961, xiii).

9. Ibid., 14.

10. Lempert (2016).

11. Goffman (1961).

12. Smith (2009, 29, 39).

13. Goffman (1961); Foucault (1977); McCorkel (2013); Lempert (2016); Middlemass (2017); Ellis (2020).

14. Davis (2003).

15. Smith (2009, 29).

16. Smith (2009, 18). Dylan Rodríguez (2006, 227) similarly argues, "the formation of the U.S. prison must be seen as inseparable from the relation of white freedom/black unfreedom, white ownership/black fungibility, that produced the nation's foundational property relation as well as an essential component (with Native American displacement and genocide) of its racial ordering."

17. Davis and Shaylor (2001); Richie (2001, 2012); Davis (2003); Rodríguez (2006); Belknap (2015).

18. Lempert (2016, 97).

19. American Civil Liberties Union (n.d.). In the video "Prison Is Abuse" (https://www.youtube.com/watch?v=nSF9VhxMorQ), Beth Richie, Monica Cosby, and Rachel Caïdor develop a detailed analysis of the ways the Power and Control Wheel, a tool commonly used by domestic violence victim advocates to explain dynamics in abusive relationships, maps onto women's prisons. In partnership with Sarah Ross, a scholar, artist, and activist, Cosby created an updated Power and Control Wheel that visually explains the parallels between abusive relationships and incarceration.

20. Flavin (2009); Roth (2017).

21. McCorkel (2013).

22. U.S. Commission on Civil Rights (2020).

23. Flavin (2009); National Research Council (2014); Belknap (2015).

24. Davis and Shaylor (2001); Davis (2003).

25. Davis and Shaylor (2001).

26. McCorkel (2013).

27. Flavin (2009); Roth (2017).

28. Johnson (2013); Cohn (2020).

29. Davis and Shaylor (2001). The documentary *Belly of the Beast* (Cohn 2020), which documents sterilization practices in California women's prisons and advocacy efforts to expose the abuse, pass legislation, and win reparations for survivors, includes footage from an interview journalist Ted Koppel conducted for *Nightline* with Dr. Anthony DiDomenico, the chief medical officer at one of California's women's prisons. Dr. DiDomenico comments that incarcerated women welcomed gynecological exams because they offered the only opportunity for physical contact with a man. See also Flavin (2009).

30. Roth (2017).

31. Adams (2022).

32. Roth (2017, 1).

33. Davis (2003).

34. Flynn (2019).

35. The U.S. criminal legal system always has relied on sexual abuse of detained and incarcerated women, particularly women of color, to maintain the intertwined systems of racial and gender subjugation. Historian Sarah Haley (2016) extensively documents the sexual nature of physical punishments Black women endured under convict leasing. Historian Danielle L. McGuire (2010) examines the sexual abuse civil rights activists such as Fannie Lou Hamer regularly experienced by correctional officers while detained following arrest for participating in civil rights protests. Both historians draw attention to the distinct vulnerabilities criminalized Black women face and show how sexual violence is a tool the state uses with impunity to keep Black women in their place. A direct thread connects slavery, convict leasing, and the Jim Crow era to the lack of bodily autonomy incarcerated women have today.

36. Amnesty International (1999); Flavin (2009); Law (2009); Fleury-Steiner and Longazel (2014); Belknap (2015).

37. Davis (2003); Richie, Cosby, and Caïdor (2020).

38. Flavin (2009, 130). Journalist Victoria Law (2009, 65) also points out that given the extreme power differential, incarcerated women lack the authority to end sexual relationships with correctional officers: "There is no consensual relationship between prisoners and staff. 'It's never over when the woman says it's over,' stated former Michigan warden Tekla Miller. 'Too many times their [the woman's] back is against the wall.'" When prison administrators discover relationships between correctional officers and incarcerated women, the woman faces formal punishment, as well as "informal retaliation by other staff members."

39. Davis and Shaylor (2001); Flavin (2009); Law (2009); Levi and Waldman (2011).

40. Davis (2003); Richie, Cosby, and Caïdor (2020).

41. Davis and Shaylor (2001, 15).

42. Ibid., 7.

43. Richie (2012).

44. Collins (2000). See also Roberts (1997, 2002); Smith (2005); Haley (2016); Ritchie (2017).

45. Ibid.

46. Patricia Hill Collins (2000), for instance, examines how the controlling image of the welfare queen—a single, unemployed Black mother who is content to live off of unearned, undeserved state benefits—provided ideological justification for regressive policies throughout the 1980s and 1990s that severely restricted public assistance and blamed Black women for alleged deviant cultural values that explained racial inequality and poverty. See also Hays (2003); Haney (2010); McCorkel (2013); Gurusami (2017); McKim (2017).

47. In 2020, the imprisonment rate for Black women (65 per 100,000) was 1.7 times the rate for White women (38 per 100,000), and the imprisonment rate for Latinx women (48 per 100,000) was 1.3 times the rate for White women. See The Sentencing Project (2022).

48. I have previously addressed the risks of voyeurism and reification when using visual research methods. See Rumpf (2017).

49. Stevenson (2014).

50. Sweeney (2010, 256).

51. From 1982 to 2017, Cook County Jail was under a consent decree that required appointed monitors to file reports on the jail's conditions twice a year with federal judges. The federal government issued the decree in response to a 1974 class action lawsuit alleging civil rights abuses at the jail. See Meisner and Schmadeke (2014).

52. Davey (2008).

53. One participant in this research project was a beneficiary of this settlement.

54. Meisner and Schmadeke (2014).

55. Political scientist Keesha M. Middlemass (2017, 60) describes incarceration as "an ongoing traumatic event" that causes post-traumatic stress disorder and shapes postincarceration experiences.

56. Martin (2018).

57. Mead (1934); Goffman (1959); Stryker (1994).

58. Research on the long-term health consequences of incarceration for women shows a strong correlation between incarceration and negative health outcomes, including mortality. It also suggests incarceration may provide some limited protective health factors, such as access to preventative care and removal from abusive relationships. Importantly, these protective factors highlight the poor living conditions and lack of resources most women experienced prior to incarceration. See Massoglia and Remster (2019); Massoglia et al. (2014).

59. Illinois legislation raised the cost of prison health care visits from two dollars to five dollars, effective January 1, 2012, placing significant financial hardship on incarcerated women. The John Howard Association's advocacy efforts culminated in new state legislation, signed into law in July 2019, that eliminated the medical copay in Illinois prisons.

60. Belknap (2015); Roth (2017).

61. Emily Widra (2017) notes that each year a person spends in prison takes two years off their life expectancy.

62. Davis and Shaylor (2001, 9).

63. Ibid., 10.

64. Lack of access to menstrual products is a widely documented problem. Incarcerated women report having to beg correctional officers for tampons and pads, using toilet paper and other items to create makeshift tampons and pads, and having to wear bloody clothes due to lack of supplies and laundry access. This degradation and humiliation have an emotional and physical toll, leading to long-term mental and physical health concerns (American Civil Liberties Union 2019).

65. Richie (2012).

66. Britton (2003).

67. The Lioness's experiences resonate with scholar-activist Mariame Kaba's (2021) analysis that Black women have "no selves to defend."

68. It seems fitting the Lioness chose a pseudonym that references a powerful, regal animal that defies the dehumanizing interpersonal and institutional violence she had endured.

69. Ritchie (2017, 36).

70. Mauer and Chesney-Lind (2002).

71. The Lioness's experience illustrates scholars' critiques about the net-widening impact of probation. See Jacobson, Schiraldi, Daly, and Hotez (2017).

72. Ann's comments about feeling threatened when the officer tried to isolate her in the elevator echoed allegations included in the MacArthur Justice Center's February 2014 proposed class action lawsuit, which alleged "correctional officers take inmates on 'elevator rides'—code for beatings out of view of security cameras." See Meisner and Schmadeke (2014).

73. Richie (2012).

74. Belknap (2015); Roth (2017).

75. Roth (2017). The way that written policies, prison staff, and medical professionals disregard incarcerated women's knowledge about their own bodies and concerns that something is wrong with their pregnancies mirrors what sociologist Tressie McMillan Cottom (2019) refers to as the assumption of bureaucratic incompetence with which Black women contend more broadly. In her essay "Dying to be Competent," McMillan Cottom situates her personal experience of pregnancy and childbirth within the larger context of the unconscionably and disproportionately high maternal mortality rate for Black women in the United States.

76. Chicago Legal Advocacy for Incarcerated Mothers (2011). In 2012, a federal court approved a $4.1 million settlement for a class action lawsuit filed on behalf of women who had been shackled during childbirth while detained at Cook County Jail. See Fettig (2012).

77. Du Bois ([1903] 1990).

78. Roberts (1997, 2002); Collins (2000).

79. Roth (2017).

80. The delayed administering of Ranisha's epidural, similar to the denial of pain medication for Corrine, may also reflect deeply engrained racist assumptions in the medical field about Black people's abnormally high tolerance for pain. See Novoa and Taylor (2018).

81. Hays (1998, 2003).

82. Lynn gave birth after 1999, when Illinois passed its antishackling legislation. She was part of the federal class action lawsuit filed against Cook County Jail for illegally shackling women during labor and began receiving payments from the settlement at the time of our interviews.

83. Roth (2017).

84. Sokoloff (2007); Flavin (2009); Law (2009).

85. Richie (2001); Welsh (2015).

86. Goffman (1961); McCorkel (2013); Lempert (2016); Middlemass (2017).

87. Davis (2003).

88. Maruna (2001); Smith (2009); Flores (2014); Ellis (2020).

3. "YOU CANNOT FIGHT NO ADDICTION WITHOUT GOD FIRST": THE PERMANENT MORAL JUDGMENT OF THE CRIMINAL-ADDICT LABEL

1. Identity projects refer to the ways people fashion and refashion the self within the context of structural arrangements that impose constraints and prohibit access to privileged statuses. See Wilkins (2008).

2. Mead (1934); Goffman (1959, 1961).

3. Foucault (1977); Bourdieu (1994); Cruikshank (1999); Brush (2003); Moore (2007); Carr (2011).

4. Carr (2011); McCorkel (2013); Cox (2015).

5. By "criminal lifestyle," I am referring to the notion that crime is not simply an act someone does but rather part of an all-consuming lifestyle in which a person has become immersed and an identity a person has developed. See Gowan and Whetstone (2012) and Kaye (2012).

6. I developed an earlier version of this argument with coauthors. See Kaufman, Kaiser, and Rumpf (2018).

7. Denzin (1993); Valverde (1998); McCorkel (2013); Tiger (2013); Sered and Norton-Hawk (2014).

8. Moore (2007); Gowan and Whetstone (2012).

9. McCorkel (2013); Miller (2014); Williams and Rumpf (2020).

10. Maruna (2001); Giordano, Cernkovich, and Rudolph (2002); Harris (2011); Opsal (2011).

11. Haney (2010); McCorkel (2013); McKim (2017).

12. Petersilia (2003); Travis (2009); Sered and Norton-Hawk (2011, 2014); Tiger (2013); Dodes and Dodes (2014).

13. Sered and Norton-Hawk (2011, 312).

14. Petersilia (2003). Twelve-Step meetings are so common in prisons in part because they are inexpensive to run and in part because they align with the correctional system's focus on promoting personal responsibility and bracketing out the social causes of incarceration.

15. Sered and Norton-Hawk (2011); McCorkel (2013); Leverentz (2014).

16. Sered and Norton-Hawk (2011); Dodes and Dodes (2014).

17. Denzin (1993); Travis (2009); Dodes and Dodes (2014).

18. Based on their review of available research studies, Lance Dodes and Zachary Dodes (2014, 53) argue that AA's success rate is surprisingly low: between 5 and 8 percent. They point out the "rate of spontaneous remission," meaning the "percentage of alcoholics [who] get better without any treatment at all," is between 3.7 and 7.4 percent, suggesting that some of AA's documented success might have little to do with AA itself.

19. Denzin (1993); Moore (2007).

20. Travis (2009, 8).

21. Tiger (2013); Dodes and Dodes (2014); Leverentz (2014).

22. Denzin (1993).

23. Alcoholics Anonymous World Services (2018).

24. I am indebted to Erica Meiners for first pointing out to me how the ubiquity of faith-based programming and 12-Step groups throughout the prison system is connected to their low or no cost to the state.

25. Sweeney (2010).

26. Erzen (2017, 7).

27. Sweeney (2010).

28. Rodríguez (2006).

29. Valverde (1998); Travis (2009); Sered and Norton-Hawk (2011); Tiger (2013); Dodes and Dodes (2014); Leverentz (2014). Indeed, the 12 Steps were a precursor to the now pervasive therapeutic self-help culture in the United States that encourages an inward focus on fixing personal flaws and strengthening one's willpower and resolve in order to attain independence, happiness, and success. The self-help industry draws specifically from the 12 Steps in prescribing clear instructions on how to do so. See Cruikshank (1999); Travis (2009); Sered and Norton-Hawk (2011).

30. Weber (1930/1992).

31. *Neoliberalism* is an expansive term that encompasses economic, political, and ideological shifts, such as deregulation of economic markets, increased privatization, the dismantling of the social safety net, reliance on market-based solutions to a host of social problems, and the devolution of the state's responsibility to provide for its members to local entities like nongovernmental organizations, faith-based groups, and private enterprises. See O'Malley (1992); Garland (2001); Wacquant (2009, 2012); Haney (2010); Miller (2014). Throughout this chapter, I focus on neoliberalism's technologies of governance, as this aspect is most relevant to my analysis.

32. O'Malley (1992); Hannah-Moffat (2000); Garland (2001).

33. Throughout this chapter, I draw on Foucault's extensive work on governmentality, meaning the discourses, interventions, programs, surveillance, and wide array of strategies the state uses to encourage people to become self-governing subjects who act in compliance with the existing social order and thereby contribute to the smooth functioning of society without the need for overt, repressive state enforcement of that order. Specifically, I build upon the work of scholars like Barbara Cruikshank (1999), Mariana Valverde (1998), and Dawn Moore (2007), who have applied Foucault's work on governmentality and the constitution of subjects to drug users.

34. Bourdieu (1994); Foucault (1977, 1994); Moore (2007).

35. Denzin (1993).

36. Valverde (1998, 11).

37. Denzin (1993, 55). See also Travis (2009); Dodes and Dodes (2014).

38. In discussing the history of Alcoholics Anonymous, which began in 1935, Trysh Travis explains that AA's cofounders, William Wilson and Dr. Robert Smith, used the framework of disease as a strategy to attract a wider group of adherents, communicate the need for urgent, ongoing treatment, and distinguish AA from other groups concerned about

alcohol use. Travis (2009, 34) concludes it was "rhetorical functionality" that "sold the co-founders on disease."

39. Alcoholics Anonymous World Services (2018, emphasis in original)

40. Tallen (1990); Sered and Norton-Hawk (2011, 2014); Leverentz (2014).

41. Rudy and Greil (1988); Tallen (1990); Travis (2009); Sered and Norton-Hawk (2011); Dodes and Dodes (2014).

42. O'Malley (1992); Garland (2001); Moore (2007); Kaufman (2021).

43. Dodes and Dodes (2014, 5).

44. Mariana Valverde (1998, 122) credits AA with "turning a disease into a full-fledged, lifelong social identity."

45. Denzin (1993, 154).

46. Travis (2009, 4).

47. Becker (1963); Goffman (1963).

48. For further discussion of the ways productive and repressive forms of power work in tandem to govern women in prison, see Hannah-Moffat (2000); for how they work to govern women on parole, see Turnbull and Hannah-Moffat (2009).

49. See Maruna (2001); Harris (2011); Opsal (2011); Miller, Carbone-Lopez, and Gunderman (2015); Miller (2016). I cannot be certain women would not have added this moral and spiritual component on their own, perhaps drawing on familial, community, and cultural values that exist beyond the criminal legal system. I am certain, however, that the state encourages this convergence of morality and spirituality with addiction and criminality by offering one dominant script for criminalized women to use to attain the intertwined projects of recovery and rehabilitation.

50. Alcoholics Anonymous World Services (2018).

51. Indeed, sociologist Ebonie Cunningham Stringer (2009) develops a rigorous analysis of the ways incarcerated mothers engage African cultural traditions and values, particularly related to religion and spirituality, to protect their mothering identities.

52. I included these photographs and an abbreviated analysis of them in an earlier publication. See Rumpf (2018).

53. Tyndale House Publishers (n.d.).

54. I also examine this interview excerpt in my forthcoming chapter with coauthor Courtney Irby. See Irby and Rumpf (forthcoming).

55. A portion of this quote is included in an earlier article. See Kaufman, Kaiser, and Rumpf (2018).

56. See Susan Sered and Maureen Norton-Hawk (2012) for an important critique of the ubiquitous presence of 12-Step programming throughout the U.S. correctional system as a potential violation of First Amendment rights.

57. Haney (2010); McCorkel (2013); McKim (2017).

58. Quintin Williams and I conceptualize the never-ending nature of rehabilitation as postincarceration burden. See Williams and Rumpf (2020).

59. McCorkel (2013).

60. Ibid., 159.

61. I am drawing on Gloria Anzaldúa's (2012) borderlands theory here.

62. I previously have examined Red's explanation of this photograph. See Kaufman, Kaiser, and Rumpf (2018).

63. Jean explained she chose this pseudonym as a reference to the X-Men superhero Dr. Jean Grey.

64. Jean's explanation of this photo is included in an earlier article. See Kaufman, Kaiser, and Rumpf (2018).

65. Denzin (1993, 162).

66. Sociologists Andrea Leverentz (2014) and Susan Sered and Maureen Norton-Hawk (2011, 2012, 2014) have extensively critiqued how the 12 Steps do not recognize the distinct challenges and demands criminalized women face.

67. Much has been written about how respectability politics uphold White supremacy and particularly deny Black women the freedom to express their insights, emotions, and selves. On this subject, I recommend Mikki Kendall's (2020) chapter "How to Write About Black Women" in her book *Hood Feminism: Notes from the Women That a Movement Forgot*.

68. Tiger (2013).

69. Gowan and Whetstone (2012); McKim (2017).

70. Sweeney (2010); Lempert (2016); Ellis (2020).

71. Ellis (2020, 757).

72. Maruna (2001).

73. Julia's photograph is included in an earlier article. See Rumpf (2017).

74. Richie (2012).

75. Davis (1998); Hays (2003); Wacquant (2009); Richie (2012).

76. Valverde (1998).

77. I am grateful to Rachel Caïdor for helping me articulate this point.

4. "I FEEL GOOD ABOUT MYSELF NOW": RECOVERING IDENTITY THROUGH EMPLOYMENT AND APPEARANCE

1. I have blocked out the mug shot photo and dates for confidentiality purposes.

2. I was glad I had helped in some small way and was confident the outcome would have been the same even if I had not been there. I was annoyed, though, that my voice carried any influence, when Ella had so thoroughly prepared for that moment for years.

3. These five components are not an exhaustive list of gendered markers of rehabilitation. I focus on these five components because they were the most prominent themes that emerged across the interviews. Additionally, scholars who study postincarceration processes have identified these areas as focal points that organizations and formerly incarcerated people use to measure and demonstrate personal transformation. See Opsal (2012); Flores (2014); Leverentz (2014); McKim (2014); Miller (2014, 2016); Welsh and Rajah (2014); Kaufman (2015); Gurusami (2017).

4. Moore (2012/2013).

5. Collins (2000).

6. Fraser and Gordon (1994, 331).

7. Ibid., 327.

8. McCorkel (2004). See also Hannah-Moffat (2000); Goodkind (2009); Haney (2010).

9. Sered (2021, 231).

10. Harris and McElrath (2012). I use "joy" to synthesize Moore's (2012/2013) discussion of enjoyment, fun, pleasure, and excitement as elements that exist on the opposite end of fear on "the emotional landscape of neoliberalism."

11. Harris and McElrath (2012, 814–15). See also Hunter and Greer (2011).

12. Moore (2012/2013).

13. Mead (1934); Goffman (1959); Stryker (1994).

14. Mead (1934).

15. Goffman (1959).

16. Cruikshank (1996, 248).

17. West and Zimmerman (1987).

18. Collins (2000, 72). See also Roberts (1997, 2002); Ritchie (2017).

19. Ibid.

20. Rafter (1985); McCorkel (2013); Leverentz (2014).

21. Rafter (1985); Hannah-Moffat (2000); Haney (2010); Hackett (2013); McCorkel (2013); Leverentz (2014); Haley (2016); McKim (2017).

22. Rafter (1985).

23. Haley (2016).

24. Ibid., 15.

25. Ibid.

26. Hannah-Moffat (2000); McKim (2008); Haney (2010); Bumiller (2013); Hackett (2013); McCorkel (2013).

27. McKim (2008); Wyse (2013).

28. Haney (2010, 13).

29. McCorkel (2013, 3).

30. Hannah-Moffat (2000); Goodkind (2009).

31. Hannah-Moffat (2000, 524).

32. As discussed more fully in the introduction, carceral scholars refer to this process as "responsibilization" and have thoroughly documented how the neoliberal state has devolved its responsibility for public safety and crime prevention to a host of nongovernmental organizations and individuals. See Garland (1996, 2001); Hannah-Moffat (2000); Goodkind (2009); Hackett (2013); Haney (2010); Miller (2014); Kaufman (2015). With regard to criminalized women, an elaborate, loosely connected network of state agencies (e.g., Child Protective Services), community-based correctional actors (e.g., parole, probation), and nonprofit organizations (e.g., drug treatment, recovery homes) form a web of surveillance and supervision that seeks to induce self-regulation on the part of the criminalized individual. Haney (2010) uses the term "state hybridity" to describe the devolved manner in which the neoliberal state operates. She explains, "Public partnerships with non-profits and private companies have led to a multiplication of actors now playing the role of the state. Quite often, these actors are disguised as community members, therapists, businessmen, or NGO activists" (Haney 2010, 16). Ultimate responsibility for reform rests squarely with the criminalized individual, however. As Hannah-Moffat (2000, 524) summarizes, "The individual prisoner is now responsible for her own discipline, which is facilitated by social science professionals upon the request/choice of the prisoner."

33. Davis and Shaylor (2001).

34. Ritchie (2017, 19).

35. Roberts (1997, 2002); Collins (2000); Richie (2012); Haley (2016).

36. McCorkel (2013); Lindsey (2022).

37. McCorkel (2013, 218).

38. Goffman (1961); McCorkel (2013); Lempert (2016).

39. Maruna (2001); Harris (2011); Opsal (2011, 2012); Leverentz (2014); Miller (2016).

40. Maruna (2001); Giordano, Cernkovich, and Rudolph (2002).

41. Maruna (2001). See also Harris (2011); Opsal (2011).

42. Harris (2011); Opsal (2012); Williams and Rumpf (2020).

43. See Hannah-Moffat (2000); McCorkel (2004, 2013); Goodkind (2009); Haney (2010); Hackett (2013); Gurusami (2017).

44. For additional scholarship on how marginalized girls and women adapt problematic available scripts to suit their needs, see E. Summerson Carr's (2011) analysis of "flipping the script," a strategy in which women in a drug treatment program perfectly spoke the therapeutic program language practitioners used, without internalizing the script; Jill A. McCorkel's (2013) analysis of "faking it to make it," a strategy used by incarcerated women in a habilitation program in which women acted as if they had surrendered to the program but remained privately critical of it; Aimee Meredith Cox's (2015) analysis of how young Black women residing in a homeless shelter in Detroit mocked and negotiated social scripts about poor young Black women's sexuality; and Megan Sweeney's (2010) analysis of incarcerated women's reading practices, specifically their selective engagement of self-help narratives in which they criticized women's submissive gender roles within families, while embracing other parts of the narrative that felt more liberatory. All of these insightful analyses have significantly informed my own.

45. I am not able to show these photographs due to confidentiality concerns.

46. Sered and Norton-Hawk (2014); Chamberlen (2017); Martin (2018).

47. Sered and Norton-Hawk (2014); Miller, Carbone-Lopez, and Gunderman (2015).

48. Flores (2014, 189).

49. Based on their extensive study with criminalized women in Boston, Susan Starr Sered and Maureen Norton-Hawk (2014, 178) also acknowledge the significant messages weight loss and gain communicate about drug use and recovery, noting "we have heard of parole officers cite weight loss as evidence of 'relapse.'"

50. Haney (2010, 250).

51. I cropped this photograph to remove the officer's face. Chicken Wing only wanted to show the Chicago Police badge, which the photograph now reflects.

52. Lempert (2016, 164).

53. McGuire (2010, 203). McGuire explains, this reality was common knowledge among Black women and girls from slavery throughout the Civil Rights Era, as sexual assault by White men was an ever-present threat and common occurrence.

54. This assault is discussed in chapter 2.

55. McKim (2014).

56. Maruna (2001); Kaye (2012); Opsal (2012); Leverentz (2014); Miller (2014).

57. Opsal (2012, 387).

58. Acker (1990); Britton (2003); Davis (2003); Wyse (2013).

59. Gurusami (2017, 435). See also Roberts (1997); Hays (2003); Haley (2016).

60. Opsal (2012, 397).

61. McKim (2008); Goodkind (2009); Haney (2010); Richie (2012); McCorkel (2013); Leverentz (2014).

62. Pager (2007).

63. Leverentz (2014). This dynamic reflects a long history in the United States of the male breadwinner family model being inaccessible to people of color, particularly Black

men and women, due to intersecting oppressions based on race, gender, and class. See Lorber (1994); Amott and Matthaei (1996); Collins (2000); Hill (2005).

64. See Petersilia (2003); Pager (2007); Natividad Rodriguez and Avery (2016); Williams and Rumpf (2020).

65. Couloute and Kopf (2018).

66. Ibid.

67. Dodge and Pogrebin (2001).

68. The ways women noted the relationship between work and their sense of self strongly echoed the narratives Tara Opsal (2012) and Andrea M. Leverentz (2014) document in their research with formerly incarcerated women.

69. Fraser and Gordon (1994).

70. Moon's linking of moral worth and employment resonates with Susila Gurusami's (2017) "rehabilitation labor" concept. In her research with formerly incarcerated Black women, Gurusami found participants faced extraordinary pressure to secure employment. Not just any job would do, however. State agents accepted only specific types of work as acceptable and as proof of Black women's "commitment to their moral—and therefore criminal—rehabilitation" (Gurusami 2017, 434).

71. Opsal (2012); Leverentz (2014).

72. My point here is not to suggest that sex work is humiliating or inferior to legal employment. Sex workers' rights organizers convincingly show how sex work often is the most dignified work option within an exploitive labor market and argue that decriminalizing sex work would enhance sex workers' safety and financial security. It is the criminalization of sex work, rather than sex work itself, that creates unsafe and further challenging conditions of this work. See the work of DecrimNY (https://www.decrimny.org) and DECRIMNOW (https://www.decrimnow.org/about).

73. Moon's experience highlights the limitations of ban the box initiatives, which remove criminal background questions from job applications. Removing the box provides applicants with a chance to secure an interview and make a positive impression on the employer by showcasing their abilities and skills, without the stigma of the criminal label clouding the employer's assessment of the applicant. Employers retain the ability to complete a background check later in the application process, however. Despite convincing an employer they are the best candidate, an applicant can lose the job once the background check is complete, particularly if the employer has a policy not to hire anyone with a criminal background. In practice, banning the box only delays discrimination in the hiring process, rather than eliminates it. Notably, Target removed criminal background questions from its job applications nationwide in 2014. It extended conditional offers to applicants, like Moon, while awaiting the results of criminal background checks conducted later in the hiring process. Despite receiving widespread praise for being a corporate leader in banning the box, Target later came under fire for discriminatory hiring practices. In 2018, Target agreed to pay $3.7 million to settle a class action that alleged its criminal background check policy disproportionately led to Black and Latinx applicants not being hired (Kumar 2018).

74. Pager (2007). See also Williams and Rumpf (2020).

75. Nyla's frustration echoes sociologist Reuben Miller's (2021) critique of reentry organizations' provision of job readiness services and certificates of completion, but no jobs. Miller recalls interviewing an administrator at a human services agency about job prospects

for formerly incarcerated men. The administrator candidly explained, "We're not keeping up our end of the bargain . . . My guys got fourteen certificates and no job" (Miller 2021, 235).

76. Nyla had asked another resident at the recovery home to take this picture of her. I am not able to include the photograph due to confidentiality concerns.

77. Nyla's photographs offer a visual representation of the often invisible "reentry work" criminalized women engage in order to meet their basic needs while navigating the competing demands of social service and carceral institutions (Welsh and Rajah 2014).

78. Gurusami (2017, 439).

79. Purser (2012); Bumiller (2013); Williams and Rumpf (2020).

80. Leverentz (2014); Garcia-Hallett (2019); Sered (2021).

81. Goodkind (2009); Purser (2012); Wacquant (2012); Bumiller (2013); Gurusami (2017).

82. Sassen (2002).

83. Wacquant (2012).

84. Lempert (2016, 189).

85. Opsal (2012, 389).

86. I am developing a parallel analysis here to Patricia Hill Collins's analysis of the "Black lady" controlling image. Collins (2000, 80–81) explains, "this image may not appear to be a controlling image, merely a benign one" since it refers to successful, professional women who "stayed in school, worked hard, and have achieved much." In addition to assessing how this image actually is an extension of the hardworking mammy and the unfeminine matriarch images, Collins details its connection to the welfare queen image. According to Collins (2000, 81), "Via affirmative action, Black ladies allegedly take jobs that should go to more worthy Whites, especially U.S. White men. Given a political climate in the 1980s and 1990s that reinterpreted antidiscrimination and affirmative action programs as examples of an unfair 'reverse racism,' no matter how highly educated or demonstrably competent Black ladies may be, their accomplishments remain questionable . . . when taken together, the welfare queen and the Black lady constitute class-specific versions of a matriarchy thesis whose fundamental purpose is to discredit Black women's full exercise of citizenship rights. These interconnected images leave U.S. Black women between a rock and a hard place."

87. Hannah-Moffat (2000); McCorkel (2004); Goodkind (2009).

88. Harris and McElrath (2012). See also Hunter and Greer (2011).

5. "GOD BLESSED THE CHILD THAT HAS HER OWN":
RECOVERING IDENTITY THROUGH DOMESTICITY AND MOTHERING

1. The Christian hymn "Amazing Grace," with its focus on personal salvation through God's love, comes to mind: "Amazing grace how sweet the sound, that saved a wretch like me. I once was lost, but now am found. Was blind but now I see." The hymn's conversion story resonated with Ann Williams's redemption narrative that began with God saving her through incarceration, as discussed in chapter 3.

2. I am specifically referring to Steps 1, 3, and 6 of the 12 Steps. See Alcoholics Anonymous World Services (2018).

3. Leverentz (2014); Williams, Spencer, and Wilson (2020).

4. Haney (2010); McCorkel (2013).

5. Petersilia (2003); Fontaine and Biess (2012); Welsh and Rajah (2014); Middlemass (2017); Keene, Smoyer, and Blankenship (2018).

6. Welsh and Rajah (2014, 336).

7. Petersilia (2003); Lipsitz (2012); Middlemass (2017).

8. Williams and Rumpf (2020).

9. Petersilia (2003); Middlemass (2017).

10. Ibid.

11. Public housing authorities often retain discretion in determining how to implement restrictions, meaning formerly incarcerated people may in fact be eligible for assistance or at least to stay with a loved one. The policies are so varied and confusing and instill such fear that someone will lose a scarce resource, however, that they effectively prohibit people from even seeking assistance. In cities like Chicago, public housing waiting lists are so long or closed that the resource is basically nonexistent, even without discriminatory policies against people with convictions.

12. Lipsitz (2012).

13. Richie (2001); Lipsitz (2012); Garcia-Hallett (2019).

14. Ibid.

15. Richie (2001, 383).

16. Lipsitz (2012); Sered and Norton-Hawk (2014); Sered (2021).

17. Welsh and Rajah (2014).

18. Sawyer and Bertram (2022).

19. Morash et al. (2020).

20. Richie (2001); Welsh and Rajah (2014); Gurusami (2019); Williams and Rumpf (2020).

21. Keene, Smoyer, and Blankenship (2018); Rosenberg et al. (2021).

22. Keene, Smoyer, and Blankenship (2018, 806).

23. Ibid., 811.

24. Fraser and Gordon (1994).

25. As discussed in chapter 2, I am drawing on Beth E. Richie's (2012) violence matrix, which offers a framework to study how Black women experience multiple types of gendered violence (e.g., physical, sexual, and emotional) across multiple contexts (e.g., intimate households, community, and the state).

26. As I discuss in the next chapter, Denise had survived an extremely violent intimate relationship and had previously lived in a domestic violence shelter.

27. Denise's reflections suggested the benefit of including a gender analysis to Rosenberg et al.'s (2021) analysis of ontological security and housing instability among formerly incarcerated people. Rosenberg et al. (2021) found the surveillance participants encountered in group homes undermined ontological security. While the women who participated in this study corroborated that finding, Denise and other women who experienced a newfound sense of safety in residential programs indicated that such programs also could enhance ontological security.

28. Haney (2010); Gowan and Whetstone (2012); Kaye (2012). Sociologist Nicole Kaufman (2015, 536) specifically identified domestic labor as one practice of prisoner incorporation, her term for "the ways in which institutional actors (especially NGOs) target, process, and route ex-prisoners to prepare them for citizenship."

29. This story is discussed in chapter 4, as part of the Lioness's reflections on her appearance.

30. Kaufman's (2015) examples of domestic labor as a prisoner incorporation strategy are strikingly similar to the domestic transformations Rose and the Lioness shared. Kaufman references a newsletter from St. Matthew House (SMH), a residential sober living facility in Wisconsin, and its feature on a resident named Jenelle. "The article states that before rehab, 'The only way to survive was sleeping on the couch of a roach and rodent infested apartment trading herself for her precious crack. Scratching her skin raw from the bugs and mice, she felt she was literally living in hell.' The newsletter features a recent picture of Jenelle with a vacuum in a main hallway, thus using a commitment to hygiene to symbolize the striking contrast between her life before and after her participation in rehab and then the SMH program" (543).

31. I am indebted to an anonymous reviewer for highlighting this connection between structural and relational needs.

32. The ability of Chicken Wing's parole officer to revoke her movement and overnight stays based on reports from Growing Stronger staff members, as discussed in chapter 3, supported Rosenberg and colleagues' (2021) argument that the impermanence and surveillance formerly incarcerated people experience in residential programs undermines ontological security.

33. Since I did not obtain written permission from Iris to include her photographs in publications, her photograph of the condo building is not presented here.

34. Hays (1998).

35. Haley (2016).

36. Collins (1994, 2000).

37. Roberts (2002). As a particularly compelling example, Black women are more likely to be drug tested during pregnancy, reported for drug use, and have their newborns removed, even when controlling for other variables such as drug use and class.

38. Ibid., 207.

39. Collins (1994); Garcia-Hallet (2019); Williams, Spencer, and Wilson (2020).

40. Brown and Bloom (2009).

41. McCorkel (2013); Gurusami (2019).

42. Brown and Bloom (2009); Welsh and Rajah (2014); De Coster and Heimer (2020).

43. Aiello and McCorkel (2018, 362).

44. Brown and Bloom (2009); Leverentz (2014); Williams, Spencer, and Wilson (2020).

45. Stringer (2009).

46. Opsal (2011).

47. Stringer (2009); De Coster and Heimer (2020).

48. Gurusami (2019).

49. Brown and Bloom (2009).

50. I examine an abbreviated version of this anecdote in a forthcoming chapter with coauthor Courtney Irby. See Irby and Rumpf (forthcoming).

51. This concern is documented in the literature on formerly incarcerated women's mothering challenges. Researchers point out that since criminalized women's children typically live in the same socially disadvantaged communities that contributed to their mother's incarceration, it is common for children to experience similar threats related to violence, hypersurveillance, and criminalization (Brown and Bloom 2009; Stringer 2009).

52. Stringer (2009); De Coster and Heimer (2020).

53. Roberts (1997); Richie (2012); Collins (2000).

6. "I'VE GOTTEN SO MUCH BETTER THAN I USED TO BE": RECOVERING IDENTITY THROUGH RELATIONSHIPS

1. Relationships are the fifth and final identity component I analyze as part of the rehabilitated woman controlling image. As noted previously, though, there likely are many more gendered markers of rehabilitation that constitute criminalized women's identity work and would be fruitful areas of future research.

2. Williams, Spencer, and Wilson (2020).

3. Ritchie (2017).

4. Sampson and Laub (1992); Maruna (2001); Giordano, Cernkovich, and Rudolph (2002); Leverentz (2014).

5. Giordano, Cernkovich, and Rudolph (2002).

6. Collins (2000); Lindsey (2022).

7. As sociologist Andrea Leverentz (2006, 2014) argues, avoiding "people, places, and things" creates a gendered dilemma for many formerly incarcerated women whose caretaking responsibilities keep them connected to the people and places associated with their drug use and criminalization.

8. Giordano, Cernkovich, and Rudolph (2002); Leverentz (2006, 2014). Jody Miller, Kristin Carbone-Lopez, and Mikh V. Gunderman (2015) found in their research with women in recovery from methamphetamine use that women articulated plans to leave unhealthy relationships, such as those with meth-using men, as part of their overall redemption narratives.

9. Ms. Fields had obtained full-time employment and a subsidized apartment through a permanent housing program. Additionally, she reflected on her changed appearance as an indication of her rehabilitation. Like Ella, as discussed in chapter 3, Ms. Fields had obtained her rap sheet, which included her mug shot. She kept the mug shot on the cover of a binder that held documentation of her various accomplishments since her release from prison, such as certificates of program completion. She used the mug shot to remind her of her past. She described looking at the "crazy" photo and thinking, "Oh, through the grace of God I don't look like that." She added, "That don't even look like me . . . My hair was all ate out, all around there, yeah . . . I just knew that that was a part of my past, you know . . . I never wanna forget where I came from."

10. This focus on working on one's self before entering into marriage resonates with findings from sociologists Kathryn Edin and Maria Kefalas's (2005, 113) research with low-income single mothers. They found that participants only felt it was suitable to marry after they and their partners had established their own, independent financial security, which would provide "some insurance against a marital failure." Additionally, the mothers viewed marriage as a long-term goal that was appropriate only after they matured and were ready to settle down.

11. Giordano, Cernkovich, and Rudolph (2002).

12. Leverentz (2006, 2014).

13. For examples of the diverse relationship discourses criminalized women engage, see Megan Sweeney's (2010) research on incarcerated women's reading practices, specifically

their engagement with urban fiction and self-help books' portrayal of heterosexual relationships.

14. Sociologists Jill A. McCorkel (2013) and Lynne A. Haney (2010) have analyzed how a drug treatment program and an alternative-to incarceration program, respectively, advanced discourses that made a direct link between women's inability to resist bad men and women's participation in criminalized activities.

15. Janet Garcia-Hallett (2019) describes a similar network of information and resource sharing among formerly incarcerated women.

16. I am referencing journalist Maya Schenwar's (2014, 48) description of how incarceration weakens community and family ties, "punching holes in the networks they [incarcerated people] left behind."

17. One Billion Rising for Justice (2014) is a global campaign started by Eve Ensler's V-Day organization to raise awareness about sexual violence against women. Beginning in 2013, groups around the world participate in coordinated events annually on February 14 (V-Day). According to the One Billion Rising website: "It is a call to survivors to break the silence and release their stories—politically, spiritually, outrageously—through art, dance, marches, ritual, song, spoken word, testimonies and whatever way feels right." A dance movement therapy intern at Growing Stronger organized this event and taught women a choreographed dance to perform. Note how this event is another example of discourses women drew upon to make sense of relationships.

18. I previously have shared Moon's photograph and reflection on it. See Rumpf (2017).

19. La Vigne, Mamalian, Travis, and Visher (2003).

20. For examples, recall Denise's exchanges with Judge Hopkins, discussed in chapter 3; Ella's process to seal her record, discussed in chapter 4; New Life's evolving relationship with Growing Stronger staff members, discussed in chapter 3 and chapter 5; Ann Williams's progression through Starting Again, discussed in chapter 5; and Chicken Wing's efforts to manage her parole officer, discussed in chapter 3.

21. Davis (1998, 11).

22. Garland (2001); Davis (2003); Bumiller (2008); Wacquant (2009, 2012).

23. Davis (2003, 91).

24. Chunky took a photograph of the organization's office placard for our PEI. I chose not to include the photograph for confidentiality reasons.

7. THE PERSONAL IS POLITICAL: MOVING TOWARD SOCIAL TRANSFORMATION

1. Of course, dehumanization is what prisons do. Since the creation of the penitentiary, the prison regime has been designed to break people down so that a new self-regulating self can emerge or, absent that, at least a controllable self that can be contained. See Smith (2009).

2. Though the tides may have begun to turn, as evidenced by policy changes like President Joe Biden's recent embrace of harm-reduction strategies, the massive investment in punitive responses to drug use has reaped social harms with which this country will be dealing for generations. Notably, the modicum of progress with regard to reforming the War on Drugs has occurred alongside increased criminalization on other fronts,

namely reproductive justice, gender-affirming care to young people, and critical education. The criminal legal system continues to shape shift in ways that support its own preservation and the preservation of the interlocking systems of White supremacy, heteropatriarchy, and capitalism.

3. McCorkel (2013).

4. Haney (2010).

5. Gowan and Whetstone (2012); Kaye (2012); McKim (2017).

6. Erzen (2017); Ellis (2020).

7. Sweeney (2010).

8. Smith (2009, 23).

9. Schenwar and Law (2020).

10. Sweeney (2010, 172).

11. Kushner (2019).

12. Sweeney (2010, 172). A review of the vast body of scholarship that outlines the fundamental values, goals, and strategies of prison abolition is beyond the scope of this concluding chapter. For particularly helpful introductions and overviews that also center gender, see Davis (2003), Kaba (2021), Purnell (2021), and Davis et al. (2022).

APPENDIX: METHODOLOGICAL TENSIONS

1. Rumpf (2017, 2018).

2. Haney (2010); McCorkel (2013).

3. Smith (1987, 105, 106).

4. Riessman (1987).

5. See also Harper (1998, 2002); Pink (2001); Collier (2001); Frohmann (2005); Gauntlett and Holzwarth (2006); Clark-Ibáñez (2007); Packard (2008); Lapenta (2011); Bell (2014); Rumpf (2017).

6. Frohmann (2005, 1398).

7. I use the term *met* here because not all participants were current clients or residents at these programs. Some worked as staff members at these organizations. Some had previously lived at or received services from these organizations but were not at the time of our interviews.

8. One participant informed me after the first interview she no longer wanted to participate in the project. I lost touch with another participant who actually took photographs in preparation for our PEI. We were in and out of touch for a few months and rescheduled the second interview multiple times but ultimately did not meet again. Two participants, who were in a relationship with each other, provided conflicting accounts of what happened to their cameras. One said her partner pawned both cameras. The other said both cameras "went missing" when they moved.

9. Weiss (1994, 77).

10. Emerson, Fretz, and Shaw (1995, 143).

11. See Rumpf (2017) for a more thorough discussion of this issue.

12. See Frohmann (2005) and Bell (2014) for examples.

13. Rumpf (2017).

14. Cerda-Jara et al. (2019).

REFERENCES

Acker, Joan. 1990. "Hierarchies, Jobs, Bodies: A Theory of Gendered Organizations." *Gender & Society* 4(2):139–58.

Adams, Char. 2022. "The End of Roe Is 'Horrific' for Incarcerated People Seeking Abortion Care." *NBC News*, June 29, 2022. https://www.nbcnews.com/news/nbcblk/end-roe -horrific-incarcerated-people-seeking-abortion-care-rcna35898.

Aiello, Brittnie L., and Jill A. McCorkel. 2018. "'It Will Crush You Like a Bug': Maternal Incarceration, Secondary Prisonization, and Children's Visitation." *Punishment & Society* 20(3):351–74.

Alcoholics Anonymous World Services. 2018. *The A.A. Group . . . Where It All Begins.* https://www.aa.org/assets/en_US/p-16_theaagroup.pdf.

Alexander, Michelle. 2010. *The New Jim Crow: Mass Incarceration in the Age of Colorblindness.* New York: New Press.

American Civil Liberties Union. n.d. "Women in Prison: An Overview." Retrieved October 30, 2021. https://www.aclu.org/other/words-prison-did-you-know.

———. 2019. *The Unequal Price of Periods: Menstrual Equity in the United States.* https:// www.aclu.org/report/unequal-price-periods.

Amnesty International. 1999. *Not Part of My Sentence: Violations in the Human Rights of Women in Custody.* New York: Amnesty International. http://www.amnestyusa.org /node/57783.

Amott, Teresa, and Julie Matthaei. 1996. *Race, Gender, and Work: A Multi-cultural Economic History of Women in the United States.* Boston: South End Press.

Anzaldúa, Gloria. 2012. *Borderlands/La Frontera: The New Mestiza.* 4th ed. San Francisco: Aunt Lute Books.

Appiah, Kwame Anthony. 2020. "The Case for Capitalizing the B in Black." *The Atlantic*, June 18, 2020. https://www.theatlantic.com/ideas/archive/2020/06/time-to-capitalize -blackand-white/613159/.

Becker, Howard S. 1963. *Outsiders: Studies in the Sociology of Deviance*. New York: Free Press.

Beckett, Katherine, and Bruce Western. 2001. "Governing Social Marginality: Welfare, Incarceration, and the Transformation of State Policy." *Punishment & Society* 3(1):43–59.

Belknap, Joanne. 2015. *The Invisible Woman: Gender, Crime and Justice*. 4th ed. Stamford, CT: Cengage Learning.

Bell, Shannon Elizabeth. 2014. "The Southern West Virginia Photovoice Project: Community Action through Sociological Research." In *Sociologists in Action: Sociology, Social Change, and Social Justice*, 2nd ed., edited by Kathleen Odell Korgen, Jonathan M. White, and Shelley K. White, 178–83. Thousand Oaks, CA: Sage.

Bourdieu, Pierre. 1994. "Rethinking the State: Genesis and Structure of the Bureaucratic Field." *Sociological Theory* 12(1):1–18.

Britton, Dana M. 2003. *At Work in the Iron Cage: The Prison as Gendered Organization*. New York: New York University Press.

Brown, Marilyn, and Barbara Bloom. 2009. "Reentry and Renegotiating Motherhood: Maternal Identity and Success on Parole." *Crime & Delinquency* 55(2):313–36.

Brush, Lisa D. 2003. *Gender and Governance*. Walnut Creek, CA: AltaMira Press.

Bumiller, Kristin. 2008. *In an Abusive State: How Neoliberalism Appropriated the Feminist Movement Against Sexual Violence*. Durham, NC: Duke University Press.

———. 2013. "Incarceration, Welfare State and Labour Market Nexus: The Increasing Significance of Gender in the Prison System." In *Women Exiting Prison: Critical Essays on Gender, Post-release Support and Survival*, edited by Bree Carlton and Marie Segrave, 52–93. New York: Routledge.

Bush-Baskette, Stephanie. 1998. "The War on Drugs as a War against Black Women." In *Crime Control and Women: Feminist Implications of Criminal Justice Policy*, edited by Susan L. Miller, 113–29. Thousand Oaks, CA: Sage.

Carr, E. Summerson. 2011. *Scripting Addiction: The Politics of Therapeutic Talk and American Sobriety*. Princeton, NJ: Princeton University Press.

Cerda-Jara, Michael, Steven Czifra, Abel Galindo, Joshua Mason, Christina Ricks, and Azadeh Zohrabi. 2019. *Language Guide for Communicating about Those Involved in the Carceral System*. Berkeley: Underground Scholars Initiative, UC Berkeley. https://undergroundscholars.berkeley.edu/blog/2019/3/6/language-guide-for-communicating-about-those-involved-in-the-carceral-system.

Chamberlen, Anastasia. 2017. "Changing Bodies, Ambivalent Subjectivities, and Women's Punishment." *Feminist Criminology* 12(2):125–44.

Chesney-Lind, Meda. 2003. "Imprisoning Women: The Unintended Victims of Mass Imprisonment." In *Invisible Punishment: The Collateral Consequences of Mass Imprisonment*, edited by Marc Mauer and Meda Chesney-Lind, 79–94. New York: New Press.

Chicago Legal Advocacy for Incarcerated Mothers. 2011. *Support HB 1958: Ban Restraints on Pregnant Prisoners*. Chicago: CLAIM. http://www.aclu-il.org/wp-content/uploads/2011/10/HB-1958-Fact-Sheet-Sept-2011.pdf.

Clark-Ibáñez, Marisol. 2007. "Inner-City Children in Sharper Focus: Sociology of Childhood and Photo-Elicitation Interviews." In *Visual Research Methods: Image, Society, and Representation*, edited by Gregory C. Stanczak, 167–96. Thousand Oaks, CA: Sage.

Coalition to End Money Bond. n.d. "The Pretrial Fairness Act." Retrieved July 10, 2022. https://endmoneybond.org/pretrialfairness/.

Cohn, Erika, director. 2020. *Belly of the Beast* [film]. ITVS and Idle Wild Films. https:// www.bellyofthebeastfilm.com/about.

Collier, Malcolm. 2001. "Approaches to Analysis in Visual Anthropology." In *Handbook of Visual Analysis*, edited by Theo van Leeuwen and Carey Jewitt, 35–60. London: Sage.

Collins, Patricia Hill. 1994. "Shifting the Center: Race, Class, and Feminist Theorizing about Motherhood." In *Mothering: Ideology, Experience, and Agency*, edited by Evelyn Nakano Glenn, Grace Chang, and Linda Rennie Forcey, 45–65. New York: Routledge.

———. 2000. *Black Feminist Thought: Knowledge, Consciousness, and the Politics of Empowerment*. 2nd ed. London: HarperCollins.

Couloute, Lucius, and Daniel Kopf. 2018. "Out of Prison & Out of Work: Unemployment among Formerly Incarcerated People." *Prison Policy Initiative*, July 2018. https://www .prisonpolicy.org/reports/outofwork.html.

Covington, Stephanie S., and Barbara E. Bloom. 2003. "Gendered Justice: Women in the Criminal Justice System." In *Gendered Justice: Addressing Female Offenders*, edited by Barbara E. Bloom, 3–24. Durham, NC: Carolina Academic Press. http://www.stepha niecovington.com/assets/files/4.pdf.

Cox, Aimee Meredith. 2015. *Shapeshifters: Black Girls and the Choreography of Citizenship*. Durham, NC: Duke University Press.

Crewe, Ben. 2011. "Depth, Weight, Tightness: Revisiting the Pains of Imprisonment." *Punishment & Society* 13(5):509–29.

Cruikshank, Barbara. 1996. "Revolutions within: Self-Government and Self-Esteem." In *Foucault and Political Reason: Liberalism, Neo-liberalism and Rationalities of Government*, edited by Andrew Barry, Thomas Osborne, and Nikolas Rose, 231–51. Chicago: University of Chicago Press.

———. 1999. *The Will to Empower: Democratic Citizens and Other Subjects*. Ithaca, NY: Cornell University Press.

Davey, Monica. 2008. "Federal Report Finds Poor Conditions at Cook County Jail." *New York Times*, July 18, 2008. http://www.nytimes.com/2008/07/18/us/18cook.html.

Davis, Angela. 1998. "Masked Racism: Reflections on the Prison Industrial Complex." *Colorlines: Race, Culture, Action* 1(2):11–20.

———. 2003. *Are Prisons Obsolete?* New York: Seven Stories Press.

Davis, Angela Y., Gina Dent, Erica R. Meiners, and Beth E. Richie. 2022. *Abolition. Feminism. Now.* Chicago: Haymarket Books.

Davis, Angela Y., and Cassandra Shaylor. 2001. "Race, Gender, and the Prison Industrial Complex: California and Beyond." *Meridians: feminism, race, transnationalism* 2(1): 1–25.

De Coster, Stacy, and Karen Heimer. 2020. "Techniques of Identity Talk in Reentering Mothers' Self-Narratives: (M)othering and Redemption Narratives." *Feminist Criminology* 17(1):3–25.

DECRIMNOW. n.d. "DECRIMNOW About." Retrieved June 30, 2019. https://www .decrimnow.org/about.

DecrimNY. n.d. "DecrimNY Home." Retrieved June 30, 2019. https://www.decrimny.org.

Denzin, Norman K. 1993. *The Alcoholic Society: Addiction and Recovery of the Self*. New Brunswick, NJ: Transaction.

Dodes, Lance, and Zachary Dodes. 2014. *The Sober Truth: Debunking the Bad Science Behind 12-Step Programs and the Rehab Industry*. Boston: Beacon Press.

Dodge, Mary, and Mark R. Pogrebin. 2001. "Collateral Costs of Imprisonment for Women: Complications of Reintegration." *Prison Journal* 81(1):42–54.

Du Bois, W. E. B. 1903/1990. *The Souls of Black Folks*. New York: First Vintage Books.

Edin, Kathryn, and Maria Kefalas. 2005. *Promises I Can Keep: Why Poor Women Put Motherhood Before Marriage*. Berkeley: University of California Press.

Ellis, Rachel. 2020. "Redemption and Reproach: Religion and Carceral Control in Action among Women in Prison." *Criminology* 58(4):747–72.

Emerson, Robert M., Rachel I. Fretz, and Linda L. Shaw. 1995. *Writing Ethnographic Fieldnotes*. Chicago: University of Chicago Press.

Erzen, Tanya. 2015. "Heart." In *Rethinking Therapeutic Culture*, edited by Timothy Aubry and Trysh Travis, 153–65. Chicago: University of Chicago Press.

———. 2017. *God in Captivity: The Rise of Faith-Based Prison Ministries in the Age of Mass Incarceration*. Boston: Beacon Press.

Ewing, Eve L. 2020. "I'm a Black Scholar Who Studies Race. Here's Why I Capitalize 'White.'" *Medium*, July 2, 2020. https://zora.medium.com/im-a-black-scholar-who-studies-race -here-s-why-i-capitalize-white-f94883aa2dd3.

Fettig, Amy. 2012. "$4.1 Million Settlement Puts Jails on Notice: Shackling Pregnant Women Is Unlawful." *News & Commentary* (blog). American Civil Liberties Union, May 24, 2012. https://www.aclu.org/blog/content/41-million-settlement-puts-jails-notice-shackling -pregnant-women-unlawful.

Flavin, Jeanne. 2009. *Our Bodies, Our Crimes: The Policing of Women's Reproduction in America*. New York: New York University Press.

Fleury-Steiner, Benjamin, and Jamie Longazel. 2014. *The Pains of Mass Imprisonment*. New York: Routledge.

Flores, Edward Orozco. 2014. *God's Gangs: Barrio Ministry, Masculinity, and Gang Recovery*. New York: New York University Press.

Flynn, Meagan. 2019. "Female Inmates Were Forced to Expose Their Genitals in a 'Training Exercise.' It Was Legal, Court Rules." *Washington Post*, July 19, 2019. https://www.washington post.com/nation/2019/07/19/female-inmates-were-forced-expose-their-genitals-train ing-exercise-it-was-legal-court-rules/.

Fontaine, Jocelyn, and Jennifer Biess. 2012. *Housing as a Platform for Formerly Incarcerated Persons*. Washington, DC: Urban Institute. https://www.urban.org/sites/default/files /publication/25321/412552-Housing-as-a-Platform-for-Formerly-Incarcerated-Persons .PDF.

Foucault, Michel. 1977. *Discipline and Punish: The Birth of the Prison*. Translated by Alan Sheridan. New York: Vintage Books.

———. 1994. *Ethics, Subjectivity and Truth: The Essential Works of Michel Foucault, 1954–84*. Edited by Paul Rabinow. New York: New Press.

Fraser, Nancy, and Linda Gordon. 1994. "A Genealogy of Dependency: Tracing a Keyword of the U.S. Welfare State." *Signs: Journal of Women in Culture and Society* 19(2):309–36.

Frohmann, Lisa. 2005. "The Framing Safety Project: Photographs and Narratives by Battered Women." *Violence Against Women* 11(11):1396–1419.

Garcia-Hallett, Janet. 2019. "'We're Being Released to a Jungle': The State of Prisoner Reentry and the Resilience of Women of Color." *Prison Journal* 99(4):459–83.

Garland, David. 1996. "The Limits of the Sovereign State: Strategies of Crime Control in Contemporary Society." *British Journal of Criminology* 36(4):445–71.

———. 2001. *The Culture of Control: Crime and Social Order in Contemporary Society*. Chicago: University of Chicago Press.

Gaskins, Shimica. 2004. "'Women of Circumstance'—The Effects of Mandatory Minimum Sentencing on Women Minimally Involved in Drug Crimes." *American Criminal Law Review* 41:1533–53.

Gaspar, Maria. n.d. "96 Acres Project." Retrieved July 10, 2022. https://mariagaspar.com/96-acres-project.

Gauntlett, David, and Peter Holzwarth. 2006. "Creative and Visual Methods for Exploring Identities." *Visual Studies* 21(1):82–91.

Giordano, Peggy C., Stephen A. Cernkovich, and Jennifer L. Rudolph. 2002. "Gender, Crime, and Desistance: Toward a Theory of Cognitive Transformation." *American Journal of Sociology* 107(4):990–1064.

Goffman, Erving. 1959. *The Presentation of Self in Everyday Life*. New York: Anchor.

———. 1961. *Asylums: Essays on the Social Situation of Mental Patients and Other Inmates*. New York: Anchor.

———. 1963. *Stigma: Notes on the Management of Spoiled Identity*. New York: Simon & Schuster.

Goodkind, Sara. 2009. "'You Can Be Anything You Want, But You Have to Believe It': Commercialized Feminism in Gender-Specific Programs for Girls." *Signs: Journal of Women in Culture and Society* 34(2):397–422.

Gowan, Teresa, and Sarah Whetstone. 2012. "Making the Criminal Addict: Subjectivity and Social Control in a Strong-Arm Rehab." *Punishment & Society* 14(1): 69–93.

Gurusami, Susila. 2017. "Working for Redemption: Formerly Incarcerated Black Women and Punishment in the Labor Market." *Gender & Society* 31(4):433–56.

———. 2019. "Motherwork under the State: The Maternal Labor of Formerly Incarcerated Black Women." *Social Problems* 66(1):128–43.

Hackett, Colleen. 2013. "Transformative Visions: Governing through Alternative Practices and Therapeutic Interventions at a Women's Reentry Center." *Feminist Criminology* 8(3):221–42.

Haley, Sarah. 2016. *No Mercy Here: Gender, Punishment, and the Making of Jim Crow Modernity*. Chapel Hill: University of North Carolina Press.

Haney, Lynne A. 2004. "Introduction: Gender, Welfare, and States of Punishment." *Social Politics* 11(3):333–62.

———. 2010. *Offending Women: Power, Punishment, and the Regulation of Desire*. Berkeley: University of California Press.

Hannah-Moffat, Kelly. 2000. "Prisons That Empower: Neo-liberal Governance in Canadian Women's Prisons." *British Journal of Criminology* 40(3):510–31.

Harper, Douglas. 1998. "An Argument for Visual Sociology." In *Image-Based Research: A Sourcebook for Qualitative Researchers*, edited by Jon Prosser, 24–41. London: Routledge Falmer.

———. 2002. "Talking about Pictures: A Case for Photo Elicitation." *Visual Studies* 17(1): 13–26.

Harris, Alexes. 2011. "Constructing Clean Dreams: Accounts, Future Selves, and Social and Structural Support as Desistance Work." *Symbolic Interaction* 34(1):63–85.

Harris, Julie, and Karen McElrath. 2012. "Methadone as Social Control: Institutionalized Stigma and the Prospect of Recovery." *Qualitative Health Research* 22(6):810–24.

Hays, Sharon. 1998. *The Cultural Contradictions of Motherhood*. New Haven, CT: Yale University Press.

——. 2003. *Flat Broke with Children: Women in the Age of Welfare Reform*. Oxford: Oxford University Press.

Hill, Shirley. 2005. *Black Intimacies: A Gender Perspective on Families and Relationships*. Walnut Creek, CA: AltaMira Press.

Hunter, Vicki, and Kimberly Greer. 2011. "Filling in the Holes: The Ongoing Search for Self among Incarcerated Women Anticipating Reentry." *Women & Criminal Justice* 21(3):198–224.

Irby, Courtney, and Cesráea Rumpf. Forthcoming. "Self-Work as a Moral Project: Gender, Faith, and Therapeutic Authority in Marriage Preparation and Reentry Programs." In *Bloomsbury Handbook: Religion, Gender, and Sexuality*, edited by Dawn Llewellyn, Sian Hawthorne, and Sonya Sharma. London: Bloomsbury Academic.

Jacobson, Michael P., Vincent Schiraldi, Reagan Daly, and Emily Hotez. 2017. "Less Is More: How Reducing Probation Populations Can Improve Outcomes." Program in Criminal Justice Policy and Management, Harvard Kennedy School, August 2017. https://www .hks.harvard.edu/sites/default/files/centers/wiener/programs/pcj/files/less_is_more _final.pdf.

Johnson, Corey G. 2013. "Female Inmates Sterilized in California Prisons without Approval." *Reveal*, July 7, 2013. https://revealnews.org/article/female-inmates-sterilized -in-california-prisons-without-approval/.

Kaba, Mariame. 2021. *We Do This 'Til We Free Us: Abolitionist Organizing and Transforming Justice*. Edited by Tamar K. Nopper. Chicago: Haymarket Books.

Kaufman, Nicole. 2015. "Prisoner Incorporation: The Work of the State and Non-Governmental Organizations." *Theoretical Criminology* 19(4):534–53.

——. 2021. "Governing through Partnerships: Neoconservative Governance and State Reliance on Religious NGOs in Drug Policy." *Critical Criminology* 29:589–611.

Kaufman, Nicole, Joshua Kaiser, and Cesráea Rumpf. 2018. "Beyond Punishment: The Penal State's Interventionist, Covert, and Negligent Modalities of Control." *Law & Social Inquiry* 43(2):468–95.

Kaye, Kerwin. 2012. "Rehabilitating the 'Drugs Lifestyle': Criminal Justice, Social Control, and the Cultivation of Agency." *Ethnography* 4(2):207–32.

Keene, Danya E., Amy B. Smoyer, and Kim M. Blankenship. 2018. "Stigma, Housing and Identity After Prison." *Sociological Review* 66(4):799–815.

Kendall, Mikki. 2020. *Hood Feminism: Notes from the Women That a Movement Forgot*. New York: Viking.

Kumar, Kavita. 2018. "Target Pays $3.7 Million to Settle Lawsuit Over Racial Disparity in Use of Criminal Background Checks." *StarTribune*, April 5, 2018. https://www.star tribune.com/target-pays-3–7-million-to-settle-lawsuit-over-racial-disparity-in-use-of -criminal-background-checks/478887513/.

Kushner, Rachel. 2019. "Is Prison Necessary? Ruth Wilson Gilmore Might Change Your Mind." *New York Times Magazine*, April 17, 2019. https://www.nytimes.com/2019/04/17 /magazine/prison-abolition-ruth-wilson-gilmore.html.

Lapenta, Francesco. 2011. "Some Theoretical and Methodological Views on Photo-Elicitation." In *The SAGE Handbook of Visual Research Methods*, edited by Eric Margolis and Luc Pauwels, 201–13. London: Sage.

La Vigne, Nancy G., Cynthia A. Mamalian, Jeremy Travis, and Christy Visher. 2003. *A Portrait of Prisoner Reentry in Illinois*. Washington, DC: Urban Institute.

Law, Victoria. 2009. *Resistance Behind Bars: The Struggles of Incarcerated Women*. Oakland, CA: PM Press.

Lempert, Lora Bex. 2016. *Women Doing Life: Gender, Punishment, and the Struggle for Identity*. New York: New York University Press.

Leverentz, Andrea M. 2006. "The Love of a Good Man? Romantic Relationships as a Source of Support or Hindrance for Female Ex-Offenders." *Journal of Research in Crime and Delinquency* 43(4):459–88.

———. 2014. *The Ex-Prisoner's Dilemma: How Women Negotiate Competing Narratives of Reentry and Desistance*. New Brunswick, NJ: Rutgers University Press.

Levi, Robin, and Ayelet Waldman, eds. 2011. *Inside This Place, Not of It: Narratives from Women's Prisons*. San Francisco: Voice of Witness and McSweeney's Books.

Lindsey, Treva B. 2022. *America, Goddam: Violence, Black Women, and the Struggle for Justice*. Oakland: University of California Press.

Lipsitz, George. 2012. "'In an Avalanche Every Snowflake Pleads Not Guilty': The Collateral Consequences of Mass Incarceration and Impediments to Women's Fair Housing Rights." *UCLA Law Review* 59:1746–1809.

Lorber, Judith. 1994. *Paradoxes of Gender*. New Haven, CT: Yale University Press.

Martin, Liam. 2018. "'Free but Still Walking the Yard': Prisonization and the Problems of Reentry." *Journal of Contemporary Ethnography* 47(5):671–94.

Maruna, Shadd. 2001. *Making Good: How Ex-Convicts Reform and Rebuild Their Lives*. Washington, DC: American Psychological Association.

Massoglia, Michael, Paul-Philippe Pare, Jason Schnittker, and Alain Gagnon. 2014. "The Relationship between Incarceration and Premature Adult Mortality: Gender Specific Evidence." *Social Science Research* 46:142–54.

Massoglia, Michael, and Brianna Remster. 2019. "Linkages between Incarceration and Health." *Public Health Reports* 134:8S–14S.

Mauer, Marc, and Meda Chesney-Lind. 2002. *Invisible Punishment: The Collateral Consequences of Mass Imprisonment*. New York: New Press.

McCorkel, Jill. 2004. "Criminally Dependent? Gender, Punishment, and the Rhetoric of Welfare Reform." *Social Politics* 11(3):386–410.

———. 2013. *Breaking Women: Gender, Race, and the Politics of Imprisonment*. New York: New York University Press.

McGuire, Danielle L. 2010. *At the Dark End of the Street: Black Women, Rape, and Resistance—A New History of the Civil Rights Movement from Rosa Parks to the Rise of Black Power*. New York: Vintage Books.

McKim, Allison. 2008. "'Getting Gut-Level': Punishment, Gender, and Therapeutic Governance." *Gender & Society* 22(3):303–23.

———. 2014. "Roxanne's Dress: Governing Gender and Marginality through Addiction Treatment." *Signs: Journal of Women in Culture and Society* 39(2):433–58.

———. 2017. *Addicted to Rehab: Race, Gender, and Drugs in the Era of Mass Incarceration*. New Brunswick, NJ: Rutgers University Press.

McMillan Cottom, Tressie. 2019. *Thick and Other Essays*. New York: New Press.

Mead, George Herbert. 1934. *Mind, Self, and Society*. Chicago: University of Chicago Press.

Meisner, Jason, and Steve Schmadeke. 2014. "Lawsuit Accuses Cook County of Allowing 'Sadistic' Culture at Jail." *Chicago Tribune*, February 27, 2014. http://www.chicagotribune.com/news/local/breaking/chi-cook-county-jail-brutality-lawsuit-20140227,0,6491372.story.

Middlemass, Keesha M. 2017. *Convicted and Condemned: The Politics and Policies of Prisoner Reentry*. New York: New York University Press.

Miller, Jody, Kristin Carbone-Lopez, and Mikh V. Gunderman. 2015. "Gendered Narratives of Self, Addiction, and Recovery among Women Methamphetamine Users." In *Narrative Criminology: Understanding Stories of Crime*, edited by Lois Presser and Sveinung Sandberg, 69–95. New York: New York University Press.

Miller, Reuben Jonathan. 2014. "Devolving the Carceral State: Race, Prisoner Reentry, and the Micro-politics of Urban Poverty Management." *Punishment and Society* 16(3):305–35.

———. 2016. "'You're in a Room Full of Addicts!' Prisoner Reentry as a Social Institution and the Making Up of the Ex-Offender." School of Social Work, University of Michigan. Unpublished manuscript.

———. 2021. *Halfway Home: Race, Punishment, and the Afterlife of Mass Incarceration*. New York: Little, Brown.

Moore, Dawn. 2007. *Criminal Artefacts: Governing Drugs and Users*. Vancouver: University of British Columbia Press.

Moore, Kelly. 2012/2013. "Fear and Fun: Science and Gender, Emotion and Embodiment under Neoliberalism." *Scholar and Feminist Online* 11(1)–11(2). http://sfonline.barnard.edu/gender-justice-and-neoliberal-transformations/fear-and-fun-science-and-gender-emotion-and-embodiment-under-neoliberalism/.

Morash, Merry, Elizabeth A. Adams, Marva V. Goodson, and Jennifer E. Cobbina. 2020. "Prison Experiences and Identity in Women's Life Stories: Implications for Reentry." In *Beyond Recidivism: New Approaches to Research on Prisoner Reentry and Reintegration*, edited by Andrea Leverentz, Elsa Y. Chen, and Johnna Christian, 151–71. New York: New York University Press.

National Research Council. 2014. *The Growth of Incarceration in the United States: Exploring Causes and Consequences*. Washington, DC: National Academies Press.

Natividad Rodriguez, Michelle, and Beth Avery. 2016. *Unlicensed & Untapped: Removing Barriers to State Occupational Licenses for People with Records*. National Employment Law Project, April 26, 2016. https://www.nelp.org/publication/unlicensed-untapped-removing-barriers-state-occupational-licenses/.

Nguyen, Ann Thúy, and Maya Pendleton. 2020. "Recognizing Race in Language: Why We Capitalize 'Black' and 'White.'" Center for the Study of Social Policy, March 23, 2020. https://cssp.org/2020/03/recognizing-race-in-language-why-we-capitalize-black-and-white/.

Novoa, Cristina, and Jamila Taylor. 2018. "Exploring African Americans' High Maternal and Infant Death Rates." Center for American Progress, February 1, 2018. https://cdn.americanprogress.org/content/uploads/2018/01/29114454/012918_MaternalInfantMortalityRacialDisparities-brief.pdf?_ga=2.109580677.1078993161.1635635210-1690229725.1635635210.

O'Malley, Pat. 1992. "Risk, Power, and Crime Prevention." *Economy and Society* 21(3):252–75.

One Billion Rising for Justice. 2014. "The Campaign." Retrieved October 2, 2021. https://www.onebillionrising.org/about/campaign/one-billion-rising/.

Opsal, Tara D. 2011. "Women Disrupting a Marginalized Identity: Subverting the Parolee Identity through Narrative." *Journal of Contemporary Ethnography* 40(2):135–67.

——. 2012. "'Livin' on the Straights': Identity, Desistance, and Work among Women Post-incarceration." *Sociological Inquiry* 82(3):378–403.

Owen, Barbara. 1998. *"In the Mix": Struggle and Survival in a Women's Prison.* Albany: State University of New York Press.

Packard, Josh. 2008. "'I'm Gonna Show You What It's Really Like Out Here': The Power and Limitation of Participatory Visual Methods." *Visual Studies* 23(1):63–77.

Pager, Devah. 2007. *Marked: Race, Crime, and Finding Work in an Era of Mass Incarceration.* Chicago: University of Chicago Press.

Painter, Nell Irvin. 2020. "Why 'White' Should Be Capitalized, Too." *Washington Post*, July 22, 2020. https://www.washingtonpost.com/opinions/2020/07/22/why-white-should-be-capitalized/.

Petersilia, Joan. 2003. *When Prisoners Come Home: Parole and Prisoner Reentry.* Oxford: Oxford University Press.

Pink, Sarah. 2001. *Doing Visual Ethnography: Images, Media and Representation in Research.* London: Sage.

Purnell, Derecka. 2021. *Becoming Abolitionists: Police, Protests, and the Pursuit of Freedom.* New York: Astra House.

Purser, Gretchen. 2012. "The Labour of Liminality." *LABOUR, Capital and Society* 45(1): 11–35.

Rafter, Nicole. 1985. *Partial Justice: Women in State Prisons, 1800–1935.* Boston: Northeastern University Press.

Richie, Beth E. 1996. *Compelled to Crime: The Gender Entrapment of Battered Black Women.* New York: Routledge.

——. 2001. "Challenges Incarcerated Women Face as They Return to Their Communities: Findings from Life History Interviews." *Crime & Delinquency* 47(3):368–89.

——. 2012. *Arrested Justice: Black Women, Violence, and America's Prison Nation.* New York: New York University Press.

Richie, Beth E., Monica Cosby, and Rachel Caïdor. 2020. "Prison Is Abuse." Posted June 30, 2020. YouTube video, 57:15. https://www.youtube.com/watch?v=nSF9VhxMorQ.

Riessman, Catherine Kohler. 1987. "When Gender Is Not Enough: Women Interviewing Women." *Gender & Society* 1(2):172–207.

Ritchie, Andrea J. 2017. *Invisible No More: Police Violence against Black Women and Women of Color.* Boston: Beacon Press.

Roberts, Dorothy. 1997. *Killing the Black Body: Race, Reproduction, and the Meaning of Liberty.* New York: Vintage Books.

——. 2002. *Shattered Bonds: The Color of Child Welfare.* New York: Basic Civitas Books.

Rodríguez, Dylan. 2006. *Forced Passages: Radical Intellectuals and the U.S. Prison Regime.* Minneapolis: University of Minnesota Press.

Rosenberg, Alana, Danya E. Keene, Penelope Schlesinger, Allison K. Groves, and Kim M. Blakenship. 2021. "'I Don't Know What Home Feels Like Anymore': Residential Spaces and the Absence of Ontological Security for People Returning from Incarceration." *Social Science & Medicine* 272:1–8.

Roth, Rachel. 2017. "'She Doesn't Deserve to Be Treated Like This': Prisons as Sites of Reproductive Injustice." In *Radical Reproductive Justice: Foundations, Theory, Practice,*

Critique, edited by Loretta J. Ross, Lynn Roberts, Erika Derkas, Whitney Peoples, and Pamela Bridgewater Toure, 285–301. New York: Feminist Press.

Rudy, David R., and Arthur L. Greil. 1988. "Is Alcoholics Anonymous a Religious Organization?: Meditations on Marginality." *Sociological Analysis* 50(1):41–51.

Rumpf, Cesraéa. 2017. "Decentering Power in Research with Criminalized Women: A Case for Photo-Elicitation Interviewing." *Sociological Focus* 50(1):18–35.

———. 2018. "Studying Women's Experiences of Incarceration and Reentry Using Photo-Elicitation Interviewing." In *SAGE Research Methods Cases, Part 2*. SAGE. https://doi .org/10.4135/9781526442239.

Sampson, Robert J., and John H. Laub. 1992. "Crime and Deviance in the Life Course." *Annual Review of Sociology* 18:63–84.

Sassen, Saskia. 2002. "Global Cities and Survival Circuits." In *Global Woman: Nannies, Maids, and Sex Workers in the New Economy*, edited by Barbara Ehrenreich and Arlie Russell Hochschild, 254–74. New York: Holt Paperbacks.

Sawyer, Wendy, and Wanda Bertram. 2022. "Prisons and Jails Will Separate Millions of Mothers from Their Children in 2022." *Prison Policy Initiative*, May 4, 2022. https://www .prisonpolicy.org/blog/2022/05/04/mothers_day/.

Sawyer, Wendy, and Peter Wagner. 2022. "Mass Incarceration: The Whole Pie 2022." *Prison Policy Initiative*, March 14, 2022. https://www.prisonpolicy.org/reports/pie2022.html.

Schenwar, Maya. 2014. *Locked Down, Locked Out: Why Prison Doesn't Work and How We Can Do Better*. San Francisco: Berrett-Koehler.

Schenwar, Maya, and Victoria Law. 2020. *Prison by Any Other Name: The Harmful Consequences of Popular Reforms*. New York: New Press.

Schlesinger, Traci, and Jodie Michelle Lawston. 2011. "Experiences of Interpersonal Violence and Criminal Legal Control: A Mixed Method Analysis." *SAGE Open*:1–14.

The Sentencing Project. 2022. *Fact Sheet: Incarcerated Women and Girls*. Washington, DC: The Sentencing Project.

Sered, Susan Starr. 2021. "Diminished Citizenship in the Era of Mass Incarceration." *Punishment & Society* 23(2):218–40.

Sered, Susan, and Maureen Norton-Hawk. 2011. "Whose Higher Power? Criminalized Women Confront the 'Twelve Steps.'" *Feminist Criminology* 6(4):308–32.

———. 2012. "Criminalized Women and Twelve Step Programs: Addressing Violations of the Law with a Spiritual Cure." *Implicit Religion* 15(1):37–60.

———. 2014. *Can't Catch a Break: Gender, Jail, Drugs, and the Limits of Personal Responsibility*. Oakland: University of California Press.

Smith, Andrea. 2005. *Conquest: Sexual Violence and American Indian Genocide*. Brooklyn, New York: South End Press.

Smith, Caleb. 2009. *The Prison and the American Imagination*. New Haven, CT: Yale University Press.

Smith, Dorothy E. 1987. *The Everyday World as Problematic: A Feminist Sociology*. Boston: Northeastern University Press.

Snow, David A., and Leon Anderson. 1987. "Identity Work among the Homeless: The Verbal Construction and Avowal of Personal Identities." *American Journal of Sociology* 92(6):1336–71.

Sokoloff, Natalie J. 2007. "The Effect of the Prison-Industrial Complex on African American Women." In *Racializing Justice, Disenfranchising Lives: The Racism, Criminal Justice, and*

Law Reader, edited by Manning Marable, Ian Steinberg, and Keesha Middlemass, 73–90. New York: Palgrave Macmillan.

Stevenson, Bryan. 2014. *Just Mercy: A Story of Justice and Redemption*. New York: Spiegel & Grau.

Stringer, Ebonie Cunningham. 2009. "'Keeping the Faith': How Incarcerated African American Mothers Use Religion and Spirituality to Cope with Imprisonment." *Journal of African American Studies* 13:325–47.

Stryker, Sheldon. 1994. "Identity Theory: Its Development, Research Base, and Prospects." *Studies in Symbolic Interactionism* 16:9–20.

Sweeney, Megan. 2010. *Reading Is My Window: Books and the Art of Reading in Women's Prisons*. Chapel Hill: University of North Carolina Press.

Sykes, Gresham M. 1958. *The Society of Captives: A Study of a Maximum-Security Prison*. Princeton, NJ: Princeton University Press.

Tallen, Bette S. 1990. "Twelve Step Programs: A Lesbian Feminist Critique." *NWSA Journal* 2(3):390–407.

Tiger, Rebecca. 2013. *Judging Addicts: Drug Courts and Coercion in the Justice System*. New York: New York University Press.

Travis, Trysh. 2009. *The Language of the Heart: A Cultural History of the Recovery Movement from Alcoholics Anonymous to Oprah Winfrey*. Chapel Hill: University of North Carolina Press.

Turnbull, Sarah, and Kelly Hannah-Moffat. 2009. "Under These Conditions: Gender, Parole and the Governance of Reintegration." *British Journal of Criminology* 49:532–51.

Tyndale House Publishers. n.d. "The Life Recovery Bible NLT—Book Trailer." Video, 1:10. Retrieved July 22, 2020. https://www.tyndale.com/sites/liferecovery/.

U.S. Commission on Civil Rights. 2020. *Women in Prison: Seeking Justice Behind Bars*. Washington, DC. https://www.usccr.gov/files/pubs/2020/02-26-Women-in-Prison.pdf.

Valverde, Mariana. 1998. *Diseases of the Will: Alcohol and the Dilemmas of Freedom*. New York: Cambridge University Press.

Wacquant, Loïc. 2009. *Punishing the Poor: The Neoliberal Government of Social Insecurity*. Durham, NC: Duke University Press.

———. 2012. "Three Steps to a Historical Anthropology of Actually Existing Neoliberalism." *Social Anthropology/Anthropologie Sociale* 20(1):66–79.

Weber, Max. 1930/1992. *The Protestant Ethic and the Spirit of Capitalism*. New York: Routledge.

Weiss, Robert S. 1994. *Learning from Strangers: The Art and Method of Qualitative Interview Studies*. New York: Free Press.

Welsh, Megan. 2015. "Categories of Exclusion: The Transformation of Formerly Incarcerated Women into 'Able-Bodied Adults without Dependents' in Welfare Processing." *Journal of Sociology & Social Welfare* 42(2):55–77.

Welsh, Megan, and Valli Rajah. 2014. "Rendering Invisible Punishments Visible: Using Institutional Ethnography in Feminist Criminology. *Feminist Criminology* 9(4):323–43.

West, Candace, and Don Zimmerman. 1987. "Doing Gender." *Gender and Society* 1(2):125–51.

Widra, Emily. 2017. "Incarceration Shortens Life Expectancy." *Prison Policy Initiative*, June 26, 2017. https://www.prisonpolicy.org/blog/2017/06/26/life_expectancy/.

Wilkins, Amy C. 2008. *Wannabes, Goths, and Christians: The Boundaries of Sex, Style, and Status*. Chicago: University of Chicago Press.

Williams, Jason M., Zoe Spencer, and Sean K. Wilson. 2020. "I Am Not *Your Felon:* Decoding the Trauma, Resilience, and Recovering Mothering of Formerly Incarcerated Black Women." *Crime & Delinquency* 67(8):1103–36.

Williams, Quintin, and Cesraéa Rumpf. 2020. "What's After Good?: The Burden of Post-incarceration Life." *Journal of Qualitative Criminal Justice and Criminology* 8(3):285–310.

Wyse, Jessica J. B. 2013. "Gendered Strategies in Community Corrections." *Gender & Society* 27(2):231–55.

INDEX

AIDS, 4
Aiello, Brittnie L., 122
Ann, 30–31
appearances, 82–83, 86

birth, giving while incarcerated, 31–36
Blackness, 33
Blankenship, Kim M., 109
bond, 15

Carmel, 82, 143–145, 150–151
Cathy, 61–62
Chicken Wing: appearance, 84; "crack ho," 84; employment, 91–92; Growing Stronger, 59–60; home ownership, 117–118; jealousy, 135, 146; and parole officers, 60–61; photographs, 24, 117–188, 133, 135; and police officer, 84, 85; relationships, 133–135, 137, 138, 139; self-description, 163; and state violence, 159; survival strategies, 25; work commute, 24
Child Protective Services (CPS), 36, 54, 122, 146–147, 166
Chunky, 25–26, 160, 161
clean/dirty dichotomy, 75–76, 100, 106, 138, 146
Collins, Patricia Hill, 21, 77, 121
controlling images: Black women, 30, 34, 73, 76, 77, 121; contesting, 89, 99, 100, 123, 132, 137; criminalized women, 109; dangerous women, 22; deviant woman, 101, 121; distanced women from, 94; gendered

governance, 8; gendered violence, 101; ideological justifications, 21, 136; race and class, 106; racist, 11, 73, 74, 118, 166; women of color, 16, 21, 76, 78, 79, 121, 122, 136. *See also* "crack ho", "welfare queen", "rehabilitated woman controlling image"
Cook County Jail: abusive environment, 22–23; Corrine, 154; Denise, 38; Division 17, 51; illegal strip searches, 159; Lioness, 28–29; Lynn, 114, 128; Nyla, 47; Ranisha, 34, 146; Tinybig, 14–16
Corrine, 31–35, 62–63, 154–155, 159, 160
Couloute, Lucious, 89
court, 39
"crack ho": Chicken Wing, 84; contesting the image of, 89, 113, 132; distanced from image of, 94; existing in opposition to, 100; ideological justification of mass incarceration, 79; images of, 137; the Lioness, 113; racist dehumanizing tropes, 74; reflecting the image of, 106; White supremacy, 78
criminal-addict identities: Ann Williams, 105; associated with sex work, 94; competing identities, 100, 106, 166; Denise, 143; leaving behind, 40, 124; past, 69, 70, 81, 96, 98, 100, 140; racialized and gendered, 101; resuming drug use, 62; reuniting with partners leading back to, 146; Rose, 64; "that look," 85; transformations to rehabilitated women, 82, 131

Founded in 1893,
UNIVERSITY OF CALIFORNIA PRESS
publishes bold, progressive books and journals
on topics in the arts, humanities, social sciences,
and natural sciences—with a focus on social
justice issues—that inspire thought and action
among readers worldwide.

The UC PRESS FOUNDATION
raises funds to uphold the press's vital role
as an independent, nonprofit publisher, and
receives philanthropic support from a wide
range of individuals and institutions—and from
committed readers like you. To learn more, visit
ucpress.edu/supportus.

Printed in the USA
CPSIA information can be obtained
at www.ICGtesting.com
JSHW011522080724
66045JS00018B/169